1300

METHUEN LIBRARY REPRINTS

THE PATTERN OF THE ILIAD

THE PATTERN OF THE ILIAD

BY

J. T. SHEPPARD

M.A., LITT.D.

FELLOW OF KING'S COLLEGE, CAMBRIDGE

BARNES & NOBLE, Inc.
New York
METHUEN & CO. Ltd
London

First Published in 1922

Reprinted, 1969
by
Barnes & Noble, Inc., New York
and
Methuen & Co. Ltd, London

Barnes & Noble SBN 389 01070 7
Methuen SBN 416 15650 9

Printed in the United States of America

TO

MY FATHER

"An Epic is not made by piecing together a series of heroic lays, adjusting their discrepancies and making them into a continuous narrative. There is only one thing which can master the perplexed stuff of epic material into unity; and that is, an ability to see in particular human experience some significant symbolism of man's general destiny. We do not appreciate what Homer did for his time, and is still doing for the world, unless we see the warfare and the adventure as symbols of the primary courage of life. And it is not his morals, but Homer's art that does that for us."—LASCELLES ABERCROMBIE, "The Epic."

"Much certainly, probably most, of what is suspected as copying by a later hand is deliberate and original; like the recurrence, with subtle variations, of the patterned figures in a tapestry or the carved figures in a processional frieze. For the genius of the epic this kind of repetition was an essential element in design."—J. W. MACKAIL, "Lectures on Greek Poetry."

INTRODUCTION

THE first object of this book is to assist the reader to enjoy the poetry of Homer. It does not discuss the origin of the " Iliad," the materials which the poet used, the exact proportion in which he mingled old traditions, earlier poetry and his own observation and invention for the making of his picture of heroic life. It takes the " Iliad " as a completed work of art, and, without asking how it got its present shape, tries to show clearly what shape in fact it has.

The Homeric Question wanes and waxes. Homer's poetry remains. If the coming generation is to have its chance of realizing how delightful an inheritance the ancient world has left us, it must be nourished not on controversy about Homer, but on Homer. Shakespeare himself was made a stranger, and an unpleasing stranger, to the present writer's schoolboy generation by the conscientious effort of the teachers to divert attention from the plays as plays, and to concentrate it on the derivation of such words as "wassail" and "welkin." A learned scholar of the University of Cambridge has been heard to say that at school he was not taught to read the " Iliad " and " Odyssey " as poems, but only as material for the solution of a tiresome Homeric problem. As if the problem mattered except to lovers of the poet's work. As if it could be solved by persons who have never thought about the poem as a poem.

The purpose of the present book, at any rate, is not controversy, but appreciation of the pleasant things which Homer gives us.   It is for convenience only, not because he thinks that he has solved the famous problem, that the writer dares to talk of Homer as the author of the " Iliad."   The book is not meant only for scholars, but for the general reader.   If a scholar thinks he can distinguish the successive stages by which a shorter poem or a series of short poems grew into the epic which we now possess, he is at liberty to substitute for Homer as many poets as his theory needs.   Only the layman must reject the scholar's theory unless it fits not simply the linguistic and the antiquarian data, but also the plain fact—of which the layman, not the scholar, is the judge—that the completed poem in its present shape is a great work of art, a poem made by a poet out of materials on which (however much of old traditional stuff he has incorporated) he has impressed the mark of his own genius.   The poem as we have it is our present theme, not the disputed process of its birth.

And yet, perhaps, the very absence of a theory about origins may lend the book some interest for some scholars.   In the controversy about Homer, the poets on the whole have been the champions of unity, and the learned critics have been advocates of dissection.   But the poet as a rule is too impatient to explain exactly why the poem strikes him as the work of one great artist, and the critic, bent upon dissection, can ignore the poet's protest as subjective, vague, unscholarly.   On the other hand a scholar who defends the poet's work too often feels obliged to spend his energy upon the dreary task of estimating and rebutting all the detailed arguments of his opponents. He will cite the testimony of the poets to the greatness of Homer's art.   But he has not time to analyse

its meaning.   He tends to be absorbed in the more
pressing duty of his controversial defence, his critical
retaliation.   The present writer, though he is a lover
of Greek poetry, is not a poet.   Though he is an
interested spectator of the scholar's learned warfare,
he has himself small claim to the title of a learned
scholar.   It may be useful even to the disputants if
such a writer tries to state, as plainly as he can, exactly
why he thinks the present "Iliad" a poem, well and
truly made.   This is what, in the following pages, he
has tried, however unsuccessfully, to do.

Poetry is, as Mr. Mackail has said, at once a
pattern and an interpretation of life.   The "Iliad" interprets both the tragedy and the comedy of life as
seen not merely by the average observer, but by a
poet with imaginative vision, braver, more clear-
sighted than his fellow-men.   And the pattern of its
poetry, like the vision which the poetry interprets, is
symmetrical, clear-cut, and simple.   It is not so plain
that readers cannot miss it if they are not looking for
it : but once seen, it is not soon forgotten.   If a reader
has leisure to peruse the "Iliad" several times, and to
ask himself at every point what reason, as an artist,
the poet may have had for his choice and his arrangement of material, he will find the details gradually
falling into place as parts, subordinate but always
relevant, of a magnificent design.   Through the story
of Achilles the poet has interpreted the life of the
heroic age as a splendid, tragic answer of humanity to
the inevitable fact of death.   And the pattern is so
cunningly designed that even minor incidents, digres-
sions, and comparisons contribute to the pathos and
the beauty of the central story.   We shall find, as a
result of our analysis, that the "Iliad," our present
"Iliad" is a work of art ; and we shall suspect that it
was put together—no matter how nor out of what

materials—by a poet who possessed in Walter Head-
lam's phrase, "the highest of artistic qualities, the
power of construction, of designing a composition from
the beginning to the end and controlling the relations
and proportions of one part to another; the power
that corresponds to strategy as opposed to tactics; or
the statesman's power as opposed to the mere poli-
tician's."[1]

J. T. S.

[1] "Cambridge Praelections," 1906; p. 112.

CONTENTS

THE PATTERN OF THE ILIAD

PROLOGUE

THE LAME METAL-WORKER'S PATTERN

" I WISH," said Hephaestus,[1] "I could as surely hide your son away from lamentable death, as he shall surely have fine armour; so fine that many men shall look on it, and every one who looks shall marvel." The pattern on the shield which the lame metal-worker forged of stubborn bronze and tin and precious gold and silver for Achilles is a pattern of the life that Homer knew and loved.

He wrought on it the Earth and the Sky and the Sea, the never-weary Sun and the full Moon, and all the signs with which the sky is crowned; the Pleiads and Hyads and the Strength of Orion and the She-Bear, which they also call the Wain: turning round in her own place, but always watching Orion, she alone of all the constellations may not dip into the baths of Ocean.

He made on it two Cities of mortal men, very lovely. In one of them were marriages and feasting, and to the gleam of torches in the upper city brides were being fetched out of their ch ibers. The marriage song rose loud. Boys, dancers, were spinning, and among them flutes and harps were sounding, while the women came and stood admiring, each at her house door.

[1] " Iliad," XVIII. 464 ff.

I

But in the public square the people were crowding; for a quarrel had arisen. Two men were quarreling about the price that was due for a man killed; the one protested he had paid in full, gesticulating to persuade the people, but the other said that he had had no payment; while both were eager to have trial of their case before a judge. The people were taking sides, cheering both parties on. There were heralds too who held back the people, and elders, sitting on seats of polished stone in solemn circle, and holding in their hands the staves of clear-voiced heralds, with which they came forward one by one and in turn gave judgment; while in the midst of all two talents of gold were lying, to be given to him who in that company should make good his cause.

But about the other City, gleaming in armour, lay two bands of fighting men. Their counsel was divided, whether to sack and destroy or to apportion in fair lots among them the wealth that was shut up in the lovely citadel. But the citizens were not yet yielding. They were arming for an ambush. On the walls stood their dear wives and their young children, for defenders, and with them the men who were bowed down by age; the rest were going out. Ares was leading them, and Pallas Athene, both wrought of gold; and their garments were golden; they were beautiful and tall in their full armour, like gods indeed, and very plain to recognise; but the people whom they led were smaller. So, when at last they came where it seemed good to them to lay their ambush, at a river where there was a watering-place for all sorts of cattle, there they set themselves, wrapped in their flashing bronze.

Then, too, apart from the mass, they had two watchmen set, waiting till they should see the sheep and curly-horned cattle. Soon they came, moving on quickly, and two herdsmen with them, merrily piping: they had no thought of the trap. The ambushers saw them first, and ran on them, and at once began to cut off the herds of cattle and the lovely flocks of white-fleeced sheep, and to kill their shepherds.   But the soldiers in the assembly where they sat disputing, when they heard far off the uproar where the cattle were, mounted their chariots and drove their wind-footed horses to the place, and quickly reached it ; and took their stand and began to fight a battle by the banks of the river.

They hurled bronze javelins at one another.   Strife and Battle-Turmoil were among them, and ruinous Fate, who had fastened on one man alive and freshly wounded ; but another she left untouched ; and yet another she was dragging by his legs, dead, through the press of the fight.   The cloak about her shoulders was red with the blood of men.

So they met and fought like living mortals in battle, and each side sought to drag away the bodies of the dead.

And he put on it a soft field, a rich ploughland, a broad field ploughed three times a year ; and in it many ploughmen turned their teams about, and ploughed it up and down.   Whenever they had turned the end of the furrow and had reached the edge of the field, a man would come and put into their hands a cup of honey-sweet wine. So they kept on turning their furrows and were eager to reach the edge of the deep-loamed field.   The field grew black behind them : it was like a real ploughed field, though it was made of gold · it was a marvel of his workmanship that he wrought.

He put on it a King's field, heavy with the harvest. Here labourers were reaping, with sharp sickles in their hands.   Part of the corn as it was cut would fall on the ground in lines behind the swathe that they were cutting ; but part the binders were tying into sheathes with ropes of straw.   There were three chief binders, and behind them boys who gathered up the corn in bundles and brought it in their arms and still kept feeding the binders. In the midst of all, the King with his sceptre stood by the swathe in silence, his heart rejoicing.

And away, under an oak apart, were his heralds, busy about the banquet. They had killed a great ox and were dressing it, while the women kneaded into cakes abundance of white barley for the dinner of the labourers.

He put on it a vineyard, heavy-laden with the vintage. It was beautiful and made of gold, but the grape-bunches were black. It was staked out with silver vine-props, and he drove a ditch of blue cyanus around it, and about it he drove a fence of tin. There was only one way that led to it, and by this the bearers came out when they had done their gathering in the vineyard.

Girls and young lads, with gentle thoughts, were carrying the honey-sweet fruit in wicker baskets ; and in the midst of them a boy played a tune of love on his clear harp, and sang to it with delicate voice the pretty song of Linus. So they beat the ground in time to his tune and his singing, and danced upon their way.

And he made on it a herd of straight-horned cattle. The cows were wrought of gold and tin. Lowing, they plunged down from their stalls to the pasture, by a murmuring river, by a shivering bed of reeds. Behind the strings of cattle went four herdsmen, all of gold, and with them nine swift-footed dogs.

But among the cows that were leading two fierce lions had fastened on the full-throated bull who bellowed loudly while they tore at him. The dogs and the young men were coming on behind ; but the lions had bitten through the great bull's hide and were sucking at his entrails and black blood. In vain the herdsmen ran, and set the dogs at them ; for the dogs turned aside from the lions and shirked biting them ; very close they stood, and barked, but still kept out of their way.

And the lame and famous craftsman made on it a pasturage in a lovely meadow-glade, a great pasturage of white sheep, with stalls, thatched cots and pens.

Also the lame and famous craftsman very cunningly inlaid on it a Dancing-Place like that which Daedalus once fashioned in wide Cnossos for the lovely-haired Ariadne, where young lads and girls worth many oxen were dancing with their hands on one another's wrists. The girls had delicate veils of linen, and the boys wore finely woven shirts that glistened smoothly with olive oil. The girls had lovely garlands, but the boys had knives of gold, hanging from silver belts.   Sometimes they would run with practised feet, quite lightly, like a wheel, running true in the potter's hand as he sits and tries it to see if it runs true.   Sometimes again, they would run in lines, one line upon another.   A great company stood round that dance of love, right merrily rejoicing.   Among them a Bard divine was playing on his harp and singing, and two tumblers in the throng, while the singer led the music, kept spinning in the midst of them.

And he put on it the great Strength of the river Ocean on the edge of the outside rim of the Shield so strongly made.

The pattern on the shield is in fact a pattern of human life: Earth, sea and sky and stars, and the river Ocean, framing the world; the gleam of torches at a wedding and men disputing in a city square; the gleam of armour and a camp with its divided counsel; an ambush by a river, and a battle with its turmoil and its dead: the ploughman and his cup of wine at the furrow's end; the harvest home in a king's field, and the dinner which awaits the reapers; the vintage when the girls and boys bring home the grapes to the tripping tune of an urchin's song; long lines of cattle swaying down to the meadows by the river, and the lions who break in, as it were, to remind us that there is war in the farm as well as in our world; a quiet sheep-run with its huts and hurdles; and last, most exquisite of all, a holiday at which the boys and girls in their best clothes dance a set measure, and the tumblers, the professionals, display their skill, while, to lead the music and to crown the festival, instead of the urchin with his pretty song of Linus, a Bard divine—no other bard than Homer—plays his harp and sings.

The poet has not told us how the strips and panels of this pattern were distributed on the shield, or how one shield could hold them all.   Hephaestus was a god and could do wonders.   If a human craftsman could paint frescoes of dancing girls at Cnossos, could inlay a sword-blade with a lion-hunt, and could emboss a metal cup with scenes of bull-trapping or of fighting round a city wall, Hephaestus could be trusted with a far more complicated design.   Whatever group of subjects, for her own poetic purpose, the Muse suggested, Hephaestus could translate in terms of stubborn bronze and tin and precious gold and silver.

But the Muse had her own poetic purpose, and it is the Muse's pattern, not the mere mechanical translation by Hephaestus, that Homer, as an artist not of metal but of words, has given us.

First, then, the Muse puts the great powers of nature at the beginning and the end, balancing one another.   At the beginning—"Earth and Sky and Sea . . . the Pleiads and Hyads and the Strength of Orion and the She-Bear . . . the only constellation that may not dip into the bath of Ocean."   At the end—"the great Strength of the river Ocean on the edge of the outside rim of the Shield so strongly made."   We hardly realize—this is how the Muse delights to play her tricks with us—that the great Strength of the Ocean draws from the Strength of Orion some of its magical power upon our hearts.   We may not know exactly why we are so touched and happy that the stream of Ocean runs all round the shield.   Part of the reason is that the Muse has cunningly told us at the outset of the constellation which may never dip into the Ocean's bath.

Homer, in fact, has a way of giving a composition symmetry by linking the beginning and the end of the scene

or paragraph.   As the stream of Ocean was thought to en-
circle Homer's world, so the human pictures of the shield
are poetically framed by the natural wonders of earth and
sky and sea.   And the human scenes are arranged on the
same quite simple principle of a free symmetry.

It is obvious, for instance, that the scene of dancing in
the peaceful city to the music of the marriage-song makes
up a pattern with the dancing of the vintagers to the urchin's
song of Linus and the concerted movement of the boys and
girls and tumblers to the singing of the minstrel in the
dancing-place.   The cup of wine which awaits the ploughman at the end of his furrow corresponds in Homer's pattern
to the dinner of the harvesters.   It is not, perhaps, so obvious
but it is also true, that the sudden battle by the river, so
violently contrasted with the quiet setting of the ambush
and the cheerful piping of the shepherds, finds its counterpart, on a smaller scale, in the affair of the two lions and
the bull by the river-side.   We may notice, in passing, that
in the ambush scene there are both sheep and cattle.   In
the sequel the cattle are put into one picture, the picture of
war in the four-footed world.   But the sheep are not forgotten.   They are the theme of the companion picture of a
peaceful farm.

The beauty and the significance of the pattern are enhanced
by skilful variation of the verbs with which the Muse begins
each paragraph of the description.   First, Hephaestus " began
to make " the shield ; then he " wrought on it " earth, sea, and
sky and stars.   The heightened verb suits the high theme.
Then, simply and strongly, " he made " the two contrasted
cities.   The first picture of the peaceful city, the marriage
festival, has no hint in it of tragedy ; but the second, though
its orderly litigation is contrasted with the crude injustice of
war, is, after all, a scene of quarrel—and the quarrel is about
the price for a man killed.   That leads us by a natural
transition to the first panel of the great contrasted scene, the
city at war.   In the besiegers' camp, as in the city square,
men are disputing.   But they are men at arms and their
dispute is about the fate of the beleaguered city.   The second
panel shows us the city walls, defended only by the old men,

women and children, while the soldiers go to their ambush.
The third panel describes the quiet ambush by the river,
and the fourth and most impressive suddenly assumes the
colours of real tragedy.   We shall not soon forget the picture
of the fight for the dead body and of Fate in her blood-red
cloak dragging her victim by the legs.   This scene of war
is vital to the poet's scheme.

Having finished his two great city tableaux, the artist
passes to lighter scenes.   Three times we hear "he put on
it. . . ."   First of a ploughing, then of a harvest home, then
of a vintage.   That the larger pattern is not forgotten, we
are reminded by the touch "it was a marvel that he wrought"
at the end of the ploughing scene ; but all three scenes are
cheerful, and the vintage culminates, as the city scenes
began, with dance and song.

Then once more we hear " he made," and as we watch
the cows swaying down the meadows by the river we feel
the spirit of the ambush scene again.   We are not mistaken.
The lions, sucking the blood and entrails of their victim,
make the panel a companion picture to the scene of battle-
havoc.   But with the sequel, the lovely sheep farm which
" he made," peace is restored.

So we pass at last to the great dancing scene on which
the poet lavished all his loving artistry.   For the first time
and the last we hear that Hephaestus " curiously inlaid the
picture."

Finally, when the whole is rounded off by Ocean, we hear
again the simple phrase " he made," but it is followed in the
next couplet by the splendid repetition " so when he had now
wrought the shield. . . ."   So, at the outset, "he began to
make the shield . . . and wrought on it the earth and the
sky and the sea."

Homer's purpose was not simply to make his design
symmetrical, nor even simply to make it beautiful. He has
contrived to make the pattern tragically significant.   It is a
pattern of life as a thing of youth and joy and music, with
conflict and the peril of sudden death lurking always in the
shadow.   And he has suggested this tragic background by
his pictures, first, of a dispute about the price of a man killed,

then of a dispute in a besieging army, then and most violently of a battle in which men struggle for men's bodies and a dead man's body is dragged by the legs.

Have not these scenes been chosen because, not crudely and directly, but no less certainly, they touch in us precisely the emotions which are stirred by thoughts of Agamemnon and Achilles, of Patroclus and Achilles, of Hector and Achilles?

The quarrel between Agamemnon and Achilles is on the point of being ended. The fight for the body of Patroclus is already over. Very soon Achilles will exact the price from Hector, and will be dragging Hector's body in the dust. And we know that with the death of Hector, death is also very near Achilles. " I beseech you," said Thetis to Hephaestus, " I beseech you to give my son a shield and helmet, greaves and breastplate, *since he is so soon to die.*" [1] Zeus had given to her more sorrows than to any other immortal. He had married her against her will to Peleus, a mortal who was now grown old, and her son was to die and was unhappy. And she could not help him. " He gave me a son to bear and rear, a son that is eminent among heroes. He grew up like a young tree. And I, who nursed and tended him like a plant in the orchard corner, sent him to Troy to fight. . . . Give me armour for my son. He is so soon to die." [2] " I wish," Hephaestus answered, " I could as surely hide your son away from death as he shall surely have fine armour."

Achilles came to Troy, knowing that he would die there. He came because he cared so much for glory. He chose glory and an early death rather than the pleasure of a long inglorious life. For his glory he quarreled with Agamemnon and prayed for the Achaean defeat. And now his glory is heaped high, but his friend Patroclus lies dead. [3] " Mother," he has said, " the Olympian indeed has granted my prayer ; but what pleasure is there in it to me since my friend is

[1] XVIII. 458 ff.   [2] XVIII. 436 ff.   [3] XVIII. 79 ff.

dead?" That is why the pattern of the shield is appropriate. At the highest moment of his glory and his sorrow, strong young and beautiful, and so near death, the hero goes to fight his battle with a shield on which Hephaestus has emblazoned both the sweetness and the uncertainty of life.

BOOK I

THE PATTERN OF THE ILIAD: FIRST MOVEMENT

CHAPTER I

THE QUARREL

IN the story of the "Iliad," no less than in the pattern of the Shield, we shall find the evidences of a masterly design.

But, before we start, it may be well to state exactly what we shall mean, and what we shall not mean, when we speak of Homer's pattern. We shall not mean that Homer had in mind a formula on which epic narrative should be constructed, and to which he felt himself as an artist bound to conform. We shall simply mean that in composing for an audience of listeners, not readers, he and his predecessors had hit upon some very simple but important discoveries, which have been made again by many lecturers and preachers since their time. We shall also say that Homer in particular has made a brilliant use of these discoveries.

First, Homer knew that if you have an ordinary human audience it is well to state the main points of your story at least twice, and if you can contrive to state them three times without wearying the listener, so much the better. If you want to make it clear that Achilles is your hero, it is not enough to ask the Muse for a song about the son of Peleus. You should begin by asking her to sing "the wrath of Achilles, son of Peleus," and then, after a taste of other matter, exclaim, as if by accident, "beginning at the moment when the son of Atreus quarrelled with the glorious Achilles." Or again, if you want to emphasize the importance of

Agamemnon's cruelty to the old suppliant Chryses, you
will let Achilles tell the story to his mother over again; but
with this difference, that Achilles adds an interesting detail.
Chryseis was taken prisoner at the sack of Thebe, the strong
city of Eetion.[1]   You will thus have driven home your point
by repetition, but avoided boredom by a slight change in
the second version.

Homer knew, then, that a phrase or incident can gain by
repetition.   He also knew that, unless the expression be
varied, there is a risk of weariness.

He was further aware that human beings have a liking
for a pattern.   He likes a pattern himself.   But here
emerges a fact of the first importance to the craftsman.
Both repetition and a pattern are an aid to the memory.
Whether or not the poet had a precious manuscript as the
chief treasure in his wallet,[2] he had to give his public
recitations with the rapt but easy fluency of a man through
whom the Muse is speaking.   A stock run of a dozen lines
about the launching of a ship, the preparation of a dinner,
or the summoning of an assembly is to such a man quite
literally a god-send.   Arrange your story in a long straight
row of incidents : you will find it very difficult to remember.
Break it up into a number of distinctly articulated groups
or episodes : let each episode have a pattern of its own, akin
to the main scheme, but also individual : you will find you
can remember the composition.

We do assert, therefore, that Homer, with all his amazing
variety and almost infinite resourcefulness, has framed his
poem in a certain symmetry.   He likes to throw his material
into a shape that is simple and quite easily recognizable.
If the scheme involves repetitions, he does not object,
but regards the fact as a positive advantage.   The
several patterns play on one another and contribute to the
beauty of the whole like the designs in some elaborate
tapestry.

The repetitions have a further merit.   They enable Homer

---

[1] I. 316.
[2] Consult Prof. Murray's " Rise of the Greek Epic; " but νῆφε καὶ
μέμνησ' ἀπιστεῖν.

not only to drive home his point to the slowest mind, but
also subtly to prepare the hearts of the more sensitive among
his audience for the great tragic moments.   When Achilles
cries to Priam, " Do not provoke me, for fear I lay hands on
you though you are a suppliant," [1] we are the more moved
because in the first book Achilles came so near to killing
Agamemnon.

But of course we shall not suggest that Homer meant his
hearers to be thinking about Agamemnon while he was
telling them about Priam and Achilles.   He did not want
his audience, like a company of Roman poetasters, to
applaud his *callida junctura*, to cry " Sophôs ! Ah, the
phrase that Thetis used a hundred lines ago !   Oh, brilliant,
novel, tragic application ! "   He simply wanted them to be
absorbed in his story.   But he knew that they, like us, were
touched by reminiscences and repetitions, even when they
were least conscious of the cause.

Nor shall we mean, when we speak of Homer's pattern,
that his grouping has the geometrical exactness, for example,
of the panels of a triptych representing the Madonna and
adoring saints.   An analogy may perhaps be found in music.
The pattern may be infinitely varied.   We can enjoy the
composition without even seeing that it has a scheme.   But
the scheme is there, and is one cause of our enjoyment.
And the themes—we do not mean *leit-motifs*—repeated,
varied, sometimes recognized and sometimes not, are yet
deliberately chosen and arranged.   By the Muse ?   Or the
Musician ?

SING, goddess, the wrath of Achilles, son of Peleus ;
accursed wrath, which laid innumerable griefs on the
Achaeans, and hurled to Hades many strong souls of
heroes, making the men themselves a prey to dogs and
to all birds, in the fulfilment of the will and counsel of
Zeus ; beginning at the moment when the strife and the
dissension first arose between the son of Atreus, King of
Men, and glorious Achilles.

[1] XXIV. 516.

Thus Homer launches his " Iliad." [1]   Achilles is the hero and his wrath the theme.   So Achilles is named first; then Zeus who will preside not over the Greek defeat alone but over the whole tragedy; then at the end again Achilles, but this time "the glorious Achilles," distinguished by an epithet which gives him something of the glory even of Zeus himself. He is linked with the chief who wronged him ; but the chief is not to be the hero of the poem.   So we only have his patronymic and official title, not his name.

"Accursed wrath, which laid innumerable griefs on the Achaeans."   The poet does not yet mention its consequences for Achilles.   He holds them in reserve.   Perhaps he also reflects that in an ordinary evening's entertainment he will not be called upon for his whole great story.   That would take at least a long day, and a day on which from morning until evening there was no hunting, no assembly, nothing to interrupt.   This exordium will serve for an occasion when the guests demand the simple story of the Quarrel, or at most the Quarrel and the Greek Defeat.   Yet it will also serve far better than a detailed catalogue of contents as a prelude to the poet's masterpiece as a whole.   The reference to the fate of the heroes' bodies will suggest to an audience, of course familiar with the legend, thoughts of the bodies of Patroclus and of Hector.

The wrath of Achilles, then, with its fatal issue is to be the theme, and the drama is to be governed by the will of Zeus.

"Which of the gods first set them to strive and fight with one another?   The Son of Leto and of Zeus . . ."

This repetition of Zeus we recognize as a touch from the hand of the great shield-maker.   As the first paragraph made a pattern of the names "Achilles, son of Peleus—Zeus —and the glorious Achilles," so the second is dominated by the words "the Son of Leto and of Zeus—Apollo—and the Son of Zeus Apollo."   That is how Homer works.

[1] I. I ff.

The Son of Leto and of Zeus. It was he who in his anger against the King sent plague upon the army—and the people were dying—because the son of Atreus put dishonour upon Chryses, his priest. He had come to the swift ships of the Achaeans to buy back his daughter's freedom, bringing with him an abundant ransom, carrying a golden staff enwreathed with the holy wreaths of Apollo, the Far-Shooter [Ominous, that epithet, for the Greeks]. And he prayed to all the Achaeans, but most of all to the two sons of Atreus, rulers of the people. "Sons of Atreus, and you, the rest of the well-greaved Achaeans, may the gods who dwell in the halls of Olympus grant you the sacking of the city of Priam and a safe return home: but release me my daughter and accept the splendid ransom, for your reverence to the Son of Zeus, Apollo, the Far-Shooter." Then the rest of the Achaeans cried assent. "Let us respect the priest," they said, "and accept the splendid ransom." But it did not please the heart of the son of Atreus, Agamemnon.

It was for this that Agamemnon's name was so long withheld, to be mentioned only at the moment of his tragic blunder.

So King Agamemnon dismissed the priest with threats and insults: "Let me not find you, old man, lingering here now by the ships, or coming here again. If I do— much good the staff and sacred wreaths of the god will be to you.[1] I will not let her go." So the old man was afraid and went away. "Sadly he stepped along the beach of the splashing sea," then went apart and prayed " to King Apollo, whose mother was Leto, lovely-haired." Apollo here is King because he is strong to punish King Agamemnon: he is also, for our pity of Chryseis, his mother Leto's son. The poet is cunningly embroidering a pattern with the names of the god. "Hear me, god of the silver bow, protector of Chryse, and of holy Killa, King and mighty defender of Tenedos;"—then (with a sudden intimacy, which touches the heart of peasant religion),

---

[1] I. 28, μή νύ τοι οὐ χραισμῇ. Cf. pp. 23, 36.

"Mouse-God, if ever I have thatched a lovely shrine for thee or burnt for thee fat thighs of bulls or goats, accomplish this my prayer.   Let the Danaans pay for my tears under thy arrows."

So he spoke, praying; and Phoebus Apollo heard him, and stepped down over the peaks of Olympus with anger in his heart.   From his shoulders hung his bow and arrows and his covered quiver : the arrows rattled on his shoulders in his anger as he moved.   He went on, like the night.   Then he sat apart, away from the ships, and shot an arrow.   Terrible was the tang of the silver bow.   He ranged at first among the mules and the quick dogs, then aimed a sharp dart at the men, and hit, and still kept hitting.   And many pyres of the dead were always burning.

That completes the Introduction.   It gets its clear-cut outline from the repetitions.   "Sing, Muse, the wrath of Achilles . . . which made the bodies of heroes a prey to dogs and birds . . . by the counsel of Zeus . . . beginning when the son of Atreus quarreled with the glorious Achilles;"[1] then, "the son of Leto and of Zeus, who was angry and sent plague upon the army, and the people were dying . . . and Phoebus Apollo heard him and stepped down with anger in his heart . . . and the pyres of the dead were always burning."   The second panel contains three themes, first Agamemnon's insolence to Apollo's suppliant, then the prayer of the old man by the sea to the son of Leto, then the vision of the god in all his splendour.

After nine days of the plague Achilles took it on himself to call an Assembly.   Hera, who pitied the Greeks, had put the thought in his heart.   He rose in the meeting and demanded that a prophet, priest or dream-interpreter be consulted—"for dreams too come from Zeus "—about the cause of Apollo's anger.   Calchas, the prophet, hardly

---

[1] Having once noticed this series (Διὸς βουλή, δῖος ᾿Αχιλλεύς, Λητοῦς καὶ Διὸς υἷος), you will feel the effect of line 74, where Calchas addresses Achilles as διΐφιλε.   Achilles (line 86) modestly transfers the epithet to Apollo.

dared to speak for fear of Agamemnon. We have seen how Agamemnon treated Chryses. Calchas also is a servant of Apollo. The promise of Achilles, "While I live no man shall lay a hand on you—no, not Agamemnon," is a hint of the coming storm.

At length, encouraged by Achilles, the prophet speaks. Apollo is angry for his priest, whom Agamemnon has insulted. He will not repent until the girl is given back freely without ransom, and a hecatomb is sacrificed to him at Chryse.

Agamemnon rises, violently angry. "His heart grew black with wrath, his eyes were like shining fire." Boding no good to Calchas, he protests that the prophet has never yet had any good to tell him. He values Chryseis more highly than his own wife Clytaemnestra. "Yet all the same I am willing to give her back, if that is better. I would rather have the people saved than let them perish. But do you make ready for me another prize, that I be not the only man of all the Argives without my prize of honour —it is not even decent."

Then Achilles, quietly, but with one insolent epithet: "Son of Atreus, lover of glory, greedy of possessions, how can the great-hearted Achaeans give you a prize of honour? There is no spare booty left over for distribution. . . . But if ever Zeus grant that we sack the well-walled Trojan city, we will give you three-fold, four-fold recompense."

That increases Agamemnon's resentment. Achilles wants to keep his own property, but thinks Agamemnon should give up Chryseis without compensation? Very well. "If the Achaeans mean to give me a present, let them see that it is worth the exchange—but if they do not give, I shall take for myself—your prize, or the prize of Ajax or Odysseus : I will go myself and take it, and the man I come to will be angry. . . ." But let that pass for the moment. Let a ship be launched and let Ajax or Idomeneus or Odysseus, or perhaps the noble son of Peleus himself, go on board with the girl and with a sacrifice for Apollo, and set sail for Chryse.

But Achilles has taken fire at the mere hint of a slight

2

from Agamemnon.   It is not the fear of being robbed that
stirs him, but a sense that Agamemnon, of all people, should
not treat the honour of his fellow-princes lightly.   "Oh,
you are shameless in your greed,"[1] he cries, "how can an
Achaean heartily obey you? . . . I did not come here to
fight because of the Trojan spearmen.   I have no quarrel
with them.   They never drove my cattle or my horses, or
hurt my crops in deep-loamed fertile Phthia.   There are
many mountains and the sounding sea between.   It was
you we followed—oh, how shameless!—for your pleasure,
to win honour for Menelaus, and for you, dog-face, from the
Trojans.   But you do not care for that at all, or regard it.
You actually threaten to take from me, to take for yourself,
my prize of valour, for which I laboured, which the sons of
the Achaeans gave me."   Very well, he will go home to
Phthia.   "Desert, if you will," says Agamemnon.   "You
will have no prayers from me to stay here for my sake."
Presently he will be humbly begging Achilles to come back.
"There are plenty here to honour me and most of all the
Counsellor Zeus."   But what if the counsel of Zeus be
directed against Agamemnon?

"You are most hateful to me of all the Zeus-nurtured
princes, because quarreling and fights and battles are
always dear to you.   If you are very strong, it was a god,
I suppose, that gave it.   Go home with your own ships
and your companions, and rule among your Myrmidons.
I do not care about you, nor about your anger.   I will
threaten you—as Phoebus Apollo takes Chryseis from
me, I will send her with my own ship and my own companions home; but I will take the lovely-cheeked Briseis.
I will go myself to your hut and take her, your prize,
that you may know how much greater I am than
you. . . ."

At that Achilles was about to draw his sword and end
the story, when Athene stopped him :—

He was drawing his great sword from its sheath when
Athene came from heaven.   She was sent by the white-

[1] I. 149.

armed goddess Hera, who loved them both and cared for both of them alike in her heart. She stood behind and seized the son of Peleus by his golden hair, appearing to him only. None of the others saw her.

The goddess bids Achilles put up his sword. He shall receive from Agamemnon for this insult compensation worth three times the value of Briseis. Achilles obeys, and the second movement of the quarrel scene begins.

The whole episode of the quarrel is designed, in fact, like a picture in three panels. The chief actors in the first are Calchas, Agamemnon, and Achilles. In the third Achilles, Agamemnon, and Nestor. The first [1] depicts the growing anger of the King and culminates in his threat to seize Briseis. The third [2] opens with the solemn oath of Achilles that he will withdraw from the fighting. The Achaeans shall pay dearly for Agamemnon's insolence. " And then much good your grieving will do you, when many shall fall dying at the hands of murderous Hector." That, by the way, is the first mention of Hector in the poem. And then, to balance Calchas in the companion picture, Nestor is introduced, with his wise old story, attempting vainly to restore the peace. The central panel, [3] which gives shape to the whole episode, contains the intervention of Athene, sent by Hera, a brilliant picture, corresponding in the larger scheme of the whole episode first to the intervention of Apollo in his anger, then to the nod of Zeus which is presently to shake Olympus. [4]

On the main issue Agamemnon is quite clearly in the wrong. His theft of Briseis is an act of gross injustice and a deadly insult to Achilles, which gives him every right to withdraw from the fighting. Achilles owes Agamemnon no allegiance, but is fighting solely for the honour of which Briseis as his prize of valour is the symbol. On the other hand, Achilles goes too far. Nestor has put the matter plainly. Both men are young, and both are behaving badly. Agamemnon ought not to take Briseis. But the son of

---

[1] I. 53-187. [2] I. 223-317. [3] I. 188-222. [4] I. 530.

Peleus should remember that a King like Agamemnon always receives more than an equal share of honour—which in terms of Achaean chivalry means booty.   He holds his sceptre from Zeus.

Nestor, however, was disregarded.   The princes still quarreled.   The assembly broke up, and while Agamemnon bade the people sacrifice to Apollo and purify themselves, and sent Odysseus off with Chryseis in a ship to Chryse, the son of Peleus went away to his huts and ships " with the son of Menoitios and his companions."   So, by a patronymic only, the hearer is first introduced to Patroclus.[1]

With Achilles back at his ships and Odysseus started on his voyage to Chryse, we embark on a new group of pictures, corresponding in the pattern to the episode of Chryses' mission, though naturally painted on a larger scale.   Chryses, it will be remembered, prayed to the sons of Atreus and to the Achaeans : his prayer rejected, he went apart and prayed on the beach to Apollo, and in answer Apollo came against the Greeks from Olympus, terrible with his arrows.   Then followed the great episode of the Assembly in its three divisions.   That episode ended, we are not surprised, though we are, I think, delighted to find that the next series touches themes foreshadowed in the Chryses episode.

First, Agamemnon's heralds take away Briseis.   She goes with them unwillingly,

and Achilles, weeping, went apart and sat away from his companions on the beach of the great sea, looking out over the water, and stretched up his arms and prayed to his dear mother. . . . So he spoke weeping, and his lady mother, sitting in the depths of the sea by her old father, heard him, and came up quickly from the grey sea, like a mist, and sat before him as he wept. . . .

We see now another reason why the poet, at the moment when Chryses prayed to Apollo on the seashore, chose to make him call the god "son born of Leto lovely-haired."

---

[1] I. 307.   The name Patroclus, with the epithet διογενίς, 337.   This proud epithet and the word φίλῳ in line 345 are the only hints the poet here allows himself to give of the love of that two friends for one another.

This prayer of Achilles to his goddess mother and her promise to carry his request for honour to the feet of Zeus in Olympus form the first panel[1] in the design of this new group of pictures.

The second panel[2] is, as usual, an interlude, which serves to make the hearer realize the long waiting of Achilles, still sitting in his hut, his anger eating at his heart. It describes the arrival of Odysseus at Chryse, the landing, the restoration of Chryseis to her father, the old man's prayer for the staying of the plague (of course in form recalling his earlier prayer for vengeance),[3] the sacrifice to Apollo, the feast and the singing of a Paean, and then the happy return of Odysseus and his crew to the Greek camp.

But all the while he sat in his anger by his swift-faring ships, the son of Peleus, Zeus-born, swift-footed Achilles. He would never go to the place of assembly, the place where men are honoured, nor ever to the field; but stayed behind and ate his heart out, and longed for the battle-cry and the fighting.[4]

Then the third panel—of course [5]—

But when at length there came the twelfth day after that, the ever-living gods went to Olympus, all of them, Zeus leading. Thetis did not forget her son's request, but came from under a wave of the sea, and went up in a mist to heaven and to Olympus, and found the far-seeing son of Cronus sitting away from the others on the highest peak of many-ridged Olympus.

The third panel then contains the prayer of Thetis to Zeus. The picture is completed when at the nod of the immortal King's ambrosial head, Olympus trembles.

About the pattern of this very simple triptych nothing more need be said. But there are two points in its narrative so important for the sequel that they must be mentioned. The first states what Mr. Lascelles Abercrombie,[6] a poet

---

[1] I. 318-427.　　　[2] I. 428-493.　　　[3] I. 37 ff., 451 ff.
[4] I. 488-492, corresponding in the pattern to 423 ff.
[5] I. 493 ff.　　　[6] "The Epic," p. 62.

appreciating a poet, has seen to be the central notion, the sustaining principle, of the " Iliad."   It was to his mother that the hero first really opened his heart, and this is what he said :—[1]

Mother, since you bore me, though I am to live for such a little time, Olympian Zeus the Thunderer ought to have given me honour.   As it is, he has not honoured even a little.   The son of Atreus, the great ruler, Agamemnon, has put dishonour on me.   He has taken my prize and has it.   He has taken it for himself.

Honour is to Achilles the most precious thing in the world. Where another man would have said, " I have lost my friend whom I love," Achilles says, " I have lost my friend whom I honoured as myself." [2]

Secondly, Achilles begs his mother to obtain from Zeus a promise that the Greeks shall be defeated until they are driven to the ships and penned up by the sea.[3]   Thetis knows that that request is excessive.   She asks, and Zeus promises, something less,[4] though in the sequel, and with tragic consequences for Achilles, Zeus gives him actually what he himself desires.

" Father Zeus," she prays, " if ever I have done thee service by word or deed among the immortals, accomplish this my prayer.   Honour my son who is short-lived above all others, for now the King of men, Agamemnon, has dishonoured him.   He has taken his prize.   He has taken it for himself.   But do thou, Zeus, counsellor, Olympian, honour him, and give the Trojans victory until the Achaeans do honour to my son and increase him with honour."

Finally, after this high converse, we are provided with a decorative panel, very light and very pleasant, to finish off what may be called the first great Rhapsody.   The scene is still Olympus, and the theme is an Olympian quarrel, the heavenly counterpact to the tragic quarrel of the Achaean chieftains.   Like most scenes in Homer's Olympus, it is

---

[1] I. 352 ff.   [2] XVIII. 81.   [3] I. 409.   [4] I. 503 ff.

amusing, graceful, irreverent, and of infinitely less importance than the tragedies of mortal heroes. Zeus and Hera are the disputants. The lame and famous blacksmith is the Nestor who in this affair succeeds in restoring every one to a good humour. It is delightful to observe that, when Zeus threatens Hera with his grave displeasure, he uses the familiar formula : " Much good all the gods in Olympus will do you if I once lay hands upon you." [1] It is pleasant also to observe that, just as Odysseus' crew, after the restoration of Chryseis, feasted and drank and " sang the whole day through a paean to Apollo," and then went off to sleep, so the Olympian gods, after their quarreling, laughed at Hephaestus puffing and panting about the hall ; then [2]

" All day long to the set of sun they feasted. Their heart had no lack of food, that was fairly shared among them, nor yet of the beautiful harping of Apollo and the song of the Muses, with lovely voices answering each other. But, when the bright light of the sun had set, they went away to bed each to his house, where the famous Hephaestus with his cunning craft had made a hall for every one of them."

---

[1] I. 566-567 ; cf. 28, etc.   [2] I. 601-608 ; cf. 468 ff.

CHAPTER II

THE CONFIDENCE OF AGAMEMNON AND
THE ACHAEAN PANIC

ABOUT the first book modern criticism has had few
complaints to make. The pattern is obvious, the
action clear, the movement rapid. First the exordium.
Achilles, glorious Achilles, is the hero, and Zeus is behind
the tragedy. Then the Introduction to the Quarrel, in the
form, "Apollo sent a plague because his priest was slighted,
and his servant prayed, and Apollo in his splendour sent
the plague." Then the Quarrel with three panels: first the
utterance of Calchas and the threat of Agamemnon, then
Athene's intervention, then, to balance the first panel,
Achilles' oath that he will leave the field and Nestor's vain
attempt to restore peace. Then the fetching of Briseis
from the hero's hut, and three more panels, of which the
first contains the hero's prayer to Thetis, the second the
placation of Apollo by Odysseus and his crew at Chryse,
the third the prayer of Thetis in Olympus and the Nod of
Zeus. Finally, to complete the Rhapsody, a quarrel between
Zeus and Hera, with Hephaestus as the peacemaker.

So the gods went off to bed, and Zeus as well as the
others. And Zeus slept, with golden-throned Hera by
his side.[1]

"Let us begin with Zeus and, Muses, end with Zeus
your singing" is a formula which may remind us that the
old religious hymns, long before Homer's day, had also
what Aristotle would have recognized as "a beginning, a
middle, and an end."

[1] I. 611.

24

We turn to the second book. The purpose of our adventure is to discover, not how our "Iliad" was composed, but what in fact it is. To what extent does the kind of pattern we have noticed pervade the whole? Has Homer made his many episodes fall into place as part of a design? And how far do the episodes, by similarity or contrast, add value to the main narrative of the hero's wrath? Has the poet made his detail relevant to the main theme?

"Zeus slept," said Homer, and his listeners felt that the first great chapter of his story had reached its perfect close. The wine-cups went round, and the poet rested. Then, when the audience was ready, he resumed his interrupted tale :—[1]

> The other gods and mortals slept all night. Zeus could not sleep. He was pondering in his heart how he should honour Achilles and destroy many of the Achaeans at the ships. This seemed to him the best plan, to send baneful Dream to the son of Atreus, Agamemnon. So he spoke winged words to him and said : " Go, baneful Dream, to the swift ships of the Achaeans. Go to the hut of Agamemnon, son of Atreus. Give him this message, exactly as I tell you. Bid him arm the long-haired Achaeans with all speed for battle ; because now he can take the broad-wayed city of the Trojans, since the immortal gods are no longer divided in purpose. Hera with suppliant prayers has bent them all to her will, and on the Trojans their doom is fastened."

So baneful Dream assumed the shape of Nestor, "whom Agamemnon honoured most of all the elders" (but whose advice, we remember, he had not taken yesterday), and stood over Agamemnon's head, and repeated the message quite exactly, except that he improved it both in shape and in persuasiveness by throwing it into the well-known pattern—

> I am a messenger *from Zeus*, who cares for you and pities you. He bids you arm. . . . On the Trojans their doom is fastened *by Zeus*.

[1] II. 1 ff.

Then he tells Agamemnon not to forget the message when he wakes.

Agamemnon woke. He sat upright, and put on a soft shirt, lovely, lately woven, and wrapped a great cloak round him, and fastened a lovely pair of sandals under his bright feet, and hung a silver-studded sword from his shoulders, and took his ancestral sceptre, everlasting [by which, we remember, Achilles had sworn that the Greeks should bitterly repent], and with it stepped out among the ships of the bronze-shirted Achaeans.

Dawn was already touching the top of Olympus, announcing a new day to Zeus and the immortals, when Agamemnon went out and bade the clear-voiced heralds call the people to assembly. The heralds called, and the people were gathering fast; but first Agamemnon held a Council of his elders at Nestor's ship. He told them quite exactly what he had dreamt, then added :—[1]

> "Come then, let us see if we can arm the Achaeans to battle. But first I will try them with words, as is right and usual. I will bid them fly in the many-thwarted ships, but do you, from your places, one here, one there, restrain them with your words."

Nestor observes that, if anyone else had told them the dream, they would have said it was false, and would have taken care *not* to do what it recommended. But, since the King has seen it, they had better " see " if they can arm the Achaeans for battle. With that the old man led the way out of the Council, and the others "rose and obeyed the shepherd of the people, staff-bearing princes as they were."

It is certainly an odd scene. As the critics do not fail to tell us, Agamemnon's conduct can only point to a disordered mind. No sane man would behave like that.

We agree. No sane man would. The story of the Dream is Homer's way of telling us that the King is now the victim of Infatuation. He is in the grip of Ate. He first fell into her clutches when he sent Chryses about his business. He was not quite sane at the beginning of the

[1] 72 ff.

quarrel with Achilles. If he had been, he would not have been angry, but relieved, to hear from Calchas that the plague, which he had caused, could be stopped so easily. And now, in spite of Nestor's good advice, he has persisted. He has actually taken Briseis from Achilles. What does Achilles matter? There are plenty to honour Agamemnon—especially Zeus.

In such a state of mind, a man is subject to hot fits and cold. At one moment he is the favourite of Zeus, sure to take Troy to-day. At the next moment the cold fit is indicated by the faltering phrase "let us see if we can arm the Greeks to battle," which Nestor gloomily underlines. Perhaps, thinks Agamemnon, it would be best to make sure of my own position. I will put responsibility for the offensive on my staff. I will appear as the wise, peace-loving monarch. I will propose evacuation—but of course I shall have arranged a patriotic Press protesting. With all the different shades of party-colour, they shall clamour for the attack. Then, if we win, I shall still have the credit. I always do, if we win. But if the offensive proves too costly, I shall not be to blame.

The method surely is familiar? What in heroic times was called a "testing of the people" is now called "propaganda." But the anonymity of the Press makes the process more plausible to-day. To-day, as three thousand years ago, such a "testing of the people" is considered by official circles "right and usual." But the method has its dangers. A wise government does not use it. The people may *bolt* for peace. Still, we can understand why an infatuated, nerve-wracked Agamemnon thinks of the device.

Nestor's view is implied, not spoken. His silence on the King's proposal is, from such a ready speaker, portentous. He knows it is no use protesting. When Agamemnon turned his back on Chryses, all the other Achaeans opposed him; but it was useless. He is the King. When Achilles was insulted, Nestor did his best, but to no purpose. The King is obviously infatuated. So Nestor says nothing, and lets Agamemnon take his course. But

Nestor leads the way out of the Council without waiting
for the King to end the meeting, a breach of etiquette
which the courtly Alexandrian scholars labelled "indecent."
But Nestor's abruptness is in fact his comment on Agamemnon's plan.

Meanwhile the people were thronging to the assembly.
Like bees, swarming from a hole in a rock, they came on,
buzzing. Gossip, the messenger of Zeus, was at work
among them, active as fire, speeding them on to the
meeting.[1]

The place of assembly hummed with them. The
earth groaned with the people taking their seats. There
was a hubbub, and nine heralds tried to restrain them,
shouting to make them cease their noise and listen to
the Zeus-nurtured princes. And they eagerly took their
seats and were restrained in their places, and stopped
clamouring.

Not a good instrument for Agamemnon's purpose. They
are all alive with curiosity and excitement. No wonder,
after what happened at the assembly yesterday. This is
no ordinary stock description of a meeting of the Achaean
assembly. It represents an army already restive, likely to
be easily demoralized.

Lord Agamemnon rose, holding the sceptre which
Hephaestus made. Hephaestus gave it to Zeus, the
King, the son of Cronos. . . .

It is the sceptre by which Achilles swore his oath,[2] and
we see now why Homer mentioned it again when Agamemnon woke and sat up and dressed. The repetition makes
the sceptre matter to us. So, leaning on the sceptre of his
greatness, by which Achilles swore his oath that the
Achaeans should suffer, the King spoke :—

Friends, heroes, Danaans, Zeus son of Cronos has en-
tangled me in a grievous Infatuation. He is cruel. He
promised me formerly and confirmed it with his nod that

---

[1] II. 93 ff.   [2] I. 234 ; II. 46, 101 ff.

I should go home as the sacker of strong-walled Troy : and now, see, he has devised an evil trick upon me, and bids me go to Argos with ill fame, because I have lost many lives of my people. . . .

Tragic irony was a device invented before Sophocles. Agamemnon played his part only too well. When at length, with a touching reference to wives and children, the King proposed evacuation, the whole scheme miscarried. The people took him at his word. There was no time for the staff with its propaganda. . . .[1]

The assembly was stirred as the waves of the Icarian sea are stirred when the South wind swoops on them from the clouds of Zeus the Father. As a cornfield moves beneath the fierce attack of the West wind, and the ears are bowed beneath the blast, so moved the whole assembly. With shouts they rushed to the ships, and the dust went up in a cloud under their feet. They were shouting to one another to take hold of the ships and drag them to the glorious sea, and were clearing out the channels, and the clamour of them, eager to go home, went up to heaven. They were taking the props from under the ships. . . .

Then would the Argives have gone home. . . . Had not what happened ?

By this time we are acquainted with the poet's method. It is with a pleasant sense of recognition that we hear the theme of the central panel—"had not Hera spoken to Athene."[2]

It is the pattern of the Quarrel series again. Agamemnon, in the first assembly, said, " I will take Briseis," and Achilles would have killed him, had not Athene, sent by Hera, stopped him. So now Agamemnon spoke, and the Argives would have gone home, had not Athene, sent by Hera, stopped them. She came to Odysseus, who of course was not launching his ship, but stood by it, hurt and indignant.

---

[1] II. 143 ff.

[2] II. 155-156 ; cf. I. 188 ff. Hera's address to Athene incidentally prepares us for a future scene by mentioning the name of Helen, the great prize for whom so many Greeks have died. The point is driven home by repetition.

She repeated what Hera had said to her, and Odysseus acted. He took Agamemnon's sceptre to show that he had the King's authority,[1] and he stopped the rout.

To eminent princes he adopts a tone of gentle protest.[2] " It does not become you to show fear, like a base-born man. Set a good example. You do not perhaps realize that Agamemnon is testing the people? Presently he will reveal his mind and crush them. And you know what it means when a King is angry !" To common people, with a blow from the sceptre,[3] " You are nobodies. Sit still, and listen to your betters talking. The rule of many is a bad thing. Let one be Master, one be King." Illogical and unfair, because after all Agamemnon had suggested flight. But they ought to have waited humbly for the end of the little comedy that their betters had arranged for them.

So the people rushed back to the assembly, with a sound like the roaring of a wave on a great sea-beach. And they sat down and were duly restrained in their places—except Thersites.

This, the first democratic agitator in our literature, was "the ugliest man that went to Troy." [4] He limped, he squinted, he stooped, and he had very little hair on his oddly pointed head. His talent was for brawling against the princes, and saying anything foolish and disorderly that he thought would make the Achaeans laugh. When Odysseus brought the sceptre down on his shoulders and he sat, half-stunned, with a tear in his eye and a great lump on his back, every one laughed. Confidence and good humour were restored. It was agreed that Odysseus had never done a better thing in his life. That is the way of the crowd. Yet this contemptible rebel had used exactly the same arguments, and often the same phrases, as Achilles used in his denunciation of Agamemnon's greed. Thersites thinks that the Greeks, if they had any spirit, would murder Agamemnon. He derives the notion from Achilles.[5] Homer himself reminds us of the fact, by saying that Thersites " was of all men most hateful to Odysseus and Achilles," [6]

---

[1] II. 186.   [2] II. 190 ff.   [3] II. 198 ff.   [4] II. 216 ff.
[5] II. 242; cf. I. 232.   [6] II. 220; cf. I. 176.

though at present he attacked King Agamemnon.   Achilles
would have been ashamed to hear his arguments advanced
by such a pleader.   The poet implies that the disorder and
the insubordination we have witnessed are due in part to
Achilles as well as to the King.

Order restored, Odysseus rises, sceptre in hand, with
Athene as a herald by his side, commanding silence.   The
picture corresponds in the pattern to the moment when
Agamemnon rose to speak.[1]   Odysseus makes of course no
reference to Agamemnon's own proposal.   The less said
about that the better.   Happily, Thersites has made it
possible to represent the movement to the ships as a re-
grettable occurrence, a breach of discipline, for which no
one in authority is to blame.   In fact, by his attempt to
exploit the situation, Thersites actually helps the princes to
gloss over Agamemnon's folly.   Very skilfully, Odysseus
adapts the King's own phrases to make every one forget the
main point of the royal speech.   "You seem to want to
bring discredit on Agamemnon," he complains.   "You are
forgetting your own promises, not to return till Troy is
sacked."   And again, "I sympathize with you in your
home-sickness.   Of course it is hard to be away so long
from wife and children."   Most cunningly spoken, without
a glance at Agamemnon![2]   The people are to feel that the
recent panic was not the sequel to the King's pathetic talk,
but a spontaneous movement, prompted solely by their own
weak hearts.   Then, having well prepared his ground,
Odysseus tells the story of an omen which Calchas long
ago interpreted as an assurance that Troy would fall this
year.

After Odysseus, Nestor.   Is it not Homer's perfect comedy
that makes old Nestor tell King Agamemnon to go on
leading his army "with firm unshaken counsel as before"?[3]
Odysseus and Nestor between them have restored the
monarch's credit.   And if Odysseus can contribute to the
general confidence by his tale of Calchas, Nestor can produce
an omen sent by Zeus himself.   So thoroughly does the

[1] II. 268; cf. 200.   [2] Cf. II. 284-290, 296-297 with III-113, 136-137.
[3] II. 344.

propaganda work that Nestor, without endangering the success of the affair, can afford a gentle innuendo at the King's expense : " Divide up the people by tribes and clans. Then you will be able really to test them. You will be able to see how each set of men behaves in battle."[1] No wonder Agamemnon wishes he had ten such counsellors. He has every reason to be grateful to his lieutenants.

Agamemnon's speech, which follows, marks an important stage in the action. The King has learnt something from his recent experience. The shock, in fact, has almost re-stored his sanity. He has not yet suffered enough to pocket pride and offer Achilles amends. But he acknowledges his mistake, and, without attempting to defend the maladroit manœuvre of his previous speech—any reference to that would have undone the good work of his colleagues—he makes a generous reference to the real cause of the army's restiveness :—[2]

> The son of Cronos, Zeus, has given me sorrows, involv-ing me in bootless strife and quarreling. I and Achilles fought and exchanged harsh words for the sake of a girl —and I was the first to be angry. If ever we are of one mind in counsel, then Troy's disaster will no longer be delayed, no, not for a little while. But come to dinner, and afterwards let every man make sharp his spear.

Agamemnon is almost himself again. That is the issue and the main purpose of the episode.

In form this second Rhapsody is designed as a parallel to Book I. Accordingly, to complete the pattern, after a shout of assent from the assembly, like the noise of a wave which the South wind drives on a great headland—the third wave-simile[3] of the group—there follow scenes of sacrifice and feasting, including a great banquet given by Agamemnon to his Council. Here Diomed is for the first time intro-duced, and Menelaus becomes prominent. After the sacri-fice Agamemnon prays. The prayer reveals that, in spite

---

[1] II. 360 ff. There is point both in 361, οὔτοι ἀπόβλητον ἔπος ἔσσεται . . . and in γνώσῃ ἔπειτ', 365.

[2] II. 375 ff.   [3] II. 144, 209, 394

of his return to sanity, he still harbours hopes of early victory.[1] But Zeus accepted the sacrifice and continued to increase his troubles.

After dinner, at a word from Nestor (corresponding in the pattern to the laconic utterance with which he took Agamemnon's story of the dream),[2] the heralds call once more. This time they call to battle, and the people go out, with Athene, not Gossip, urging them on, putting strength in their hearts and making battle seem more sweet to them than a homeward voyage. Then, with a series of magnificent similes (corresponding in the pattern to the simile of the bees),[3] the army gathered, glittering in arms like a fire, with a noise as of flocks of birds, as numerous and persistent as flies about pails of milk. Their captains go among them, ordering the ranks, like goat-herds with their flocks; and among them Agamemnon, like Zeus, like Ares, like Poseidon—as a bull in a herd of cows, was Agamemnon made conspicuous by Zeus that day.

The pattern is completed by the Catalogue of the Greeks and of the Trojan allies. On the one side Achilles and his horses, on the other side Glaucus and Sarpedon, are given special honour. But the problem of the Catalogues is too complicated for discussion here. For us it is sufficient to have seen how this second episode, which began with the infatuated Agamemnon, deluded by a dream from Zeus, ends with the same Agamemnon sufficiently restored to be the noble leader of a noble army, and made pre-eminent by Zeus. But Agamemnon had yet to suffer and be humbled.

---

[1] II. 412 ff.   [2] II. 434 ff.; cf. 79 ff.
[3] Contrast the whole passage 441 ff. with 87 ff., the corresponding panel.

CHAPTER III

THE FIRST DAY OF BATTLE

W E pass to the elaborate and ingeniously constructed narrative (Books III-VII) which describes the first day's fighting. Its place, as the central panel in the first narrative of the poet's decorative scheme, is perhaps by this time obvious. Of its relevance and importance, as heightening the significance of the main tragedy, we shall say something here, though the full effect of Homer's very careful preparation is not felt until we reach the crisis of the fates of Hector and Patroclus and Achilles.

First, then, a word about the pattern. We shall indicate the main lines only, leaving the reader to discover for himself many delightful details which reveal the craftsman's subtlety, variety, and freshness.

There are three chief panels : first a duel between Paris and Menelaus, the two disputants for whose cause the larger quarrel, the whole war of Greeks and Trojans, is being waged ; then as a central panel, which is itself a skilfully constructed rhapsodic period, the long episode of Diomed's heroic exploits ; thirdly, as we expect, a second duel, but between champions more eminent as fighters, Ajax and Hector : the one to be the bulwark of the Greek defence in the great rout, the other, as we know, the great antagonist of Achilles.

That is the main scheme ; Paris-Menelaus, Diomed, Ajax-Hector ; but in connection with the Paris-Menelaus episode the poet introduces us to Helen and to Priam ; in connection with the Diomed series he has brilliantly asserted the importance of the Lycian heroes Glaucus and Sarpedon ;

34

and in the Ajax-Hector episode he shows us Hector's wife
Andromache.   Then, when night separates the fighters, to
complete the formal beauty of the composition, Agamemnon
makes a sacrifice and feast at which old Nestor, as before,
gives moral and strategical advice.   There is a Trojan and
a Greek assembly.   At the former, a proposal to surrender
Helen is shipwrecked on the opposition of Paris : in the
latter, Diomed's enthusiasm defeats the Trojan offer of a
compromise.   A truce is, however, arranged for the burial
of the dead, and the day ends with funeral pyres on both
sides burning.   As Nestor has advised, the Greeks employ
the respite for the building of a great defensive wall—a poor
defence, when Zeus intends that they shall be defeated.   The
pattern ends (like that of the first Rhapsody) with feasting
and the drinking of wine ; but this time Tragedy is im-
minent :—

> All night the long-haired Achaeans feasted, and so did
> the Trojans and their allies in the city.   All night the
> Counsellor Zeus devised evil for them, terribly thunder-
> ing.   And pale fear seized them, and they poured wine
> from their cups upon the ground : no man dared to drink
> before he had made libation to the mighty son of Cronos.
> Then at last they slept, and took the gift of sleep.[1]

Thus, after the main pattern of the duels and of Diomed's
great exploits, there is a kind of coda, using to new purpose
the familiar themes of the Introduction—assembly, Nestor's
counsel, funeral pyres, feasting and omens ; and marking
clearly enough (though a staff-reporter would no doubt have
explained with greater accuracy how such a tactical result
had been attained) the fact that in the first day's fighting
the Greeks, though they had done great deeds, had substan-
tially admitted a defeat.

The opposing armies advance,[2] the Trojans with a noise
"as of a flight of cranes," the Achaeans " silently, breathing
courage, determined to help one another."   The dust they

---

[1] vii. 476 ff. ; compare and contrast i. 467 ff., 601 ff. ; ii. 430 ff.
[2] iii. 1 ff.

raise is like a mountain mist, "not dear to shepherds, but better than night for a thief." In front of the Trojan ranks is the god-like Paris, clothed in a leopard-skin, with bow and arrows and two spears which he brandishes, challenging the Achaeans.

When Menelaus saw him he rejoiced [1] "as a lion when he is hungry, and has come on some great beast, a stag or a wild goat, which he will devour, no matter how the swift hounds and the strong young men may chase him."

That simile is the first of a long series not unimportant in the pattern of the " Iliad." Paris retired, as frightened as a man who has met a snake on a mountain road.[2] Hector cried :—[3]

"Beauty, cheat, womaniser, this is the sort of courage that you showed when you went to a foreign land and brought away a lovely woman—to be a sister to your soldier brothers, a calamity to your father and your city and to all your people, a joy to your enemies, and a shame to yourself ? Could you not face the war-like Menelaus ? He would have shown you what is the spirit of the man whose lovely wife you are keeping. Much good your harp and your gifts from Aphrodite, your hair and your beauty, will do you, when you are laid in the dust. Nay, the Trojans are cowards, else you would already have put on a shirt of stones—stoned to death for the wrongs that you have done them." [4]

Paris answers in effect that the heart of Hector is of iron :—[5]

"Your heart is always like a hard axe, which a carpenter who is cutting a ship's timber drives through the plank, and the axe increases the man's strength ; so is the mind in your bosom, inflexible. Do not reproach me with

[1] III. 23 ff.
[2] III. 31, see XXII. 93 ff. for the tragic development of this theme.
[3] III. 39 ff.
[4] III. 54 f. οὐκ ἄν τοι χραισμῇ . . . and 56 ἀλλὰ μάλα Τρῶες δειδήμονες. . . . The poet is using, with intention, the familiar themes; cf. I. 28, 232, 242, 566; II. 241.
[5] III. 60 ff.

the lovely gifts of Aphrodite : the noble gifts of the gods may not be rejected when the gods themselves give you them, though a man would not take them of his own free will."

Paris, in fact, with his harp and his beauty and his fatal love of Helen, has his own place in the poet's vision of our tragic human destiny.

Homer intends to make the quarrel of Achilles and the King for the girl Briseis the most significant event of the whole war.   To that end, the greater quarrel of the Greeks and Trojans for Helen is made a part of the decorative background.   Of that greater quarrel the duel between Paris and Menelaus is the symbol.

So Paris offers to meet Menelaus in single combat.   " Let an oath be sworn by both sides that the issue of the war shall be decided by this duel."   Menelaus accepts, and heralds are sent to summon Priam for the solemn swearing of the oaths.

That gives the poet his chance for the introduction of Helen, a real and charming woman, but the perfect type of the vanities for which men are content to live and die.   When Iris fetches her to watch the duel—" Paris and Menelaus are to fight for you with long spears, and whichever wins will call you his dear wife "—she is touched by longing " for her former husband, her city and her parents." [1]

At once she put on a white veil.   She went out quickly from her chamber, weeping delicately : not alone, two handmaidens went with her.   They came to the Scaean gate, where Priam sat with his old councillors.   Old age had stopped their fighting, but they were good talkers still, like cicadas that sit on a tree in a wood and chirp with their lily-like voice.   So they sat, the elders of the Trojans ; and when they saw Helen coming to the tower, they very quietly said to one another : " Small blame to the Trojans and well-greaved Achaeans that they suffer a long time for such a woman ; she is strangely like the immortal goddesses to look at.   Yet for all that, though she be as

[1] III. 140 ff.

she is, let her go in the ships and not leave sorrow for us and for our children after us." So they spoke, but Priam called her to him : " Come here, dear child, and sit by me, to see your former husband and your relatives and friends. I do not call you to account. It is the gods I hold responsible, who have brought on me this grievous war with the Achaeans. Tell me, who is that mighty man, so beautiful, so majestic; he is like a King?"

Of course it is Agamemnon. The poet has not scrupled to let Priam fail to recognize him in the tenth year of the war. He does so, partly for the sake of Helen's answer: " A good king and good fighter, Agamemnon, and once—to my shame I speak—my husband's brother ; " but partly also for the sake of the old man's comment, which is relevant to the last scenes of the poem :—[1]

" Ah, happy son of Atreus, child of destiny, blessed in your fortune, how many sons of the Achaeans own your sway. I visited Phrygia once and saw the hosts of the Phrygians . . . but they were not so many as the Achaeans."

The day will come when Priam shall be lying at the feet of Achilles, and Achilles shall say, " And you, Sir, they tell us were once happy, and ruled over all the people between the Hellespont and Phrygia."

Then in succession we are given the memorable character of Odysseus, and the slighter references to Ajax, the great bulwark of the Achaeans, and to Idomeneus the Cretan; and the episode ends with Helen's touching thought that perhaps her brothers, whom she misses from the field, are ashamed to fight because of her disgrace. They are really lying dead in Sparta.[2]

Meanwhile the sacrificial beasts are ready, and the heralds fetch King Priam. He shivers as he rises, then drives out through the Scaean gates, down to the plain. This picture is the poet's subtle preparation for Priam's visit to Achilles.

---

[1] III. 182 ff.; cf. XXIV. 544 ff.
[2] III. 236 ff. This incident contributes to the effect of XXII. 436-446.

After the sacrifice and oath-taking, Priam drives back to Troy, and Hector and Odysseus prepare the ground for the duel.

The two men fought and Paris would have perished, had not Aphrodite snatched him from the clutches of his enemy, and set him down safe at home, and fetched Helen to him. So the scene ends, with Aphrodite casting her spell on the weak unhappy victims. But Menelaus in the field was raging up and down like a wild beast, looking for Paris.[1]

Agamemnon claims that Menelaus has won, and indeed a suggestion is made by the Father of gods and men himself that perhaps the war might be allowed to end on that assumption. Helen might be surrendered, and the city of Priam saved. " Never ! " cries Hera. Zeus is teasing her.[2] He has not really forgotten his promise to Achilles. " I hate those Trojans so, I would rather see one of my own dear cities, Argos, Sparta or Mycene, sacked, than miss the sack of Troy. . . . Let Athene go," says Hera, " and make the Trojans break the truce." Nothing loath, Zeus lets Athene go, and she induces Pandaros to shoot treacherously at Menelaus. Agamemnon cries : " I know it now, a day will come when Troy shall perish." [3] That marks a further step in Agamemnon's process of recovery. His anxiety about Menelaus is charming, and is characteristic of King Agamemnon in his better moments. The little scene in which Machaon,[4] the physician, applies his soothing drugs is again the first of a great series not unimportant in the poet's design.

But the truce is broken : Agamemnon, with a good conscience, can order a general attack. He reviews his forces, going on foot from group to group. The fact that he can do so after what has happened shows how perfectly Greek discipline has been restored. But the poet's object in describing this review is to draw attention to the character of Diomed, whom he means to play a great part in the

---

[1] III. 449.   [2] IV. 5.   [3] IV. 163.   [4] IV. 200 ff.

battle. The episode has touches of delightful humour, hints of the character of Agamemnon as a respectable but testy general ; he is, in fact, a great king, but a very human officer. As the inspection proceeds, we see his temper wearing thin : " Up Greeks," he says, " these Trojans are liars, and we shall beat them. Have you no shame ? Are you waiting till they reach the ships ? " [1] To Idomeneus the Cretan : " There is no man that I honour more in the battle or the feast ; " to the Ajaxes : " I need not give you orders, you yourselves are an inspiration to the rest. If my men were all like you, Troy would soon fall." Then to Nestor, who is lecturing his men on chariot tactics, Agamemnon says, with a first touch of irritation, " I wish your strength were equal to your spirit." [2] To which the old man replies : " The gods do not give all their gifts at once to any of us. I may be old—old enough indeed to have fought and killed Ereuthalion ; but I can still give counsel." Agamemnon rejoices in his heart, but he can hardly have failed to see what Nestor has in mind. Anyhow, when he comes to Odysseus, he raps out a random criticism which receives a well-earned rebuke. " Wait and see in the battle," says Odysseus, " you will not find the father of Telemachus at fault. Anyhow what you say is foolish." [3] The officer apologizes, but when he reaches the young Diomed, son of Tydeus, we observe that both old Nestor's talk about the good old days of fighting and Odysseus' reference to young Telemachus have gone home. " What, son of Tydeus, are you shirking ? You are not the man your father was." [4] Agamemnon, in fact—and this is why the whole scene was invented—insults young Diomed as gratuitously, though not so grossly, as he has insulted great Achilles. But Diomed, unlike Achilles, bows to authority. His squire may cry, " Agamemnon, you are lying, and you know it ; " [5] but Diomed will bid him to keep silence, " Respect the general officer, and take your orders from me." That is the introduction to the story of Diomed's heroic exploits ; it is designed to show this hero as a modest foil to Achilles, and

---

[1] IV. 242 ff.   [2] IV. 313 ff.   [3] IV. 350 ff.   [4] IV. 370 ff.   [5] IV. 404.

the modesty of Diomed is an essential element in the story
of his valour, which is now to be developed.[1]

"Tush," Diomed cried,[2] " be silent ; take your orders
from me. I do not blame Agamemnon, shepherd of the
people, for rallying the well-greaved Achaeans to the fight.
His will be the glory if the Achaeans destroy the Trojans
and take Troy, and his the great grief if the Achaeans are
destroyed. Come, then, let us too be mindful of our
bravery." He spoke, and leapt from the car in his full
armour to the ground. Terribly rang the bronze on the
hero's breast as he rushed on ; even a strong brave man
would have feared it. And as a wave of the sea, driven
by the blast of the west wind, moves incessantly upon a
resounding beach ; first out at sea it lifts its head, then
breaks on the land with a great roar, and curves and rears
about the headlands, and spits out sea-foam ; so then the
companies of the Danai moved on incessantly, stubbornly,
to war."

It is the climax of the series of wave similes ; but, unlike
the waves, the Achaeans moved silently. The Trojan battle-
cry—for Homer is a Greek—was like the bleating of great
flocks of sheep. The Greeks were led by Athene, and the
Trojans by Ares ; and in the midst was Strife, the sister of
Ares, " who is but small when first she rises, but afterwards
she hits the heaven with her head, though she walks on the
earth." [3]

So the armies clashed, with the noise of two mountain
torrents meeting. But Achilles was not fighting.

The poet's first pictures of the general battle are designed
to remind us that Achilles is not there. The pattern falls
into three small panels, of which the second is the most
elaborate and important. In the first, Antilochus, the son
of Nestor, killed a Trojan Echepôlos, and there was a

[1] I have discussed this aspect of the Diomed episode in a paper on "The
Heroic *Sophrosyne* and the Form of Homer's Poetry," in the "Journal of
Hellenic Studies," 1920, vol. XI. p. 47 ff.
[2] IV. 412 ff.   [3] IV. 441 ff.

struggle for the spoils.[1]   In the third, the Thracian Peiroos
kills Dioreus, who is killed in turn by Thoas as he tries to
take his armour, and there is a fight over both bodies.[2]
But the central panel is what matters :—[3]

> Then Telamonian Ajax hit the son of Anthemion (the
> flower-man), a young man and flourishing, Simoeisios,
> whose mother came down from Mount Ida and bore him
> by the banks of the river Simoeis ; she had gone with
> her parents on a visit to the flocks : that was why they
> called him Simoeisios.   But he did not pay his parents
> back a child's return for nurturing ; short was his span of
> life ; he was cut off by the spear of the great-hearted
> Ajax.   As he moved in the front rank, he was hit in the
> breast by the right nipple ; the brazen spear passed on
> through the shoulder.   He fell on the ground in the dust,
> like a black poplar that grows in a low-lying meadow
> pasture, a smooth trunk with branches growing at the
> top ; a wood-cutter has cut it down with the bright iron,
> to bend it into a felloe for a beautiful car, and it lies
> there drying by the river banks : such was Anthemides
> Simoeisios, when he was killed by Zeus-born Ajax.

Can we doubt that all this beauty—the flower-name,
the river-birth, the simile of the poplar—is lavished on the
Trojan youth because he was short-lived ?   And can we
doubt that, when we hear such music as this, we are meant
to think of Achilles ?   At any rate, Achilles is in Homer's
mind.   Let Homer take up the story :—

> Antiphos, of the bright breast plate, son of Priam,
> aimed at Ajax and missed him, but hit Leukos, the good
> companion of Odysseus, in the groin, as he was dragging
> off the body (of Simoeisios) ; and he fell in a heap and
> loosed his hold of the body.   But Odysseus in his heart
> *was very angry for his friend* that was killed, and strode
> through the ranks of the first fighters, helmed in bright
> bronze, and went very close, and stood and aimed his
> flashing javelin, looking round for his mark—and the
> Trojans drew back before the hero as he shot.   He did

[1] IV. 457-472.   [2] IV. 517-538.   [3] IV. 473-517.

not shoot in vain, but hit Democoon, a bastard son of
Priam, in the forehead, *in his anger for his friend who had
been slain.*

And at that moment Apollo, grudging the Greeks their
triumph, shouted from the citadel of Troy : " Up Trojans,
do not yield to the Greeks ; they are made of flesh, not
stone or iron ; and Achilles, son of lovely Thetis, is not
fighting."

If we remember Simoeisios, and the beauty with which
Homer has invested him to remind us of Achilles, we shall
be saved from much mistaken criticism as we proceed with
our analysis.

So the battle raged, and many Greeks and Trojans lay
in the dust, and Athene put strength and courage into the
son of Tydeus.   Fire flashed from his shield and helmet,
" like the light of an autumnal star, fresh from the bath of
Ocean ; so fire flashed from his head and shoulders." [1]
There was a Trojan nobleman, a rich man and a priest of
Hephaestus, Dares : he had two sons, Phegeus and Idaios
(son of Oak and son of Ida), both skilful fighters.   One of
them Diomed killed ; the other was saved by Hephaestus,
" that the old man might not be altogether sorrowful." [2]

Athene persuaded Ares to withdraw with her from the
field : the Greeks were winning ; Agamemnon killed his
man, so did Idomeneus ; Menelaus killed Scamandrios [3]
(Simoeisios is not forgotten)—"the good hunter whom
Artemis herself had taught to shoot all the wild creatures
that feed in the mountain woods.   But little good to him
that day was Artemis, who delights in hunting, or his far-
shooting, in which formerly he was so eminent.   The son
of Atreus killed him as he fled. . . ."   Meriones killed
Pheroclos, son of the clever carpenter who made the fatal
ships in which Paris sailed to Greece.[4]   Meges killed Pedaios,
" who was a bastard ; but bright Theano tended him as
lovingly as her own children, to please her husband." [5]
And last, to complete the pattern, Eurypylos killed

[1] v. 4-6.   [2] v. 24.   [3] v. 49 ff.
[4] v. 69 ff.   [5] v. 70-71.

Hypsenor, son of another priest, "Dolopion, who was priest of the Scamander, and was honoured like a god by the people."[1]

As for the son of Tydeus, you could not have told on which side he was fighting, so swiftly he raged over the plain, like a torrential river that breaks down all the bridges and the fences, when the rain of Zeus has filled it. Pandaros saw him, and shot an arrow and wounded him, but did not stop his career: "Athene," cried the hero, "if ever you showed favour to my father Tydeus, help me now."[2] Diomed had not forgotten Agamemnon's insult. And the goddess came to him with a promise and a strange command: "Fight boldly; I have put in you the spirit of your father. I have taken the mist from your eyes, that you may know gods from men. If any of the immortals comes against you, do not fight—unless it be the goddess Aphrodite." So Diomed raged three times more violently than before, like a wounded lion.[3] He killed Astynoos and Hyperion, but left them where they lay and pressed on after Abas and Polyeidos, "the two sons of Eurydamas, an old man, an interpreter of dreams. They did not go home for the old man to interpret them their dreams; the mighty Diomed slew them."[4] He pressed on after Xanthus and Thoon, "the two sons of Phaenops, both late born: sad old age afflicted him; he did not beget another son to leave as heir to his possessions."[5] Diomed killed them both; the father was not to welcome them home alive. Last, he killed two sons of Priam in one chariot; and of course, to complete the pattern, he leapt on them, as a lion leaps among a herd of cattle and breaks the neck of a heifer or a cow.[6]

Aeneas now joins Pandaros, who observes that, if he gets home safe, he will burn his bow and arrows—"my head be chopped off if I don't."[7] He has drawn blood both from Menelaus and from the son of Tydeus, but has only made them more violent. He wishes he had brought his horses

---

[1] v. 77 f.   [2] v. 115.   [3] v. 136 ff.   [4] v. 149 ff.
[5] v. 152 ff.   [6] v. 162 ff.   [7] v. 215.

and chariots from home, where he has plenty. He wishes he had followed his father's counsel and brought a chariot with him: the son of Lykaon, we notice, in his own small untragic way, suffers like the great son of Peleus, for not following an old father's good advice. So Aeneas takes him up in his chariot (drawn by a marvellous pair of horses, from the stock Zeus gave to Tros for Ganymede), and the pair drive on against the son of Tydeus. Sthenelos, the squire, suggests retreat—" Aeneas is the son of Aphrodite." " It would not be like my father's son to run away," says Diomed, " nor would it please Athene." [1]

Pandaros of course is killed (Athene guides the spear of Diomed through his perjured tongue[2]); the marvellous horses are captured, and Aphrodite throws her arms about Aeneas. Diomed sees the goddess, rushes in and wounds her; and the poor lady, "lover of smiles," must needs fly off in tears to Olympus, where she gets the same poor consolation that is all we humbler mortals can expect: "You are not the first to suffer: fighting is not your gift; your business is with marriage; leave fighting to swift Ares and Athene." [3]

Some critics have complained that Diomed's great exploits overshadow the achievements of Achilles. If they refer to his wounding of the goddess Aphrodite, our reply is that this exploit is delightful comedy, magnificent perhaps, but neither war nor tragedy.

But the incident is certainly a trial to the modesty of Diomed:—[4]

He leapt upon Aeneas, although he knew that Apollo's arms were defending him. He did not respect even that great god, but still pressed forward to kill Aeneas and to rob him of his famous armour. Thrice he leapt on, eager to kill; and thrice Apollo thrust his bright shield aside; but when the fourth time he rushed on like a dæmon, Apollo, the Far-Worker, shouted terribly, and spoke to him: "Take care, son of Tydeus, and yield. Conceive not that you are equal with the gods. The race of the

[1] v. 253.   [2] v. 292.   [3] v. 382 ff.   [4] v. 432 ff.

immortal gods and of men that go on earth was never yet the same." So he spoke, and the son of Tydeus gave way a little, to avoid the wrath of the Far-Shooter, Apollo.

That incident, as we shall see, was not designed for the sake of Diomed only. It relates his exploits to the main tragedy. Diomed's self-control under Agamemnon's insults made him a foil to Achilles; his behaviour in his encounter with Apollo leads up to the last scene in the life of the hero's friend, Patroclus.

The second exploit of the son of Tydeus is the overthrow of Ares. Having wounded Aphrodite, the cause of the whole trouble, Diomed is to defeat the god of War himself. And, in fact, immediately after the encounter with Apollo, Ares begins to stir himself and exhorts the Trojans to fight bravely. But, before Diomed meets Ares, there is an interlude, not unimportant for the sequel. Sarpedon, the Lycian hero, whose death is to give glory to Patroclus, must be introduced to us early if the glory of Patroclus is to matter. But the poet has another reason for putting him precisely here in the pattern. After overthrowing Ares, Diomed is to meet a human fighter, Glaucus, and the interview with Glaucus is to give significance to the whole of Diomed's exploits and to relate them to the poet's vision of Achilles. So Sarpedon, the friend of Glaucus, is given his place here in the central panel of the series.

Aeneas, as we have seen, has been bearing the brunt of battle, and Sarpedon rallies Hector on his inactivity. The terms he uses recall (and the poet meant them to recall) Achilles' protest that he had no quarrel with the Trojans.[1] Like Achilles, Sarpedon and his Lycians are fighting for a cause that is not their own. "The citizens," says Sarpedon, "are shirking; they are like hounds afraid to attack a lion."[2]

"And we allies do the fighting. For I, too, am an ally from a distant country. Lycia is far off on the banks of swirling Xanthos, where I left my dear wife and my infant

<hr>

[1] I. 152 ff.   [2] v. 475 ff.

son, and great riches such as every poor man longs for.
Yet, for all that, I urge my Lycians to battle, and am
eager myself to fight my man—though I have nothing
here that the Achaeans could carry off or plunder—while
you are idle, and are not even ordering the others, your
own people, to stand fast and help their mates."

That brings Hector into the field. The battle sways, but
the Greeks stand fast. We are warned that we are starting
on the second part of Diomed's adventures by a miniature
review with which the poet makes the great Greek heroes
rally their men.[1]

Odysseus, Diomed, and the two Ajaxes were urging on
their men . . . and the son of Atreus went up and down
the ranks, with many exhortations : " My friends, be men.
Take a brave heart. Respect each other in the battle.
Where men, because of that respect, stand fast, more of
them live than die ; but, when men fly, they have neither
glory nor strength."

We are beginning a new episode, and again, in the description of the introductory fighting, we hear the river
music which reminded us of Achilles. When Agamemnon
has duly rallied his men, Aeneas kills two noble Greeks—

The two sons of Diocles, Crethon and Orsilochus,
whose father lived at prosperous Phera and was rich ;
their race was sprung from a river, from Alphaeus who
flows loudly through the country of the Pylians. Alphaeus was the father of Orsilochus, a king over many
men ; and Orsilochus was father of great-hearted Diocles ;
and from Diocles came these two sons, Crethon and
Orsilochus, skilled in all kinds of fighting, who went to
Ilion, land of horses, in the black ships with the Argives,
to win honour for the sons of Atreus, Agamemnon and
Menelaus. But death gathered them instead. They
were reared up like two young lions on the mountain
peaks, reared by their mother in the thickets of a deep
wood ; together they go hunting the cattle and fine sheep,
and ravage the settlements of men, until they themselves

---

[1] v. 519 ff.

are killed by the hands of men with the sharp bronze. Such were they when they fell, slain by the hand of Aeneas ; like lofty pine-trees. And the war-like Menelaus pitied them when they had fallen ; and strode through the rank of the first fighters, helmed in bright bronze.

Antilochus joins Menelaus, and Aeneas, when he sees the two, retires. Diomed, we remember, did not yield to Pandaros and Aeneas. Antilochus and his companion do their killing, until Hector, with the aid of Ares, rallies the Trojan ranks. Diomed sees the God and shivers ; "as a man runs back when he sees a river rising in flood," so Diomed retires, and shouts to his men that Ares is with Hector. For the moment Hector triumphs. He kills two men in one car. Ajax, on his side, kills a man, but cannot strip him. He retires fighting with a stubbornness that is a hint of the part he is presently to play.

So the battle swayed until "Fate caused the son of Heracles, Tlepolemos, to meet the god-like Sarpedon."[1]

Of Tlepolemos we learn from the Greek catalogue.[2] The son of Astyocheia, a woman captured by Heracles from one of the many cities that he sacked, this youth began his career by killing his father's uncle Likymnios, an old man and a soldier. He collected a company of adventurers and fled to Rhodes, where he settled, "as an exile, suffering." The island was then colonized by three divisions of his followers : "they were loved by Zeus, who reigns above gods and men ; the son of Cronos showered great wealth upon them." Such is the hero who is chosen by the poet as the fit antagonist for Sarpedon, the very son of Zeus. He is suitable, not only for the sake of the rhetorical challenge : " They lie, Sarpedon, who say you are the son of Zeus ; very different was my father, Heracles ! ;" not only because Heracles himself sacked Troy ; but also because, in the pattern of the epic as a whole, Homer has systematically employed

[1] v. 628.   [2] II. 653 ff.

the myth of Heracles—a story from an earlier generation of heroes—as a significant recurring theme. Even Zeus is subject to the weaknesses and limitations of his human puppets—to limitations, at any rate, which resemble theirs in kind if not in degree. When Zeus desires to cheat the Fates and save some favourite, Hera reminds him of the birth of his heroic son. When Heracles was born, Zeus was himself the victim of "Infatuation." The theme is introduced at the beginning of the poem, when Hera's inclination to defy her lord and master is checked by the reminder from Hephaestus :—[1]

"Bear up, dear Mother, and control yourself, in spite of your annoyance, lest I see you, dear as you are to me, being beaten before my eyes : and then it is little good that I can do you, sorry as I shall be. For the Olympian is a hard god to oppose. Once before, when I was anxious to come to your aid, he took me by the legs and hurled me from the wondrous threshold of Olympus. All day I fell, and at sunset I reached Lemnos with little spirit left in me ; "

and Hera smiled at the memory.

Again, in Book XIV, when Hera is inviting Sleep to help her in deceiving Zeus, Sleep remembers how he suffered for acceding to a similar request from Hera "on the day when the high-hearted son of Zeus was sailing from Ilion, when he had sacked the city of the Trojans."[2] Hera had persuaded Sleep to help her then. Zeus had slept, and Hera had driven Heracles out of his homeward course. But when Zeus woke, he was angry, "throwing the gods about the house." Yet, in spite of such memories, Sleep's uneasy scruples are again overcome; Hera promises him one of the Graces for his wife. So Zeus sleeps in Hera's arms, and the Greek defeat is for the moment averted. But, when Zeus wakes, he reminds his consort of that same incident :—[3]

"Do you not remember when you were hung up on high, and I hung two anvils from your feet, and

[1] i. 586 ff. [2] xiv. 250 ff. [3] xv. 18 ff.

4

put a golden chain, unbreakable, about your arms; so there you hung in the upper air and clouds? And, though the gods were angry throughout high Olympus, they could not loose you. Any one of them that I caught, I seized and threw from the threshold, till he came to earth all fainting."

The victim, we know, was Hephaestus.

But the story of Heracles has a graver application than these extracts may perhaps suggest. Agamemnon makes it the theme of his great speech at the moment of reconciliation with Achilles.[1]

"It is to the son of Peleus I shall show my heart; but do you, other Argives, attend and mark well each of you the words that I shall say: they are words which the Achaeans have often used to me, and used them with reproaches; yet it is not I who am responsible, but Zeus and Fate and the Fury who walks in mist, who put grievous Infatuation in my heart in the Assembly on that day when I took away Achilles' prize of honour for myself. What could I do? A god accomplishes all things. Infatuation, the accursed, Infatuation ruins all men. She is an elder daughter of Zeus; her feet are soft, for she does not touch the ground as she moves but steps along the heads of men. Why, Zeus himself was once infatuated, and he, they say, is best of men and gods; when he was cheated by Hera, a woman, with her cunning, on the day when Alcmena was to bear the mighty Heracles in Thebes, city of the lovely ramparts. He boasted, and he said among all the gods: 'Hear me, ye gods and all ye goddesses, that I may say what my heart bids me say. To-day the goddess of birth-travail shall bring to the light a man who shall be king over all the dwellers round about, a man and hero of the race that is sprung from my stock and my blood.' But the lady Hera spoke to him with cunning: 'You will be proved a liar. When the time comes you will not fulfil your word. Come, swear me a great oath, Olympian, that in very truth

[1] xix. 83 ff.

the man of thy stock and blood who shall to-day fall between the feet of a woman shall rule over all the dwellers round about.' "

Zeus swore the oath, and Hera, having got his word, delayed Alcmena's delivery and hastened on the birth of Eurystheus. "That," says Agamemnon, "is why Zeus threw Infatuation out of Heaven and bade her henceforth trouble us mortals."

Heracles, then, throughout the poem, is the symbol of the limitations of Zeus. His tale is a supreme example of the paradox which alone makes the Homeric theology "sympathetic." "I care about them though they perish," says Zeus.[1] But he will not, indeed he cannot, any more than Hephaestus, "hide away Achilles from death when his dread fate comes to him."

When Sarpedon meets and kills Tlepolemos, the son of Heracles, we expect a reference to Sarpedon's own mortality; and we find that reference relevant not only to Sarpedon's tragedy, but also to the main theme of the poem, human life, as embodied in Achilles, its nobility and its transience, so strangely interdependent. In other words, we expect the sort of music that we heard at the death of Simoeisios. Nor are we disappointed. After the insult of Tlepolemos, "You are no son of Zeus. Heracles sacked Troy, and you, as Troy's defender, are of little use to her," Sarpedon kills the challenger. He is wounded himself, though "his Father saved him from death" for the moment. In his weakness he calls for help to Hector whom so lately he was reproaching, and Hector, without a word, gives the best answer by pressing on against the enemy.[2]

Then his bright companions laid the god-like Sarpedon under a lovely oak, the tree of Aegis-bearing Zeus. And strong Pelagon, who was his dear companion, drew the ashen spear from his thigh. His spirit left him, and a mist came over his eyes; but he revived, and the north wind blew on him and refreshed him as he painfully struggled for his breath.

[1] xx. 21.   [2] v. 689 ff.

Presently, when Sarpedon and Patroclus are facing one another, Zeus will pity them and say to Hera :—[1]

"Ah, woe is me! now that Sarpedon, dearest of men to me, is fated to be killed by Patroclus, son of Menoitios ; my heart is divided within me : shall I snatch him alive from the fearful fight, and set him down safe at home in the rich country of Lycia, or slay him now at the hands of the son of Menoitios?"

And Hera will answer : "Dread son of Cronos, what is this word that you have spoken? Will you save from lamentable death a man who is doomed, and whose fate was long ago decided?"

If Zeus breaks his own rules, other gods and goddesses will break them. But this much, says Hera, he can do for Sarpedon if he will :—[2]

"When his life and spirit have left him, send Death and sweet Sleep to carry him until they come to the country of broad Lycia, where his brothers and his kinsmen shall bury him with the honours of the grave : that is the prize of honour of the dead."

In that passage there is no mention of the tale of Heracles ; but critics who desire to understand the art of Homer will not forget that Hera, only a little while before, was talking to some purpose with "Sleep, the brother of Death."

So, at last, we shall hear how Apollo,[3] at a word from Zeus, "stepped down over Ida's mountain to the dread battle, and lifted the bright Sarpedon away from the weapons, and carried him a long way off. He washed him in the waters of a river, and anointed him with ambrosia, and put immortal garments on him ; then gave him a swift escort to carry him to his home, Death and Sleep, who quietly laid him down in Lycia's rich country."

This little episode of the meeting of Tlepolemos and Sarpedon is relevant first to Diomed's story ; because in the pattern it makes a fine companion picture to the meet-

---

[1] XVI. 133 ff.   [2] XVI. 453 ff.   [3] XVI. 676 ff.

ing of the son of Tydeus with Sarpedon's friend. It is also relevant to the main story of the "Iliad" because (with other touches) it makes significant the meeting of Patroclus and Sarpedon. Take away Sarpedon's beauty, and you rob Patroclus of his tragic greatness. And, finally, the beauty with which the poet has invested his Sarpedon is meant to add to the significance not only of Patroclus, but of Hector, and above all of Achilles. But, of course, if you believe that the last movement of the "Iliad" is a late addition—unnecessary to the poem as a work of art—you can as easily get rid of Glaucus and Sarpedon as of any other of the poet's minor characters. The gifts of the gods we needs must carry. But the meanest of critics can reject, if he likes, the gifts of the Muse.

Sarpedon, then, lies wounded, but Hector and Ares are raging. It is time for Diomed's second great adventure. This is heralded by a magnificent Olympian intervention. Hera bestirs herself, prepares her marvellous war-chariot, and calls Athene. Athene, nothing loath, puts on her aegis with the Gorgon's head, surrounded by the shapes of Rout, Strife, Courage, and Battle-cry. Zeus himself, having no great love of Ares, gives permission, and the goddesses drive down to the battle-field. Hera with a great shout, inspires the Achaeans. Athene seeks out Diomed. She finds him resting, a little tired by his wound, needing a stimulus. He receives it: "You are not like your father Tydeus. He was a little man, but he could fight."[1] She bids him face even Ares, and herself takes the reins from Sthenelos and drives the hero's car. So the modest Diomed at last wounds Ares, who flies to Heaven and gets small comfort from the Father of the Olympians, but is duly tended by Paieon, the divine physician.

Ares wounded, the gods retire, and leave mortals to fight out their quarrel alone. Ajax kills Akamas. Diomed kills Axylos, "a friend of man," with his charioteer; his riches and his hospitality avail him nothing. Euryclos kills Drysos and Opheltios, and then strives after Aisepos

[1] v. 800.

and Pedasos, "whom a Naiad bore to Boukolion; in secret wedlock she bore him; Boukolion mingled with her in love and wedlock when he was shepherding his sheep." And many others killed and were killed.

Menelaus took Adrastos alive, and would have spared him when he offered ransom, had not Agamemnon sternly forbidden it: "Let no Trojan escape—not even the child in the mother's womb." The savage cry stands in sharp contrast to the scenes of human friendship with which the story of the first day's fighting is to end. Finally, having sent off Hector to Troy to arrange for solemn supplication (the prelude to his scene with Andromache), Homer is ready to complete the Diomed episode.

In the prelude, the review, Diomed showed his modesty and self-control under Agamemnon's insults. His first exploits culminated in the wounding of Aphrodite. The meeting with Apollo was the sequel. In the second series of his exploits he has wounded Ares, and his modesty is again to be put to the test. It is not found wanting. After Hector has left the field, Diomed meets a human antagonist who bears himself very nobly. It is the Lycian Glaucus, Sarpedon's friend. "Who are you?" Diomed asks. "If you are mortal, I will fight you." [1]

> " But I will not fight against the gods of heaven. Even great Lycurgus, son of Dryas, who strove against the gods of heaven, did not live long. He chased the nurses of the raging Dionysus over the rocky mountain of Nysa; they dropped their sacred emblems as the murderous Lycurgus lashed at them with an ox-whip. And Dionysus fled and dived beneath a wave of the sea; Thetis took him into her bosom, all trembling in his terror at the shout of the man. But afterwards the easy gods were angry, and the son of Cronos made Lycurgus blind, and he did not live long."

Does not the reference to Thetis bring a thought of Achilles? [2] Anyhow, the dialogue that ensues, though it is humorous as well as charming, is illuminated by the same tragic vision of life that makes us care for Achilles.

[1] VI. 123 ff.   [2] Cf. XVIII. 394 ff.

The bright son of Hippolochus replied: " Great-hearted son of Tydeus, why do you ask my lineage? As the generations of the leaves, such are the generations of men. The leaves are scattered by the wind on the earth, and the living wood brings other leaves to birth, and the season of the spring comes on again: so one generation of men springs to the birth, and another ceases. Yet if you wish to learn my origin—that you may know it well —there are many men who know it. There is a city Ephyra in Argos . . . where once lived Sisyphos, the craftiest and most gainful of men. . . ."

So Glaucus tells the story of his great ancestors, particularly of his grandfather Bellerophon. The tale might serve, as Homer very well knew, to illustrate a sermon on the text of Achilles' apologue about the two Jars of Zeus. Bellerophon, after his life's adventures, became a homeless wanderer " eating his heart out and avoiding men," like the unfortunate to whom Achilles said, " the gods give their bad gifts only;" and the crown of his misfortune was that Ares killed his son in battle.[1]

But Diomed, when he heard the story, rejoiced, and planted his spear in the ground, and spoke to Glaucus kindly:—

" You are a friend!" he says. " We are friends through our fathers. Oeneus, my grandfather, once feasted yours, Bellerophon. My father Tydeus I do not remember; he left home to go fighting when I was a child. Anyhow we are friends—I am your host in Argos and you mine in Lycia. Let us avoid each other in the battle. We will exchange our armour that the others may know that through our fathers we are friends."

So they embraced and pledged their friendship. " And the son of Cronos on that day robbed Glaucus of his sense; for he exchanged his armour with the armour of the son of Tydeus; gold for bronze, the worth of a hundred oxen for the worth of nine."[2] And Glaucus was descended from the craftiest and most gainful man that ever lived!

The humour is delightful, but the poet never forgets that

---

[1] VI. 203 ff. [2] VI. 234 ff.

he intends to make Patroclus wear the armour of Achilles, nor that his poem is to end with the meeting of two enemies strangely united by their sense that one is a father and the other a son.

The final panels of this noble story of the first day's fighting need not long detain us.   It will be remembered that the narrative began with the challenge of Paris to Menelaus, the truce, and the abortive duel.   We were introduced to Priam, and we saw the loveliness of Helen.   The corresponding panels, at which, after Diomed's great exploits, we are now arrived, are similar in form; certainly they are not less beautiful, and they owe something of their beauty to reminiscences of the earlier panels.   Hector returns to Troy and meets Hecuba, his mother.   She begs him to drink, but he refuses.   He bids her go with the Trojan women in solemn supplication to Athene.   So she took from her treasure-chest a lovely broidery, a robe of Sidonian workmanship which Paris brought with him when he came home with Helen, and offered it to Athene in her temple. But the goddess rejected her prayer.

In the pattern this little scene of Hecuba's prayer corresponds to the Priam scenes of the earlier panel.   Hector, meanwhile, has gone to the house of Paris, calling Paris back to the field.   He listens for a moment to Helen's self-reproaches—as graceful as they are flattering to the hearer : she could wish that, "since the gods devised such evils for her, she had been the wife of a better man"—of whom but Hector ?[1]   But he has no time or inclination for such talk.[2]

"Do not ask me, Helen, to sit down.   Though you are so fond, you will not persuade me.   My heart is already eager to be back helping the Trojans who sorely miss me.   But do you stir up Paris; or rather let him make haste himself, so that he catch me while I am still in the city; for I am going home to see my household, my wife and my infant son.   I do not know if I shall come back to them again."

Then follows the famous interview with Andromache at

[1] VI. 350.   [2] VI. 360 ff.

the Scaean gate. When he reached the Scaean gate [1]—by which he was to go out to the battle, and at last to his death—

His wife, the wife of many gifts, came running to meet him, Andromache the daughter of great-hearted Eetion. Eetion who dwelt under woody Plakos in Thebe under the hill, ruling among the Cilicians : it was his daughter that was wife to Hector of the brazen helmet ; and she met him, and with her came a handmaiden carrying a child on her bosom, a gentle-hearted boy, a baby, the beloved son of Hector, like a beautiful star. Hector called him Scamandrios, but the others called him Astyanax, defender of the city, because it was only Hector who saved Troy.

It was from the sack of Thebe by Achilles that Agamemnon took the child of Chryses prisoner, and Achilles took Briseis. The poet knows his business.

Andromache speaks :—[2]

" Sir, your own courage will destroy you. You have no pity for your little son, and for me, unfortunate, who soon shall be your widow . . . better for me to die when I lose you. I shall have no other comfort when you meet your fate, but only grief. I have no father and no lady mother. My father bright Achilles killed, who sacked the prosperous city of the Cilicians, high-gated Thebe, and killed Eetion. But he did not strip and rob him—his heart was modest and prevented that ; he buried him with his shining armour and reared a mound of earth above him. And nymphs of the mountains, daughters of Aegis-bearing Zeus, planted about it elm-trees. But my brothers, who were seven in the palace, all went to Hades in one day. All of them the swift-footed bright Achilles slew, with their shambling cattle and their white-fleeced sheep. But my mother, who was queen under woody Plakos, he brought here with other possessions, but returned her home, taking abundant ransom for her, so that she died in her father's halls by a shaft from the goddess Artemis, lover of archery. You, Hector, are my father and my mother."

Such are Andromache's memories of the man who is to kill her husband. The poet means Achilles not only to kill Hector, but to drag his body in the dust : and he means it to be tragic that Achilles of all people should thus treat him. He also means his bright swift-footed hero to give the body back, in the end, to Priam. Is not all this devised by the poet of Simoeisios, the poet of Sarpedon, and the poet of the Shield ? Andromache begs her husband to behave like a cautious general. " Stay here," she says, " on the tower, and marshal the people by the wild fig-tree, where the city is most approachable, the wall most open to attack." [1] Presently Hector is to stand at the Scaean gate, and Achilles is to come on him like a race-horse, like a baleful autumn star. When Priam, telling him of all the sons he has lost, begs him to pity his grey hairs and to come in ; when Hecuba bares her breast and entreats his pity, Hector will stand firm. But he will run at last, and his enemy will pursue him [2] " by the watch-tower and the wild fig-tree, until they come to the springs of the Scamander, where the wives of the Trojans and their lovely daughters used to wash their shining garments, in the days of peace before the Achaeans came." It is at the watch-tower and the wild fig-tree that Andromache now begs Hector to remain.

Hector's reply is no less vital for the sequel than Andromache's appeal. It gives him his own nobility and makes him the worthy antagonist of Patroclus and Achilles. He fights for honour, knowing that the fight is useless. He cannot shirk, because he cannot bear it that the Trojans and their wives should see him shirk. But he knows, however he may fight, that the day will come when Ilion shall fall and Priam and his people perish. His only hope is to die before he sees his wife a prisoner.

So, with the exquisite scene of the baby frightened at the helmet, the father's prayer for his son, the mother's unforgetable smiles and tears, Andromache goes back to her loom and Hector to his fighting. Paris, in fresh bright armour, joins him, prancing like a well-fed, well-groomed

---

[1] VI. 433 ; cf. XXII. 6 ff.   [2] XXII. 145 ff.

horse. They meet, and this time it is without reproaches from Hector, "just as Hector was about to turn away from the place where he had talked with his wife." The sweet word ὀαριστύς,[1] which describes the talk of lovers, is to come to Hector's mind in the fight, and again at the crisis of his fate.

For the last scene of the day, Athene and Apollo join hands to stop the battle. They agree that Hector shall be induced (by a word from the prophet Helenus) to challenge the Achaean champions to a duel, and they take their places as spectators " like birds, like vultures, on a high oak, the tree of Aegis-bearing Zeus." [2]

Hector challenges, and the terms of his challenge are pro-phetic—whichever wins shall take his enemy's armour ; but let the body of the vanquished be given up for burial. Menelaus volunteers to meet him, but Agamemnon will not let him go. "Even Achilles," he says, "avoids Hector in battle." For a moment no one stirs. Then Nestor cries, "Shame on us : how grieved would Peleus be, who took such pleasure in my account of the Argive heroes. I wish I were as young as when I killed Ereuthalion." [3] It is a story Nestor is proud to tell ; we remember he contrived to mention it to Agamemnon in the morning, at the review. That is how Homer weaves his pattern.

Nine champions volunteer; lots are cast and Ajax is chosen. He arms and the people pray to Zeus that he may at least prove equal to his great opponent, but as he strides into the field he is so terrible and so grim that the Trojans tremble. " Hector's own heart beat faster but he could not fly nor go back into the press of men, because he was the challenger." [4] That touch also is prophetic. So is the shout of Ajax : [5] " Now Hector, you shall know in single combat, what good men there are among the Danaans be-sides Achilles, the breaker of men, the lion-hearted."

The fight of course is equal. Neither of these great warriors is a Paris or even an Aeneas, to be snatched to ignominious safety by an Aphrodite. At nightfall they are still fighting and the heralds have to part them. Hector,

[1] VI. 515.   [2] VII. 59 ff.   [3] VII. 124 ff. ; cf. IV. 319.
[4] VI. 216.   [5] VI. 226 ff.

who does not stand on form, gives Ajax the technical advantage by first proposing that the duel should end. So the day's fighting ends with courtesy and an exchange of gifts between these two great champions. If Homer's patriotism makes him insist that the Trojans are relieved to see their Hector safe escaped from Ajax, we do not complain. He contrives to give the honours of the field to the Achaeans, and yet makes it plausible that the Trojans, who used to hide from Achilles behind their walls, now boldly treat the plain as their proper battle-field.

We are not surprised to find that the day's story ends with the repetition of a scene with which it began. Agamemnon sacrifices and Nestor gives advice, " Let a truce be arranged for burial of the dead, and let the time of truce be used for the building of a wall and trench to defend the camp." The Trojans held an assembly (noisy, we are told, like the Greek assembly of the morning) at which the wise Antenor proposed that, since oaths had been broken and Menelaus had really won, Helen should be surrendered. Paris refused, but proposed a compromise; he would not give up Helen, but would surrender all the property he had brought with him from Argos. To that proposal Priam weakly assented. It would have been better for him to have made Antenor's view prevail. But the poet, who assumes that his hearers have an ear for such matters, does not think it necessary to drive home the point. The compromise is of course rejected by the Achaeans. Diomed by this time—you may be sure it is not Agamemnon—is certain that Troy's fate is fastened on her; but Agamemnon agrees that a compromise is worthless; a truce for the burial of the dead is all that can be granted. So, in the morning, the two sides meet, washing the traces of battle from their bodies in the river. Both armies bury their dead and the Greeks are building their new defences, Poseidon watching them suspiciously.

And when the sun set both sides ate and drank—some ships had just arrived with wine from Lemnos for the Achaeans—but as they feasted Zeus the Counsellor devised evil for them and pale fear seized them.

CHAPTER IV

THE SECOND DAY OF BATTLE AND THE GREEK DEFEAT

THE first day's battle ended with a sense of impending misfortune. The building of the wall and trench is the material expression of the Greek anxiety. The second battle brings the first serious defeat. Homer has given us the exploits of Diomed partly to make us feel that his Greeks are better fighters than the Trojans, partly to make us care for their defeat when it comes. The defeat itself is not unnaturally described in a comparatively short episode, vigorous in movement, it is true, but neither in length nor in elaboration rivalling the narrative which began with Agamemnon's dream and ended with the truce. Its themes are many of them variations on themes from that great story, to which it is related somewhat as are the two assembly scenes of Book II to the assembly scenes of Book I. In the pattern of the "Iliad" as a whole this episode falls naturally into place as the end of the first battle-movement, the introduction to Agamemnon's offer of amends. On the other hand, many of its themes strike for the first time chords which we are to hear, with all the more emotion because we are thus prepared, in the tragic battles of the sequel.

The day begins with a formal Olympian assembly, summoned and addressed by Zeus. He forbids the gods and goddesses to interfere at all in the coming fight. Any who dare to intervene will come back to Olympus shamefully mauled, or Zeus himself will hurl them down to Tartaros, "as far below Hades as the sky is above the earth." If they doubt his power to carry out his threat, let all the immortals unite against him, tie a golden chain to the sky and try to drag him down.[1] He, by himself, will drag them up, earth, sea, and gods and goddesses, twist the chain round a crag of Olympus, and leave them hanging helpless in the air. The gods and goddesses are appalled and silent. But Athene, who is her father's favourite, contrives to win a concession from him. Although the gods may not actively take part, they may help their friends with counsel. Of this permission Hera presently avails herself.

So Zeus, in golden armour, drove off in his miraculous car to Ida, where he took his seat to watch the battle.

The fight begins with an equal struggle :—[2]

While it was morning and the strength of the day was still increasing, so long the weapons of both sides were shot at one another, and the people were falling. But when the sun was bestriding the mid heaven, the Father stretched his golden scales, and put in them two fates of death that lays men low, one for the horse-taming Trojans, the other for the brazen-shirted Achaeans. He held his balance in the middle, and weighed them ; and the day of destiny for the Achaeans turned the scale. Zeus himself from Ida thundered terribly, and threw a blazing bolt among the people of the Achaeans. When they saw it they were afraid. Pale fear took hold of them all. Idomeneus dared not stand his ground, nor Agamemnon. Nor did the Ajaxes stand, those servants of Ares. Nestor alone remained . . . not willingly: his horse impeded him: it had been hit by an arrow from bright Paris, lovely-haired Helen's husband.

It is a happy inspiration. It amuses us that this should happen to Nestor, who has shown himself so proud of his chariot-tactics, so anxious to assure us that his age does not discount the value of his lectures on that theme. But

[1] VIII. 18 ff.   [2] VIII. 66 ff.

it is serious enough for Nestor. Hector's horses are bearing down on him, and "he would have perished had not bright Diomed quickly noticed it."[1]

Diomed shouts to Odysseus for help; but Odysseus, in his hurry, does not hear him. So Diomed takes the old man into his own car, and together the two face Hector. Diomed actually kills Hector's charioteer, and so great is his spirit that he would have driven back the Trojans and cooped them up in Troy had not Zeus intervened again.

He thundered, and he hurled a terrible white-hot thunderbolt. In front of Diomed's horses he hurled it to the ground. Terrible was the flare of the brimstone burning.

"We must fly," says Nestor. "Zeus is with Hector to-day." "Yes," answers Diomed, "but I cannot bear to think of Hector boasting that I fled from him." "No one will believe him," Nestor answered. But when Diomed consents to go, Hector shouts after him,[2] "The Greeks have honoured you. Now they will scorn you. You are no better than a woman. Begone, girl, puppet. . . ." The son of Tydeus was divided in his mind. Should he turn back and fight? Thrice he hesitated, and three times Zeus thundered from Mount Ida.[3] Hector was confident. He shouted that Hera was with him. Much good their walls and trench would do the Greeks. "My horses will leap lightly over the trench; and when I reach the ships, remember to have fire ready, that I may burn the ships with fire and kill the men." He is too confident. It is not to be so easy as that. He presses on with a word to his horses which reminds us exquisitely of Andromache.[4] He is eager for booty. He hopes to get the golden shield of Nestor, and to take "from Diomed's shoulders the flashing breastplate that was made for him by Hephaestus."[5] These are the first notes of the tragedy of Hector.

That is the end of the first panel. At that moment Hera intervenes. Just as the Quarrel of the two great princes

---

[1] VIII. 90 f. [2] VIII. 162 ff. [3] VIII. 179 f.
[4] VIII. 186 ff. [5] VIII. 195.

fell into two parts, with the intervention of Athene, sent
by Hera, marking the division ; just as Athene, sent by
Hera, intervened between the two scenes of the second
day's assembly, so in this battle-story there are two main
scenes, and between them Hera's intervention.

Could she have persuaded Poseidon to help her, she
would have openly defied the command of Zeus. But
Poseidon, though she jumped in her seat with anger [1] and
shook the whole of Olympus, declined the perilous adventure.   Still, she was able to inspire her Greeks, and
that, for the moment, would serve :—

> Hector,[2] the son of Priam, like swift Ares, was driv-
> ing the Greeks before him, and he would have set alight
> the ships with blazing fire, had not Hera put it into the
> heart of Agamemnon to bestir himself and rally the
> Achaeans.   He strode along the huts and ships of the
> Achaeans, gripping his great purple robe in his huge
> hand ; and stood on the vast black ship of Odysseus,
> which was in the middle, best for shouting both ways,
> and shouted very clearly—"Argives, disgraces, splendid
> only in your beauty, where are your vows and boasts of
> the days when we said we were great fighters ; when in
> Lemnos you would talk and boast, as you sat and ate
> much flesh of straight-horned cattle, and drank your
> bowls of wine, and promised you would each of you be
> worth a hundred or two hundred Trojans in the fight ?
> And now you are all not worth this one ! "

Then he prayed to Zeus that his army might not perish,
and Zeus a little relented.   He sent an eagle as a sign of
it,[3] and the Greeks rallied.

Though Diomed was first out and over the trench, nine
others followed, and the ninth was Teucer.   He was an
archer, and he serves in the pattern as a less treacherous
counterpart to Pandaros.   When he had shot his man,
Teucer would run back and take shelter under the shield of
his brother Ajax, "like a child running to its mother." [4]

---

[1] VIII. 199.   [2] VIII. 215 ff.   [3] VIII. 247.   [4] VIII. 271.

He shot eight times, and each arrow found its target, but the ninth, which was meant for Hector, missed :—[1]

He hit Gorgythion, a noble son of Priam, child of the lovely Castianeira, like the goddesses in beauty. As a poppy bows its head, when it is heavy with seed and with the rains of spring, so he drooped his head on one side, under the weight of his helmet.

Again Teucer aimed, and missed. But this time he hit the charioteer of Hector. And Hector had to find another, Cebriones, whom we are to meet so often in the sequel. In the first panel, we remember, Diomed killed Hector's charioteer. The repetition of incident calls attention to the importance of Cebriones. Then Hector hurled a great rock at the archer as he was aiming yet another arrow, and broke his arm. "Ajax did not fail his brother, when he fell, but ran and stood over him and covered him with his shield." [2]

So the rally is at an end. Hector is again driving back the Achaeans, cutting off stragglers "like a hound that worries a beast it is pursuing." [3] The Achaeans are rushing madly behind their defences, shouting and praying, while "Hector, with the eyes of a Gorgon or of Ares the destroyer of men, goes driving his horses with their lovely manes amid the tumult."

Hera could bear it no longer. She appealed to Athene. "Is it not monstrous that the Greeks should be destroyed by one man's violence? Hector is raging most furiously." The crisis recalls the moment when the Queen induced Athene to go down with her against Ares. Athene then was a willing second to Hera, and Zeus approved. This time Athene takes the lead, and cunningly encourages the indignant Hera to defy her husband. She uses for the purpose, very subtly, the hated name of Heracles. [4] "Hector raging?" she asks. "No, it is my father who is mad. Hard-hearted he is! Always crossing me! And ungrateful too—often enough I used to help his son in his troubles with Eurystheus. But for my aid he would never have got back

---

[1] VIII. 302 ff.   [2] VIII. 331 ff.   [3] VIII. 338 ff.   [4] VIII. 358 ff.

5

from Hades, where he was sent to fetch up Cerberus.   Zeus
has forgotten all that.   I am nothing to him now.   He
thinks of nothing but Thetis and her prayers for Achilles.
Very well.   A time shall come when Zeus shall love me
again.   Meanwhile, let us defy him.   Get ready your car.
Let us arm and go down to battle!"   And the white-armed
goddess did not disobey her.

Of course this is a doublet of the scene in the Diomed
episode.[1]   But both scenes are Homeric.   The change of
emphasis which makes Athene here the leader, and the
delightful malice of her appeal to Hera's well-known hatred
of Heracles, stamp the work as Homer's.   So the car is
brought, and the goddesses arm, and down they drive—
but Zeus sees them, and sends Iris with a warning.   If the
goddesses persist, he will send a thunderbolt that will lame
the horses, turn the two rebels out of their chariot, and leave
them so much damaged that for years they will not recover,
"that the grey-eyed goddess may know what it means to
fight against the Father : with Hera I am not so angry.
. . . It is her habit to rail against what I say." [2]

This message was enough for Hera, and the rebels drove
home.   The Hours stabled their horses and put up the car,
and the goddesses sat down on their golden couches with
the other gods, vexed and grieving.

Zeus too drove home from Ida, and Olympus shook beneath his feet.   This time Athene was silent, but Hera
made her protest.   Zeus answered with a revelation—but
only a partial revelation—of his plan :—[3]

> At morning, if you will, you shall see the son of Cronos
> dealing yet more destruction on the great host of the
> Argive spearmen.   For to-morrow is the day when they
> shall fight in a dread press about the body of Patroclus,
> who shall fall.   The ruinous Hector shall not cease from
> fighting till the swift-footed son of Peleus rise up from
> the ships.   My word is spoken.   I care nothing for your
> anger.

To this pronouncement Hera has no answer.

[1] v. 711 ff.   VIII. 406 ff.   [3] VIII. 470 ff.

The bright light of the sun fell into Ocean, drawing down black night over the fertile earth. Reluctantly the Trojans saw him set, but to the Achaeans the black night came welcome and thrice prayed for.

This time, then, there is no help for the Greeks. A second Trojan Assembly, held by the river in the plain, not in the city, marks the triumph of the day. Hector deplores the darkness which has stopped him in his victorious career. But the Trojans shall spend the night in the plain. Watch shall be kept to prevent an Achaean evacuation. The city walls shall be manned by the old men and young boys, and the women shall kindle great fires in the houses to light up the city and prevent an ambush or an entry of the unguarded town.

Thus the Greeks are now the besieged, the Trojans the besiegers. The watch-fires in the plain and in the city complete the perfect pattern. Poetically they derive much of their splendour from the many pyres of the dead that "were always burning" while Apollo shot his arrows, and from the funeral pyres that marked the end of the first day's battle.[1]

[1] I. 52 ; VII. 427 ff. ; VIII. 554 ff.

CHAPTER V

THE MISSION OF THE ACHAEANS TO ACHILLES

ONE thing only is wanting to complete the Achaean discomfiture and to make Agamemnon ready to humiliate himself before Achilles. He has already admitted his mistake, but has not yet been ready to make amends. His admission, we remember, was wrung from him by the panic which followed his ingenious speech in the assembly.[1] Now, with the Trojans waiting eagerly for morning and for their chance of final victory, "while the Trojans kept their watch, the Achaeans were a prey to panic, the companion of defeat." [2] The grief and the distraction of their leader is compared to the effect of two winds, the North wind and the South wind, fighting one another over a stormy sea. The comparison is chosen because it adds one more to the series of wind and wave-similes we noticed in the tale of Agamemnon's "testing of the people."

The heralds are again to summon an assembly. But this time they are to do their office without shouting, fetching each man very quietly. Agamemnon works hard himself at the same task.

The people take their seats, dejected. Agamemnon rises "like a dark waterfall that pours its black water down the face of a sheer rock." [3] He repeats in earnest the proposal of evacuation which he made " to test the people " in his time of arrogance. All are silent. For a long time the people sit listless, depressed. Then Diomed speaks, Diomed, who made no answer when Agamemnon called him a coward before the first day's battle. He has refuted the charge, as all

[1] See p. 32.   [2] IX. 4 ff.   [3] IX. 14.

the Achaeans, young and old, can testify.   And he dares to say that the King's proposal is too cowardly to be accepted.[1]

Fly, if you will.   The way is open.   But we other Achaeans will remain, until we have sacked Troy.   Or if the others go, let them go with their ships to their own fatherland.   We two, I and Sthenelos, will fight on.

That cheers the people, and Nestor, not forgetting the fact that he is old and Diomed young, approves the spirit of the young man's protest.   He adds the practical suggestions that the army should take supper, and that guards be set, and that Agamemnon should convene a Council in his hut.

Accordingly seven companies of a hundred men each are sent on guard, the Council meet, and Nestor, not without careful preparation—"Great King, with you I will begin and with you end my speech [2] . . ." urges Agamemnon to approach Achilles.   He puts his advice as delicately as possible.   But he need not be anxious.   Agamemnon, who is never finer than in this moment of humiliation, seizes the hint and eagerly proposes to make Achilles generous amends.[3]

Your story of my infatuation is too true.   I was infatuated.   I do not deny it. . . . But I am willing to make amends and give abundant compensation . . . seven new tripods, ten talents of gold . . . many slave-women, besides Briseis . . . my daughter for his wife, and seven of my cities to rule over . . . if he will leave his anger. Let him yield.   Hades is stubborn and yields to no prayers : and therefore Hades is the god most hateful to mortals. Let him admit how much greater a King I am than he, how much higher than his my lineage.

It is a generous offer, but the touch of pride at the end helps us to sympathize and understand when Achilles makes his tragic blunder of refusing.   Nestor, in spite of his loquacity, has a way, as we have noticed, of implying more than he says.   Somehow we feel that he is not very hopeful of

[1] IX. 32 ff.   [2] IX. 97.   [3] IX. 115 ff.

the issue, though he pursues his mission of conciliation with all energy :—[1]

> The gifts that you now offer to the prince Achilles no one can carp at.   But come, let us send picked messengers to the hut of Achilles, son of Peleus.   I will take charge myself.   Let them take their word from me.   Phoenix first—let Phoenix, dear to Zeus, lead the way : and then great Ajax and the glorious Odysseus : and of the heralds let Odios and Eurybates go with us. . . .

He will not take the two heralds who were sent by Agamemnon for Briseis.

So, after due libation to Zeus, the son of Cronos, the deputation starts.[2]

> They stepped along the beach of the plashing sea, with many prayers to the Earth-Holder, the Earth-Shaker, that they might easily persuade the great heart of the son of Aeacus, and they came to the huts and the ships of the Myrmidons.   They found Achilles delighting his heart with a clear harp, beautiful, curiously wrought, and the bridge of it silver, which he took from the spoils when he laid waste the city of Eetion.   With this he was delighting his heart, and he was singing songs of the famous deeds of heroes.   Only Patroclus was with him, sitting opposite him, silent, waiting for the son of Aeacus, until he should finish his song.

It was from Eetion's city that Achilles took Briseis.   It was there that he provided for the burial of his enemy, the father of Andromache, and took her mother prisoner, only to set her free for ransom.

Cut out this scene if you will, as immaterial to the poet's original design.   You will not only spoil the formal pattern of the " Iliad ; " you will not only cut away the hero's tragic blunder ; you will also lose your sense of the hero's greatness, and above all of his love for Patroclus.   Formally, the reception of these peace-makers by Achilles recalls the hero's

---

[1] IX. 164 ff.   [2] IX. 182 ff.

courtesy to Agamemnon's heralds, when they came to fetch Briseis :—[1]

I give you good greeting, heralds, messengers of gods and men. Come near. It is not you I hold responsible, but Agamemnon who has sent you for the girl Briseis. Zeus-born Patroclus, come, bring out the girl and give her to them.

So now Achilles rises with Patroclus and says to Nestor and Odysseus :—[2]

I give you both good greeting. You come to me as my friends. It needs must be so, because, for all my anger, you are the dearest to me of the Achaeans.

So he led them in and bade Patroclus bring a large bowl and mix a stronger cup of wine for them. " He spoke, and Patroclus obeyed his dear companion."

When they have eaten and drunk, they deliver their message.[3]

Ajax nodded to Phoenix, but the bright Odysseus noticed, and filled a cup with wine and pledged Achilles. "Give you good greeting, Achilles. There is always a portion for you at the feast, in Agamemnon's hut, or here. But our business is not now with the delights of feasting. Zeus-nurtured prince, we see before us a very great disaster, and we are afraid. There is doubt, if you do not put on the spirit of battle, whether the well-benched ships will be saved or lost. The proud Trojans with their famous allies have pitched their camp near the wall and ships, and they say they will not stop but will attack the ships. The son of Cronos is flashing his lightning, and showing them favourable signs, and Hector, greatly exulting in his strength, is violently raging, trusting confidently in Zeus. He honours neither gods nor men. It is a mighty rage that possesses him.

There are here three rhetorical themes : first the passing reference to Agamemnon, then the admission of the great

[1] I. 334 ff.   [2] IX. 197 f.   [3] IX. 223 ff.

need of the Greeks, then the appeal to pride and indignation, based on Hector's insolence.   The orator is skilful, and
his matter is not casually arranged.   This first part of his
speech is quiet, and introduces, as if accidentally, these three
main themes, which he intends to develop in his third and
final paragraph.   For his speech, like so many of Homer's
episodes, will fall into three main panels, of which the third
repeats with heightened effect the topics of the first.   The
central panel contains the most moving appeal of all, and
matters more than all the rest to the tragic development of
the whole poem.

First, then, the preparation, which we have already heard:
You are honoured in Agamemnon's hut as here: our need
is very great: Hector is insolent and triumphant: our need
of you is great.   Then this:—[1]

Come, then, if you are minded, though late, to save the
sons of the Achaeans in their distress from the havoc of
the Trojans.   You yourself will be very sorry afterwards,
and there is no way to find a cure for the evil, once it is
done.   Nay, take thought in time, before it comes, to ward
off the evil day from the Danaans.   Dear friend, your
father Peleus told you on the day when he was sending
you from Phthia to Agamemnon, "My child, Athene and
Hera will give you strength and victory, if they will.   But
check the passion of your great heart in your breast, for
loving-kindness is better.   Cease from quarreling, which
works evil, that the Argives, young and old, may honour
you the more."   That was the old man's charge to you,
but you are forgetting.   Yet even now draw back.   Let
go your anger which hurts the heart.   Agamemnon gives
you gifts that are not unworthy . . . if you will cease
from your wrath.

That is the central appeal of the great speech.   It is duly
followed by the development of the opening themes.   First
Agamemnon—a full list of his splendid gifts of honour;
then the appeal for the Greeks in their distress—"Even if
Agamemnon is more hateful to you than death, himself and

---

[1] IX. 247 ff.

all his gifts, yet pity all the Achaeans." Then, as the last incitement to the spirit of a proud Greek soldier, " Now you can get great glory, because now you can beat great Hector. He will come very close to you since he is seized with fatal madness. He says that there is no equal to him among all the Danaans whom the ships brought here."

It is a fine speech. The appeal is genuine and moving. But it rather irritates than conciliates Achilles. The arrangement of the material, the psychological *finesse* are just a little too accomplished. That is why he answers, courteously, but with the air of breaking through a cobweb,[1]

> Zeus-born son of Laertes, Odysseus, man of many devices, I must answer this your speech with a refusal, plainly stated, just as I think, and as my action will be, that you may not sit there murmuring at me in your places. I hate the man—I hate him as the gates of Hades — who says one thing and hides another thing in his heart. For my part I will speak my thoughts.
>
> I do not think the son of Atreus Agamemnon will persuade me, no, nor the other Danai, because I find there is no pleasure in fighting always continuously against the enemy. Stay behind, and you get the same portion as if you battle hard. The brave man and the coward are held in the same honour. The do-nothing and the man who has done much, both die. I have no advantage for the trials I have endured, always staking my own life in battle. Like a bird that brings her unfledged young a choice morsel, when she gets one, but herself fares badly, so I have spent many sleepless nights and worked through bloody days in battle, fighting with men for the sake of your good company. I have fought with the ships, and sacked twelve cities of men : and on land I tell you I have sacked eleven in the fertile Trojan country. Out of all these I took my great treasures, and I brought them all to Agamemnon son of Atreus ; and he, who stayed behind by the swift ships, would take them and divide up a little portion, but keep most for

---

[1] IX. 308 ff.

himself. But the other prizes of honour that he has given to the princes and kings are theirs: they have them still. Only from me of all the Achaeans he has taken, and he keeps, a bed-fellow well-pleasing. So let him sleep with her and take his pleasure. Why should the Argives fight against the Trojans? Why did the son of Atreus muster the people and bring them here? Was it not for lovely-haired Helen? Are the sons of Atreus the only men who love their women? Why, any man who is a man sound-hearted, loves his own and cares for her as I loved this one from my heart, though she was got with my spear. But now, since he has taken my prize and cheated me, let him make no trial of me, who know too well. He will not persuade me.

No, Odysseus. Let him take counsel with you and the other princes for the keeping of the enemy fire from the ships. In fact, he has already done much labour without me. In fact, he has built a wall, and dug a trench about it, broad and great, and has stuck stakes in it. Even so he cannot hold strong, murderous Hector. So long as I was fighting with the Achaeans, Hector was never willing to give battle away from the walls. He would come as far as the Scaean gate and the oak. There he once waited for me, when I was alone, and barely escaped my onset. But now, because I do not chose to battle against bright Hector, to-morrow, when I have sacrificed to Zeus and all the gods, and loaded well my ships and drawn them to the sea, then, if you wish and if it matters to you, very early in the morning you shall see my ships sailing the fishy Hellespont, and the crews very eager to row ; and if the famous Earth-Shaker gives me good voyage, on the third day I should come to fertile Phthia. There I have my possessions, which I left when I came on this fool's errand ; and others I shall take back with me from this place, gold and red copper and well-girt women and grey iron, which I have won. But my prize has been taken back in insult by the man who gave it, by Lord Agamemnon, son of Atreus. Tell him everything I say. Tell it

him as I charge you, openly, so that the Achaeans may
be angry too, if he still hopes perhaps to cheat some
other Danaan, dressed as he always is in shamelessness—
but he would not dare, insolent dog, to look me in the
face. I will not join in any counsel with him, nor in
any act. He has cheated me. He has done basely.
And he shall not again come fumbling at me with words.
Enough of him. I will not trouble him. Let him go
his way to ruin. Zeus the Counsellor has taken away
his sense. I hate his gifts. I honour him not a hair.
Not if he gave me ten times, twenty times what he now
promises, or what he can gather together from the whole
world: not for all the riches that go into Orchomenos
or Egyptian Thebes, where most wealth is stored up in
the houses, a city of a hundred gates through each of
which two hundred men can pass with horses and with
chariots; not if he gave me treasures innumerable as the
sand or dust, not even so could Agamemnon persuade
my spirit before he shall pay back in full my spirit's pain
and anguish. I will not marry a girl that is Agamemnon
son of Atreus' daughter, not even if she were to rival
golden Aphrodite in beauty and Athene in industrious
skill. Not even so will I marry her. Let him take
some other Achaean for her, one who suits his mind, and
is more royal than I, for if the gods preserve me and I
come safe home, Peleus himself shall find me a wife.
There are many Achaean women in Hellas and in Phthia,
daughters of princes who defend their cities; from them
I will take whichever one I wish and make her my dear
wife. My strong heart is very eager to be home and
there to marry a true wedded bed-fellow, a proper wife
for me, and enjoy the possessions that old Peleus has acquired. My life is worth more to me than all the wealth
that they say belonged to Ilion, that prosperous citadel,
in the days of peace, before the sons of the Achaeans
came; and more than all the wealth that the stone
threshold of the Archer, Phoebus Apollo, guards at rocky
Pytho. Cattle and rich flocks of sheep can be lifted as
booty. Cauldrons and heads of lovely maned horses can

be had for the taking. But a man's life is not to be got again nor brought back as booty, when once it has passed out through the fence of his teeth. My mother Thetis, the silver-footed goddess, tells me that I carry with me to my end two fates of death. If I stay here and still fight round the city of the Trojans, my safe return is gone, but I shall have undying fame. If I go home to my dear fatherland, that good fame is gone, but I shall have long life.

I advise the rest of you to sail off home. You can no longer hope to see the end of lofty Ilion. Zeus has greatly put his arm round her, and her people has taken heart. So go, and take my message to the leaders of the Achaeans—that is the honourable office of you elders—bid them try and think of some other plan for saving the ships and the people of the Achaeans at the ships, because this that they now have thought of, this plan that I should leave my wrath, will not serve them. Let Phoenix stay and make his bed with us, that he may go with me to-morrow with our ships to our dear country, if he will. I shall not compel him.

" So he spoke, and all of them were silent, touched with awe : for very strongly he had refused."

Unlike the studied utterance of Odysseus, this speech is poured out with the spontaneous vigour of long pent-up indignation. Homer's art has contrived that effect. But there is a pattern here as well, designed to make us feel the magnificence and the tragedy of the hero's pride. The pattern is thus devised : Prelude : I hate a liar. I will give you a plain honest answer. First series : Brave men and cowards, it seems, all fare alike : the good get no more honour than the bad : all of them die in the end. I have suffered : other men have taken the booty. Are the Atreidae the only men who love their women ? I loved Briseis. Central panel : They have built their wall, but in vain : Hector is now triumphant : it was different when I was fighting. Third series : I will go home. I have plenty of wealth of my own. I would not take the wealth of Egypt from Agamemnon. I would not marry the daughter

of Agamemnon if she were as lovely as Aphrodite . . .
Peleus shall get me a wife. The wealth of Troy or Delphi
is not worth my life. Thetis told me it was a choice of life
or honour. I will go home. Afterthought: Phoenix may
stay here and go with me, if he will. I shall not compel
him.

The theme which is impressed by this design on the
hearer's mind is the theme of honour and short life, the
keynote of Achilles' tragedy. He gave up life and wealth
and marriage, and fought for honour. His honour once
outraged, he has become so bitter against Agamemnon
that no offer of material compensation can satisfy him.
He now wants vengeance. He wants to see Agamemnon
suffer, not merely offer amends. To see Agamemnon
suffer, he is willing to sacrifice the Greeks. To see
Agamemnon suffer, he thinks at this moment he will go
back even on his choice of honour. At this moment, in
fact, the hero who chose glory rather than long life, prefers
vengeance even to glory. The mood is not to last. It
will be modified before the end of the present interview.
The afterthought—" Phoenix may go with me : I shall not
compel him," prepares us for the change, and gives this old
friend and servant his opportunity.

The long appeal of Phoenix serves a double purpose.
First, by the intimacy and the simple details of the old
man's reminiscences, the poet makes us feel that Achilles,
after all, is neither more nor less than human, a man who
was once a baby. He himself cannot feel it at this moment.
Secondly, the whole speech is a discourse on the sanctity
of suppliants, the wisdom and the solemn duty of respect
for a suppliant's appeal. The pattern shows with what importance Homer means to invest this theme.

First, then, " If you go, I must go with you." [1]

Dear child, how could I stay behind alone, and let you
leave me? When Peleus sent me with you, on the day
when he sent you to Agamemnon from Phthia, you were
still a child, who knew nothing yet of the fight with its

[1] IX. 434 ff.

equal chances or the assembly where men win honour. That is why he sent me here, to teach you to be a speaker of words and doer of deeds: and so, dear child, I could not be left behind and let you leave me, not even if a god were himself to promise me to take away my old age and make me young and strong again, as I was when I first left Hellas, the land of lovely women, seeking exile away from a quarrel with my father Amyntor.

This reference to his own history introduces the second theme, the solemn duty of respecting the suppliant's appeal, which is developed in a curious story of the quarrel between son and father about a concubine, of the father's anger and the son's first impulse to kill him, and then of the son's determination to leave home. His kinsmen came as suppliants and begged him not to go. They set a watch on him, but at last he eluded them, and escaped to Phthia, where Peleus welcomed him as a suppliant, and treated him as kindly as a father treats his son. So naturally does Homer contrive to develop his theme. This second topic leads back, almost as if by accident, to the repetition of the first, more intimate theme, ''You are my child. . . .''

I have made you what you are, godlike Achilles, because I loved you. You would never go to the feast or eat in hall with any other than me. In the old days, when I would set you on my knee and put the wine-cup to your lips or cut off some savoury morsel and feed you with it, you often wetted the shirt on my chest by spitting out your wine in your helpless babyhood. So much trouble, yes, such care and trouble I have undergone for you, thinking this, that the gods had not given me a son of my own. I made you my son, godlike Achilles, that some day you might save me from an old age of shame and hardship. Nay, Achilles, conquer your great passion. The gods themselves are turned by prayer. . . .

Thus the repetition of the first theme in its heightened form leads on again to the magnificent development of the

second. This intimacy makes us feel that the great, the
tragic Achilles is a human baby, like ourselves. Aeschylus
knew and loved the scene. His nurse in the " Choephoroe," [1]
with her talk of the spoilt baby-linen, contrives to make
Orestes at the moment when he is about to kill his mother,
neither more nor less important, neither more nor less responsible, neither more nor less lovable, than any other human
baby.

The theme of the suppliant's prayer is developed at length.
We know the poet's reason. In the epic as a whole, the
prayers of Chryses to Agamemnon and Apollo, the prayer
of Achilles to Thetis and through her to Zeus, the present
supplication of Agamemnon, through his messengers, to
Achilles, and, at the end, the prayers of Priam, form a
sequence, not without tragic value.

> For Prayers too are the daughters of great Zeus,
> though they are lame and wrinkled and blear-eyed.
> They go behind Infatuation, healing the hurt that she
> has done. . . . If a man rejects them they pray to Zeus
> to send Infatuation to him, and he is harmed.

The apologue, of whose significance we have already spoken,
forms the central panel of the old servant's appeal. First,
the gods themselves are moved by prayer; then, the
daughters of Zeus, who go behind Infatuation; then, "even
the hearts of heroes are moved by prayer." Meleager,
like Achilles, was begged by his friends to help them in
distress. Gifts were offered him, and he refused them.
But at length, when the strain became intolerable, he returned. But he came too late. He helped them in the
end, but he missed the presents he might have had.

That last touch in the old man's appeal is a mistake.
Nevertheless the speech has had its effect. "Come back
now," says Phoenix. "Do not wait until the ships are
burning. If you do, you will have less honour, for you
will not get the gifts." The answer shows at any rate that
Achilles will not go home.[2]

> Phoenix, old father, Zeus-nurtured, I do not need that

---

[1] 747 ff.   [2] IX. 607 ff.

sort of honour. My thought is to be honoured with the honour that Zeus gives: that is the honour that will keep me by the ships so long as breath is in me, so long as my limbs still move.

Clearly enough, Achilles will not go, though he ends his speech as if the question were still undecided. Perhaps he thinks it is.

"Lie down and rest, and at dawn we will consider whether we shall go to our own place or stay." He spoke, and nodded over his eyebrows silently to Patroclus to make up a bed for Phoenix, that they might at once on rising think about their return. Then Ajax, godlike son of Telemon, spoke among them: "Zeus-born son of Laertes, Odysseus, man of many devices, let us go."

Ajax, the plain man, sees that the mission has failed, and that further talk is useless. In his curt summary of the situation he uses phrases to which the sequel gives a touching significance:—[1]

Achilles is passionate, cruel and hard-hearted. He does not give any thought to the friendship of his comrades, the love with which we honoured him above all others by the ships. He is pityless. Why, even from the murderer of his brother a man has taken compensation, or for his own son dead. . . .

To which Achilles replies, "It is all true. But my heart still swells with anger when I think of the insult Agamemnon put on me."[2]

He treated me in the presence of the Achaeans as contemptible, as an outcast who has no honour. So go, and tell him my message. For I will not think again of bloody battle until the son of the wise Priam, the bright Hector, reaches the huts and ships of the Myrmidons as he slaughters the Argives, and sets the ships on fire. At my hut and my own ship I think that Hector, eager as he is for fighting, will be stopped.

That is the end of the interview. The envoys return.

[1] IX. 629 ff.   [2] IX. 645 ff.

Odysseus tells Agamemnon nothing of the hint that
Achilles will remain and at least defend his own ships if
the enemy reaches them.   He reports exactly the formal
answer of Achilles to Agamemnon's formal proposition.[1]
Achilles will have nothing to do with Agamemnon and his
gifts, and says he will go home to-morrow.

The episode ends, as it began, with Diomed.   The rest
are silent, but Diomed speaks bravely.   Achilles is adamant.
Very well.   Let us take supper and go to bed, and to-
morrow let Agamemnon lead us into battle.[2]

So they poured libations and withdrew, every man to
his hut, and went to bed, and took the gift of sleep.

[1] IX. 677 ff.   [2] IX. 707 ff.

6

THE LAY OF DOLON

WITH the failure of the Embassy the first great movement of the "Iliad" is completed. It falls sym-
metrically into five chapters, of which each is in itself an
elaborate and symmetrical design.

First, what we have called the Quarrel Rhapsody, which
includes not only the great scene of the quarrel in the
assembly and the epilogue of the Olympian quarrel but the
prayers of Chryses to Agamemnon and Apollo, the prayer
of Achilles to Thetis, the placation of Apollo by Odysseus
and his crew, and the prayer of Thetis to Olympian Zeus.

Secondly, the dream of Agamemnon and the second
assembly, the panic which follows Agamemnon's ill-advised
attempt to test the people, and, as its consequence,
Agamemnon's first admission that he has been in the
wrong.

Thirdly, the great central story of the first day's battle.
This begins with Paris-Menelaus and ends with Hector-
Ajax. In connection with the first episode we are introduced to Helen and Priam; and in connection with the
last to Andromache and Hecuba. But the main theme of
this central movement is the heroic modesty and success of
Diomed, into which is woven, again by a device of symmetry,
the theme of Glaucus and Sarpedon.

Fourthly, the second day of battle, with the Greek defeat
and panic, and, as its consequence, Agamemnon's readiness
to make amends.

Fifthly, and lastly, with elaborate speeches, corresponding in the pattern to the speeches of the first assembly, the
mission to Achilles, the attempt of Agamemnon to make

good the wrong, and the hero's fatal refusal to accept the appeal.

Everything falls into place. No episode can be spared. The whole series as it stands makes a complete design and a good story. We shall see when we consider the sequel that, without this first movement, we should miss a great part of the tragic splendour of the later scenes. For the moment it is enough if we observe that we have reached a point at which the pattern is, as it were, provisionally finished. With Book XI, when Agamemnon leads his forces into a more desperate battle, a fresh movement, a new treatment of the pattern, begins.

Between the two parts of his great design, Homer inserts an Interlude. Book X is generally criticized because it forms a comparatively independent episode. The poet, working with the method we have been considering, has deliberately marked the pause in that way. The episode is clear-cut, the theme grim, but touched with humour. Its manner, though this point may easily be exaggerated, is different from that of the main story. The book has a style of its own, and the characters behave with a mixture of savagery and slyness which would be out of place in the great battles of the day, but suits the atmosphere of the night watches, the encounter of spies with spies. Just as the heroes, when they go man-hunting at night wear rough skin garments instead of their flashing armour, so their behaviour here is less magnanimous, or at any rate less polished, than in the fight which brings men honour.

That is precisely what the poet requires for his purpose. He wants an episode, clearly designed as an interlude, though not quite irrelevant to the main theme, a decorative panel, marking the point at which the introductory series is completed and the tragic sequel is about to begin. Achilles has made his fatal choice. The knot is tied. The development of the tragedy will begin when Agamemnon takes the field. Between the two great movements the poet has set the lay of Dolon.

But the episode is not irrelevant to the main theme.

Some Greek exploit is urgently needed if the army is to take the field for to-morrow's battle in fine spirit.   To start the battle with the Greeks dispirited would be artistically fatal.   The distress which led to Agamemnon's offer to Achilles was crushing in its effect.   The rejection of the appeal is a serious matter.   Something must clearly happen before the army can be ready for a confident attack.   So Diomed and Odysseus, the two soldiers of Athene, so prominent in the first series, are united in a brilliant nocturnal raid.

Again, although the treatment gives the story its own character, the details are contrived to suit the larger scheme. There are touches both of reminiscence and of anticipation. Neither are the result of carelessness or clumsy imitation. These touches are deliberate, and serve to paint the central panel in colours relevant to the main design.   The Diomed of this story is the familiar son of Tydeus, and Dolon's infatuation about horses prepares us for the rôle that will be played in the main tragedy by the horses of Achilles.

We begin with a reminiscence of the beginning of Book II, that is, a reminiscence of the moment when Agamemnon rose to the highest point of confidence and self-deception. With that moment the present crisis is deliberately contrasted :—[1]

The other princes of the whole Achaean host slept by the ships all night : soft sleep overcame them : but sweet sleep did not hold the son of Atreus, Agamemnon, shepherd of the people.   He was full of anxious thoughts. Like the lightning-flashes that are darted by the husband of the lovely-haired Hera when he means to make a great and marvellous storm of rain or hail of snow—and the fields are besprinkled with it—or when he means to open a great mouth of cruel battle, so quick were the pangs of grief with which the spirit of Agamemnon groaned deep in his bosom, and his heart was divided within him. When he looked to the plain of Troy, he marvelled at the many watch-fires burning before Ilium and at the

[1] x. i ff.

sound of flutes and harps, and the hubbub of men: but when he looked to the ships and the people of the Achaeans, he would tear his hair by the roots from his head in prayer for them to Zeus on high, and his noble heart would groan aloud. And this seemed to him the best counsel, to go to Nestor before any other man.

So Agamemnon rose, put on a shirt and sandals and a lion-skin, and took a spear—when Menelaus appeared. Menelaus also could not sleep.

On his eyelids also sleep would not sit, for the fear of disaster to the Argives, who for his sake had come so far over the sea to wage brave war.

The first paragraph drives home, by a clear contrast with the beginning of Book II, the situation of Agamemnon: the second couples with him Menelaus, for whose cause the war is waged. So Book II, which was devoted to the psychology of Agamemnon, is followed by the duel between Menelaus and his rival in Book III.

Agamemnon bids Menelaus help him in collecting a few chiefs for consultation. His instructions to his brother are effectively contrasted with his own behaviour on the occasion of his grand Review.[1]

Speak as you go, and bid the men be wakeful, calling each man according to his lineage and by his father's name, honouring them all: do not bluster or swagger.

"So he spoke as he despatched his brother. He gave him good instructions." He himself went off to Nestor's hut. The old man heard him moving in the darkness, propped himself up on his elbow in bed, and challenged him :—

Who goes there? Who are you, going through the ships at night when other men are asleep? Are you searching for a mule or a man? Speak. Do not come in to me without speaking. What do you want?

The answer comes in words which remind us of Achilles :—[2]

Nestor, son of Neleus, great glory of the Achaeans, you will recognize me—Agamemnon, son of Atreus, whom

[1] x. 67 ff.   [2] x. 87 ff., cf. ix. 610.

above all men Zeus has involved in troubles continuously, so long as there is breath in my body and so long as my limbs can move.

They are the words, heard by us but not by Agamemnon, in which Achilles half-unconsciously revealed the fact that he could not in the long run keep away from the fighting. Odysseus reported to Agamemnon only the formal message that Achilles meant to go home. Nestor, who was present at the whole interview, said nothing. This loquacious greybeard's silence is often as significant as his speech. The more one reads Homer the less one is inclined to scoff at Nestor, though in Nestor, as in all his characters, Homer can see and can affectionately paint the humorous defects that go with all our qualities. Nestor was silent in the interview with Achilles, and said nothing to diminish the effect of the unfavourable answer. But he does not think Achilles should be absolutely despaired of. He has comfort for his chief's private ear :—[1]

Most noble son of Atreus, Agamemnon, King of Men, the Counsellor Zeus will not fulfil for Hector all his thoughts and his many hopes. His troubles will be more than his hopes if Achilles turns his heart from his cruel rage.

We have here a series of light reminiscences, each emphasizing an important point in the main story : first Agamemnon's psychology, then Menelaus as the main disputant of the war, then Agamemnon's psychology again, then Nestor's hint that Achilles is not altogether lost to the Greek cause. After that the Menelaus theme is further developed.

Nestor criticized Menelaus.[2]

I blame Menelaus. I make no secret of it, though he is my friend and I respect him, and though you may be indignant—for shirking so and leaving you to do the work alone. He ought to be at work himself among all the princes, like a suppliant to them. . . .

[1] x. 103 ff.　　　　[2] x. 114 ff.

That repeats the effect of Menelaus' own words to Agamemnon. And in Agamemnon's reply we hear again the note of the King's new modesty :—[1]

> There are times, sir, when I even ask you to reproach him, for he is often slack and backward in the work, not because he is a shirker or light-minded, but because he looks to me and waits for me to give the lead. But this time he woke before me and came to me. . . .

Again, when Nestor goes to wake Odysseus first, then Diomed, who protests delightfully against the old man's more than youthful energy,[2] we are meant to taste the pleasant parallel and contrast with Agamemnon's interview with these three heroes in his grand Review.

Nestor takes the lead at the informal Council which is held outside the trench. He calls for a volunteer to go and reconnoitre the enemy. Diomed offers himself, but asks for a companion. "If two go together, one thinks for the other what is best : but if one thinks alone, one's mind is slow and one's counsel weaker."[3] There are many offers, and Agamemnon, though with more tact, as we should expect, than on an earlier occasion,[4] cannot help hoping that Menelaus will not be accepted. "You will of course chose your companion freely," he says to Diomed. "But do not, from respect for rank, chose a worse man and leave a better man behind." It is a light and charming reminiscence of the scene before the duel of Hector and Ajax.

Diomed chose Odysseus both for his good sense and because he was the favourite of Diomed's own patroness Athene. The company contrived to provide some sort of equipment, good enough for a night-raid, and the adventurers set out. Athene sent a heron as an omen for their encouragement. Both heroes prayed for success, and Athene heard their prayer.[5]

And they stepped out through the black night like two

---

[1] x. 120 ff.   [2] x. 164.   [3] x. 223 ff.
[4] VII. 107 ff., x. 234 ff.   [5] x. 295 ff.

lions, through the blood and the dead bodies, treading among weapons and black blood.

Meanwhile Hector on the Trojan side was arranging a similar enterprise. Dolon, who volunteers, has a character of his own, not without a familiar touch of Thersites :—[1]

> He was the son of a herald and he had much gold and bronze. He was ugly, but he could run : he was an only brother among five sisters.

He was fool enough to think that he could make his way as an eavesdropper to Agamemnon's hut ; but demanded, as the price of his boldness, an oath that Hector would present him with the horses of Achilles. Hector swore it—a false oath " but it made him go." The assumption, of course, was that Hector would capture them to-morrow. So confident were the Trojans.

Dolon sets out, and passes Diomed and Odysseus without noticing them. They see him, but at the suggestion of the cunning Ithacan, they let him pass. Then, when he is well caught, they turn back on him. He thinks at first they are Trojans. Then he realizes, and he runs. There is a chase : " Like two hounds after a young deer or a hare, they pursued him." [2] Presently we are to witness a more tragic man-hunt. Dolon is not heroic. They bring him to a stand, " pale with terror, his teeth chattering," and he offers them a great ransom if they will take him alive. Odysseus gives him no sort of promise. " Cheer up. Do not worry about your death : but tell me quite exactly. . . ." It is just enough to make the coward think that he can save himself by treachery. Accordingly he tells them not only about Hector's dispositions but about his own infatuated notion that he might some day drive the horses of Achilles. His enthusiasm for horseflesh is genuine ; but Homer also wanted another reference to the horses for his pattern. Finally Dolon, who by this time feels almost comfortable, informs his captors about Rhesus and the Thracians, all unguarded at the edge of the Trojan camp, with horses [3] " the most lovely and the biggest that ever I

---

[1] x. 315 f.   [2] x. 360 f.   [3] x. 436 ff

saw, whiter than snow, and like the winds for running ; and he has brought a chariot with him, well turned out with gold and silver, and armour of gold, wonderful, a marvel to see."

" Now tie me up here," he says, " and do not release me until you have fetched the booty and assured yourself that my tale is true." In answer, Diomed kills him just before he has time to assume the posture of a suppliant and so get a reasonable claim to mercy. It is brutal enough, of course, but it is the usual way with spies. The panel is completed by a dedication of spoils and a prayer from Odysseus to Athene.[1]

They proceed to Rhesus and his horses, kill the King and thirteen of his men, then, while they are wondering what further damage to do, Athene stops them. They must get back to safety. So they drive away the marvellous horses, and the Thracian camp is roused by Apollo, only to find the mischief done.

So back they come, and the pattern of the little episode is duly rounded off. Nestor, the organizer, is the first to hear the horses and to welcome the heroes home.[2] Odysseus makes his report, and the Achaeans are delighted and encouraged. Critics who grudge the heroes their bath and supper on the ground that they have supped already at least twice to-night, do not realize how hungry even heroes may be made by such adventures. We prefer to leave the heroes to their bath and supper, noticing with satisfaction, not only for its piety but for its perfect fitness in the poet's design, the fact that they end their exploit " by taking honey-sweet wine from a full bowl and pouring a libation to Athene."[3]

[1] x. 461.   [2] x. 531.   [3] x. 578-579.

BOOK II

THE PATTERN OF THE ILIAD:
SECOND MOVEMENT

CHAPTER I

THE WOUNDING OF THE ACHAEAN HEROES

Dawn rose from the bed of Tithonus, and Zeus sent Strife to the ships, terrible, with the portent of battle in her hands. She stood at the great ship of Odysseus and shouted, and put courage into the hearts of the Achaeans, making them strong and eager for the battle.

THEN the son of Atreus armed. His breastplate, given him by Cinyras, the King of Cyprus, was a marvellous work of gold and cyanus and tin, adorned with three blue cyanus snakes " like rainbows which Zeus shows as a portent on the clouds." [1] His sword, studded with gold, sheathed in silver, hung from a golden belt; his great round shield had two circles of bronze, twenty bosses of tin, and in the middle a great boss of black cyanus—a Gorgon's head flanked by Terror and Rout. The shield-belt was adorned with a three-headed blue snake. When he shone in his fine armour, Hera and Athene " thundered to do honour to the King of Mycenae, rich in gold."

The horses and men were mustered; there was a great shout as they moved. And the son of Cronos sent Battle-Havoc among them and a shower of rain with drops of blood in it " because he was about to hurl to Hades many strong heads." The form of this magnificent prelude will

[1] XI. I ff.

at once be recognized.   " Sing of Achilles . . . Zeus . . .
glorious Achilles . . . Apollo sent plague . . . Chryses
prayed . . . Apollo came in anger . . . and the pyres
were burning."   So here " Zeus sent Iris with a portent of
battle, and the son of Atreus armed . . . on his armour
were snakes, like rainbows displayed as a portent by Zeus
. . . Athene and Hera thundered to honour the King of
Mycenae, and Zeus sent Battle-Havoc and rained blood."
The last line, " because he meant to hurl to Hades many
strong heads," is of course a reminiscence of the famous
exordium, " Accursed Wrath, which hurled to Hades many
strong lives of heroes."

But the pattern of this second Introduction is not yet
completed.   On the other side the Trojans mustered about
Hector and Polydamas and Aeneas.   Hector in the first
rank with his shield, was " like a baneful star, which shines
out brilliantly, then sinks again into the shadowy clouds." [1]
He flashed in his bronze armour, like a lightning flash from
Zeus the Father.

Zeus—Zeus—Zeus—Zeus, and these two mortals, Agamemnon in his marvellous snake-adorned equipment, and
Hector shining in his armour like lightning, like a star that
is seen and vanishes behind the clouds.

Thus the second movement of the " Iliad" begins with
a new Introduction, similar in form to the Prelude of the
whole work.   But in the second Introduction the central
figures are Agamemnon and Hector, and the moment
chosen is the moment of their armings.   When the movement draws to its close, we shall find that the poet had a
reason.   This picture of the arming of the heroes is the
anticipation of two greater scenes, the arming of Patroclus
and the arming of Achilles.   Again, if Zeus rains drops of
blood at dawn, " because he means to hurl many strong heads
to Hades," in the heat of the day the drops will become a
shower, when Zeus abandons his own son, Sarpedon, to
death at the hands of Patroclus.   The first sound of the
new day is the shout of Strife at the ships of the Achaeans,
rousing the heroes to battle.   It is the first shout of a

[1] XI. 62 ff.

series, which will culminate in the great shout of Achilles
from the trench, when the body of Patroclus shall be
brought home.   Nor are these the only indications that the
poet has designed his second movement on the principles
with which our study of the first part of the "Iliad" has
acquainted us.   But for the moment it is sufficient to observe that the second movement ends when the tragic consequences of the hero's obstinate refusal to be reconciled
with Agamemnon have ensued.   Patroclus is dead.   And
just as the first movement ended with the tragic choice of
Achilles, his rejection of the good advice of the Achaean
suppliants, so the second movement draws to its conclusion
when, after sunset, Hector, who is to be the tragic victim
of Achilles in the final movement, has rejected, for the last
time, the good counsel of his friend, Polydamas.

Between the second movement and the last there is an
Interlude, the exquisite description of the Shield.   This, it
is true, is not so clearly marked an interlude as was the
"Doloneia."   The second movement and the third form
parts of one continuous tragic development.   Nevertheless,
the description of the armour made for Achilles by Hephaestus, inserted, as it is, between the end of the great day's
battle and the dawn of the new day on which Achilles takes
his vengeance, serves also in the pattern as a decorative
and contrasted panel between the second movement and
the third.

Finally, the design of the second movement is akin to
that of the first.   The first, we remember, had five main
divisions: the prayers and quarrels of Book I, the panic
in the Assembly, and the first hint of Agamemnon's repentance, in Book II, the great digression in which Diomed
and Athene delayed the Greek defeat, the second day of
battle and the Greek discomfiture, and finally the vain attempt of the Achaeans to be reconciled with the offended
Hero.   As we have seen, the first chapter corresponds in
the design with the fifth, the second with the fourth, and
the third and central "digression" was itself composed on
the same principle, as a design made up of panels sym-
metrically balanced.

The second movement has the following design : First, the arming of Agamemnon, the wounding of the Achaean heroes, and the triumph of Hector and Sarpedon, the storming of the Achaean wall.   In connection with this first chapter, as a central panel in this first symmetrical design, Patroclus at the hut of Nestor, listening to the exhortation which will make him eager to return to battle.

Then the central digression, the intervention first of Poseidon, then of Hera.   Idomeneus, in this digression, whose function is again to delay the Greek defeat, corresponds to Diomed in the first movement.

Then the Achaean rout, the appeal of Patroclus to Achilles —corresponding, we may notice, in the pattern, to the interview of Nestor and Patroclus—the arming of Patroclus, his triumph over Sarpedon, and his death at Hector's hands. The fighting over the body of Patroclus draws significance from its repetition of motifs used already both in the preliminary fighting and in the central digression ; and throughout the movement the recurrent similes are so chosen and arranged as to mark clearly, in spite of the great multitude of detail, the outline of the pattern we have just described.

Strife shouted, Agamemnon armed, and Zeus rained blood. Hector too armed, and led his men into the battle.   Two pictures next describe the armies fighting.   First :—[1]

So the armies met like lines of reapers facing one another as they cut a swathe of barley or of wheat in the field of a happy man ; and the sheaves fall thick on the ground ; so the Trojans and the Achaeans leapt on one another and cut, and neither thought of baneful flight.

The battle was equal, they were like wolves ravaging.   Strife rejoiced.   Then this :—[2]

While it was morning, and the strong day was still growing, they shot their weapons at one another, and the people were falling.   But at the time when a woodcutter prepares his dinner in the mountain-glade, because his arms are tired of felling trees, and satiety has come on him,

[1] XI. 67 ff.   [2] XI. 84 ff.

and a longing takes him for sweet food—at that hour the Danaans broke the enemy phalanx by their valour.

That sounds familiar. On the second day of the earlier fighting—"while it was morning . . . they shot . . . and the people were falling: but when the sun bestrode the middle of the heaven, the Father stretched his golden scales. . . ." [1] Why does the picture of the woodcutter here so intimately move us? Is it not because of Simoeisios and those others? Simoeisios lay "like a black poplar in a marshy meadow, cut down by a waggon-maker, to be bent into a felloe for his lovely car." [2]

We shall meet that theme again and yet again. When Hector and Patroclus reached the last stage of their struggle, "the Trojans and Achaeans leapt on one another ravaging, and neither thought of baneful flight." [3] Their fight was like the strife of the West wind and the South wind in the glades of a mountain, when they shake the forest, oak, ash, and broad-leaved cornel, with a great crashing of the branches against one another; and there is a noise of the breaking of branches. [4] So they fought for the body of Cebriones :—

"And so long as the sun was bestriding the midst of the heavens, [5] so long they shot their weapons at one another, and the people were falling. But when the sun turned to the hour when the ox is loosed from labour, then . . . to Patroclus appeared the end of life. He met Apollo in the battle."

And even that is not the climax, as we shall presently learn. For the moment we return to the equal battle.

The Trojan phalanx broken, the usual pursuit and slaughter followed. Agamemnon killed the Prince Bienor, with his companion Oileus, and left them "with their breasts gleaming naked, because he had stripped them of their brazen shirts." [6] Then he pursued Isos and Antiphos "two sons of Priam, both in one car." It is the second pair (as often) that matters. [7] "Two sons of Priam . . .

---

[1] VIII. 66 ff., see p. 62.   [2] IV. 457 ff., see p. 42.   [3] XVI. 770 f.
[4] XVI. 765 ff.   [5] XVI. 775 ff.   [6] XI. 100.   [7] XI. 101 ff.

whom once Achilles, on the hills of Ida, bound with the shoots of a young plant, when he caught them shepherding among the sheep, then released them for a ransom." But the son of Atreus did not spare them. He recognized them, for he had seen them when Achilles brought them in from Ida ; and now, as a lion snatches the tender whelps of a hind in its strong teeth, and easily crushes them to death—little good their mother can do for them—so Agamemnon killed these sons of Priam. All the Trojans could do nothing for them.

Achilles, as the generous captain who releases his prisoners for ransom, is already known to us. These examples, so easily worked into the pattern, have a cumulative effect ; they prepare us for the moment when Achilles in his fury, meets again a son of Priam whom he formerly released, and will not spare him.[1] For Agamemnon's sternness we have also been prepared. When Menelaus took Adrastos alive and would have spared him, it was Agamemnon who prevented it.[2] Homer has not forgotten that incident. Agamemnon catches a third pair of victims, Peisander and Hippolochus, whose father was the most insistent of the Trojans that Helen should not be surrendered. He had been bribed by Paris. When his sons, in words which recall the appeal to Menelaus of Adrastos, beg for their lives and offer a great ransom,[3] Agamemnon answers : " If you are the sons of Antimachus, who urged the Trojans in assembly to kill Menelaus, you shall pay for your father's crime." Thus the poet has recalled the earlier episode, but has given it new value by making Agamemnon's motive his great love for Menelaus.

Agamemnon has disposed of three pairs of men. The Greek pursuit is furious. " Footmen killed footmen as they fled, and horsemen, horsemen . . . and Agamemnon pressed on, still killing, still encouraging his Argives : as when destructive fire falls on a virgin wood, and the wind carries it

---

[1] XXI. 99 ff.   [2] VI. 55.
[3] XI. 131 ff. ; cf. VI. 46 ff. One of these men, Peisander, though hit on the breast and hurled from the chariot here, survives, to be killed by Menelaus, XIII. 620 ff.

and rolls it through the forest ; the bushes suddenly collapse, as if uprooted by the onset of the fire ; so fell the
heads of the flying Trojans at the hands of Agamemnon,
son of Atreus.   Many fine horses rattled the empty cars up
and down the bridges of war, mourning for the lack of their
noble drivers.   But the drivers lay on the ground, much
dearer to vultures than to their wives." [1]

Clearly enough we have completed the first panel of
the exploits of King Agamemnon.   If our experience has
taught us anything of Homer's method, we shall expect at
this point some Olympian intervention, followed perhaps
by further exploits from the King of Men.   And, since
Agamemnon and Hector were the two outstanding figures
of the prelude, we shall expect to hear of Hector soon.   In
fact, for anyone who knows the poet's method, the last
words—"much dearer to vultures than to their wives "—
suggest Andromache.   Anyhow, this is Homer's sequence :—[2]

> The drivers lay on the ground, much dearer to vultures
> than to their wives.   But Hector Zeus withdrew from
> the weapons and dust, the killing and the blood, and the
> confusion, while the son of Atreus made his way, still
> vehemently urging on the Danaans.   The Trojans,
> making eagerly for the city, rushed across the middle of
> the plain, past the tomb of the ancient Ilos, son of Dar-
> danos, past the wild fig-tree ; and still the son of Atreus
> made his way shouting, and his unconquered hands were
> blood-bespattered.   But when they came to the Scaean
> gate and the oak, they rallied, and they waited for one
> another.

They fled past the wild fig-tree ; they rallied at the
Scaean gate and the oak.   Does the reader need to be reminded of Andromache's appeal to Hector, at the Scaean
gate, to withdraw his men and marshal them at the wild
fig-tree ? [3]   Perhaps, but the effect of that appeal, and of
the present rout and rally will be felt, however little we

---

[1] XI. 150 ff.   [2] XI. 162 ff.   [3] VI. 433, p. 58; cf. XXII. 6 ff.

may know the reason, when Hector is pursued by the son of Peleus.   The oak and the wild fig-tree, by that time, will somehow seem to be bound up with Hector's destiny. That is what Homer intends.

The Trojans rally, then, at the Scaean gate and the oak ; but some of them are still straggling out on the plain—

> like cows, which a lion drives in panic, when he comes in the dead of night and frightens the whole herd : but to one of them, instant death appears.   He grips her in his strong teeth and first breaks her neck, then sucks the blood and all the entrails : so the son of Atreus followed close on them, still killing the last stragglers as they fled.[1]

It is a heightened repetition of the simile of the lion and the whelps of the poor hind.[2]   But it has developed in a very notable way.   Here is a *motif* of the Shield again.   Just as the reapers in the happy king's field will recall the armies of the Greeks and Trojans, facing one another and still cutting ; so the picture on the Shield of the trailing cows and the bull seized by the lions, who suck his blood and his black entrails, is foreshadowed in this simile of Agamemnon killing Trojan stragglers.[3]

We expected, at this point, not only a reference to Hector, but also an Olympian intervention.   We shall not be disappointed.   The Trojans are still flying, when Zeus, seated with his thunderbolt on Ida, sends Iris to the son of Priam.[4] Hector is to rally the people, but to hold himself in reserve, until Agamemnon be wounded.   Agamemnon once wounded, he may himself advance, and Zeus will give him victory "until he come to the ships, and the sun sets, and darkness falls."[5]   Hector obeys.   He leaps from his car and encourages his men.   They stand firm, and the battle is joined again, Agamemnon still eager and still first in the fight.

The second group of Agamemnon's exploits begins with the formula : " Tell me, Muses, who first came to meet

---

[1] XI. 171 ff.   [2] XI. 113, p. 95.
[3] XVIII. 550, XI. 65 ; XVIII. 579, XI. 171.
[4] XI. 182 ff.   [5] XI. 193-194.

Agamemnon?" It differs from the first, because the poet now means Hector and Andromache to be in our thoughts. That purpose dictates his choice of Agamemnon's victims. First Iphidamas, a son of Antenor, strong and tall, brought up by his uncle, who was the father of the lovely-cheeked Theano, and who gave him his own daughter to wife. He had come straight to Troy from the bridal chamber. He died at Agamemnon's hands " far from his wife of whom he had no pleasure, though he paid a heavy price for her." [1]

Coon, another son of Antenor, grieved for his brother [2] (a pretty touch recalling Agamemnon's feeling for Menelaus), wounded Agamemnon in the arm; but Agamemnon killed him and fought on.

At length, when the blood stopped flowing, the King felt his wound. His pains were like the pains of a woman in travail. [3] The poet is still thinking of Hector's wife. Agamemnon shouted to encourage his men, as he shouted at the beginning of the battle, and was carried by his horses, willing, sweating, dusty, from the field.

Hector's moment has come; it is his turn to shout. With a cry that Zeus is with him, he enters the fight. A new simile shows at once that a new episode is beginning, but that its place in the main design is not forgotten. Hector, like Ares, rouses his men against the Achaeans "as a hunter sets his quick-footed dogs at a wild boar or a lion." [4] Agamemnon, throughout his exploits, has been compared to a lion; the wild boar we shall understand very soon.

Whom, Muses, did Hector kill? Nine chiefs of the Danai, duly named, but without elaborate description; and then a mass of nameless men— [5]

as when the breath of the south wind scatters the clouds, and a great wave swells and rolls high, but the foam is scattered by the blast of the gusty wind; so fell the heads of the people at Hector's hand.

Terrible would the sequel have been for the Achaeans, had

[1] XI. 243.   [2] XI. 250.   [3] XI. 268 ff.
[4] XI. 292 ff.   [5] XI. 304 ff.

not Odysseus called to Diomed.[1] For anyone who knows the first part of the " Iliad," this is the obvious pair. But what if we had cut out the Diomed episodes and the " Doloneia " ?

Each kills his man, and the two heroes press on.

> Turning upon the Trojans they destroyed them, like two wild boars that proudly fall on the hunting dogs.[2]

Each killed a pair of men. Diomed killed the two sons of a prophet, Merops, who was eager to keep his sons from the war because he knew : but they disobeyed : " the fates of black death drew them." [3] Odysseus killed Hippodamos and Hypeirochos. The battle became more equal. Diomed wounded Agastrophos, who could not escape because his chariot was not there to pick him up. " He had been greatly infatuated ; he left his horses apart with a servant, and went rushing himself on foot among the front-rank fighters, until at last he lost his life." [4] That touch is a preliminary to the different infatuation which made Asios, son of Hyrtakos, take his horses over the trench.

Hector saw what happened, and came up to the rescue. " Here is trouble coming for us," said Diomed to Odysseus —"the dread Hector. Come let us stand and fight him." With that he aimed at Hector and hit his head. But Hector's helmet, a gift from Apollo, saved him.[5] Stunned for the moment, he recovered while Diomed was hurrying to pick up the spear, leapt into his chariot, and escaped.

So Diomed turned to strip Agastrophos of his armour, and in the act, was wounded by an arrow from Paris, who took aim at him from the tomb of the ancient Ilos.[6] He was hit in the heel, a touch which reminds us of the legend of Achilles. Diomed, though he is wounded and has to leave the field, has time to pour his scorn on Paris, in terms which form a brilliant sequel to the scattered references we have noticed to the wives of heroes :—[7]

" Archer and wastrel, girl fancier, bow-string nobleman, were you to try my valour face to face with a

---

[1] XI. 312.   [2] XI. 324.   [3] XI. 332.   [4] XI. 339 ff., see pp. 115, 133.
[5] XI. 352-353.   [6] XI. 369 ff.   [7] XI. 385 ff.

soldier's weapon, much good your bow and feathery
arrows would do you! But now you have scratched my
heel, and you make a boast about it. I care no more
than if a woman or a silly boy had hit me. There is no
sting in the shaft of a coward and a ne'er-do-well. Very
different is the pain of a weapon of my wielding: if my
spear touches ever so little it quickly pierces a man, and
his wife's cheeks are torn in her mourning, and his sons
are orphaned. Rotting he lies on the ground, making it
red with blood, and there are more birds than women
round him."

So Odysseus helped Diomed to his car, and was left to
face the enemy alone. He debated anxiously with his
great heart. Should he run? Cowards may run; brave
men take their chance. The Trojans came on; he was
surrounded, and he stood like a great boar at bay among
the hounds and the young huntsmen.[1] He wounded one;
he killed two; he killed a third; then he wounded Charops
the brother [2] of the noble Sôkos—and Sôkos came to the
rescue. A brother, we notice, helping a brother again.
Sôkos wounded him; and though Athene saved his life,
and he was able to kill Sôkos, Odysseus was forced to retire. As he went, he shouted three times for help. Menelaus heard him, and came up with the two Ajaxes.

They found Odysseus, dear to Zeus, and round him the
Trojans, "pressing like yellow jackals round a wounded
stag, that a man has wounded with an arrow . . . and the
hungry jackals worry him in the mountains in a shady
glen: but some daimôn brings up a lion, ravening: the
jackals run: it is the lion who does the worrying." [3] So
Ajax appeared to the Trojans. Menelaus led away
Odysseus, and Ajax killed a son of Priam, wounded four
other men, and, "like a brimming river that rushes to the
plain in a torrent out of the mountain, full of the rains of
Zeus, taking with it many dry oaks, and many pines, and
much rubble which it rolls with it to the sea," so was
Ajax with the Trojans.[4]

[1] XI. 414 ff.   [2] XI. 427.   [3] XI. 474 ff.   [4] XI. 492 ff.

What are these pines and dry oaks that the torrent carries with it to the sea ? They are the tree-trunks, felled by the wood-cutter, and left to dry by the bank of the peaceful river. When it swells to a torrent it carries them away. With this simile the great rally of Ajax culminates. If we look back, we shall perceive the poet's design, and once perceived, it will not quickly be forgotten.

The armies meet at first like lines of happy reapers : but they are reaping human lives. Then, at midday, when a wood-cutter's arms are tired of felling the tall trees, and he turns to take his pleasant dinner in the mountain glade, the Trojan phalanx breaks, and Agamemnon leaps to the pursuit. He kills a prince with his dear companion. He kills two sons of Priam whom Achilles spared when he caught them tending sheep ; he is like a lion that has caught the whelps of a hind. He kills two sons of a Trojan who had treacherously advised the murder of Menelaus. He is like a fire rolled by a great wind through a thick wood : beneath its blast, the forest suddenly collapses.

His victims lie on the field, dearer to vultures than to their wives. His hands are covered with the blood and filth of the fighting. The Trojans fly from him past the fig-tree, but rally at the oak. He catches the stragglers, as a lion catches a cow from a frightened herd. Then Zeus sends Iris to Hector. The Trojans stand their ground at last ; but Agamemnon still leaps on them. Who first meets him ? A newly wedded husband, whom, like a lion, he kills. But the elder brother of the dead man comes to avenge him, and wounds Agamemnon. He pays for it with his life, but Agamemnon, suffering as a woman suffers in travail, has to leave the field. The horses that carry him away are covered with sweat and dust.

Hector leads on his Trojans, loosing them as a hunter looses his dogs at a wild boar or a lion. Himself he rages like a tempest. He kills the princes, and the common people are scattered by him as the foam of a wave is scattered by the tempest. But Diomed and Odysseus face him, like boars that turn on the hounds. They kill a pair

of princes; Diomed kills two sons of a prophet, whose
father would have kept them from the war; Odysseus kills
another pair of princes. Diomed kills Agastrophos, a fool
who has left his chariot behind; but Hector comes to the
rescue of the body. They stand their ground and Diomed
hits Hector, who is stunned, but able to withdraw. Then
as Diomed stoops to take the spoils from Agastrophos, Paris
shoots him in the heel. Paris shouts, "I wish I had killed you,
before whom the Trojans are as goats afraid of a lion." But
Diomed answers: "Your arrows scratch; my spear can kill;
when it hits, a wife is desolate, sons orphaned, and a man lies
rotting, with birds not women to attend him." But Diomed
has to go.

Odysseus is alone. He stands his ground, but is like a
boar at bay among the huntsmen. He wounds one; he
kills two; he kills a third; then he kills the brother of Sôkos,
and Sôkos comes to the rescue and wounds him. Sôkos
pays his life as the price, and Odysseus cries, "When I die,
the Greeks will bury me with honour. The birds will tear
your body; your mother and father will not bury you."

But Odysseus has to yield. He shouts thrice, and
Menelaus with the two Ajaxes comes to the rescue. The
Trojans are like jackals worrying a wounded hind on the
mountains. But Ajax, when he comes, is like a raging lion,
scattering the jackals.

He slays, he is like a flooded river that turbulently carries
to the sea rubbish and tree-trunks . . . the filth of battle,
the bodies of dead men.

It is time for Hector to be brought back into the
picture :—

> Hector had not learnt yet what was happening, be-
> cause he was fighting now on the left of the whole battle,
> by the banks of the river Scamander, where most the
> heads of men were falling, and the battle-shout, unquench-
> able, was loud.[1]

His chief opponents were Idomeneus and Nestor (thus the
poet prepares us for the moment when Idomeneus will be

[1] xi. 497 ff.

the mainstay of the Greeks). And the Greeks would not have yielded had not Paris wounded the physician, prince Machaon, with an arrow.[1] Nestor drives off with the wounded man to the huts. A physician, says Idomeneus, is worth many ordinary men.[2] The pattern itself makes the incident matter to us. Why it is made important, we shall presently learn.

Paris, who retired when he had shot Diomed, has found his way after Hector to the left of the field. (Thus the poet is still developing his pattern. Hector was stunned by Diomed, and Diomed shot by Paris ; then Ajax came to the rescue of Odysseus. Now Hector reappears in another part of the field and Machaon is shot by Paris.)

With Machaon wounded and Nestor gone with him to the huts, the Greek resistance in this part of the field is weakened. Cebriones, Hector's charioteer, points to Ajax in the distance, and begs Hector to bring help where it is more needed :—[3]

I know him well, because he has a broad shield on his shoulders. But let us two drive our car and horses there, where the horsemen and footmen are most violently fighting and destroying one another; where the battle-shout, unquenchable, is loud.

The repeated phrase marks the beginning and the end of this subordinate, but not unimportant panel. We expect the second Ajax panel to begin.

Ajax, in fact, is the theme of the next paragraph. Hector and Cebriones drive over bodies and weapons to the place where he is fighting. The axles of the car and the chariot-rails are blood-bespattered.[4] But so terrible is Ajax that Hector, though his coming daunts the Greek a little, avoids him and attacks the rest. That is dictated by the poet's patriotic heart. Also he is reserving the great clash of Ajax with the son of Priam for a more important crisis. For the present—[5]

[1] XI. 505. [2] XI. 514.
[3] XI. 523 ff. ; cf. XI. 497 ff., quoted above.
[4] XI. 534. [5] XI. 544 ff.

Hector attacked the others . . . and avoided Ajax. But Zeus the Father, throned on high, sent panic on Ajax. He stood amazed, and put behind him his shield of seven ox-hides, and fled; looking about him to the throng, like a wild beast, still turning back, and yielding step by step.

He was like a lion,[1] kept away from a farm by the rustics, who have watched all night with their dogs; he is hungry and tries hard to get his prey; but they drive him off with javelins and burning fagots; and at morning, dejected, he goes. So Ajax very unwillingly retired before the Trojans. "He was like a stubborn ass driven by boys out of a corn-field; they cudgel him, but all their strength is nothing; but they chase him very eagerly, once he has taken his fill of food, and he goes."[2] So Ajax went, but kept turning back on the enemy.

Do not these admirable similes, familiar as they are, gain fresh significance, when we see them not as isolated pictures, but as part of Homer's design? This lion, driven from the farm by men and dogs, spears and torches, is the noblest of a very noble family. And the ass in the corn-field, homely, exactly true to life; have we forgotten that this pattern began with the reapers in the cornfield of death?[3]

Again there follows a subordinate panel; and again it fits the pattern; and again it is important for the sequel. When Eurypylos saw Ajax in distress, he ran up to help him, and hit Apisaon, and stooped to strip the body; and as he stooped, Paris drew his bow and shot him, and he left the field. He is the archer's third victim: the first was Diomed, wounded in the heel; the second was Machaon, the physician; the third is Eurypylos.[4] So Eurypylos left the field, and Ajax still fought on.

So they fought like blazing fire, and, bathed in sweat, the Neleian mares were carrying Nestor from the battle;

---

[1] xi. 548.   [2] xi. 558 ff.   [3] See p. 93.   [4] xi. 583.

they were taking in Machaon, shepherd of the people;
and swift-footed bright Achilles saw and noticed.[1]

It was for the sake of this moment that the whole great
series of the exploits and the wounding of the Achaean
heroes was composed.

[1] XI. 596 ff.

CHAPTER II

PATROCLUS AT NESTOR'S HUT

ACHILLES saw, and noticed :—[1]
He was standing at the prow of his vast ship, looking
out to the sharp struggle and the tearful rout. And
quickly he spoke to his companion, to Patroclus, calling
to him from the ship. From the hut Patroclus heard,
and came out like Ares—for him it was the beginning of
evil. The brave son of Menoitios was the first to speak.
"Why do you call me, Achilles? What is your need of
me?" And swift-footed Achilles spoke and answered
him : "Bright son of Menoitios, delightful to my heart,
now I think the Achaeans will stand in supplication at
my knees: for the need that is on them is past bearing
now. But go, Patroclus, dear to Zeus, ask Nestor who
is this man that he is bringing in wounded from the fight.
From behind he is very like Machaon, son of Asklepios ;
but I did not see his eyes; the mares flashed past too
quickly; they were running so well." So he spoke; and
Patroclus obeyed his dear companion, and stepped out,
running, among the huts and ships of the Achaeans.

Achilles is learning for the first time what revenge is
really like. He is not glad when he sees Machaon wounded.
At this moment, what would happen if the Greeks came to
him again as suppliants? He would probably grow hard
again; but he cares for the Greeks after all. He wants to
be certain that the wounded man is Machaon. He is remembering the friendship of the Achaean heroes. So
Patroclus shall be sent to Nestor's hut.

[1] XI. 599 ff.

The old man who is attending his physician patient, doctoring him with drink from a great cup,[1] which Nestor can lift easily, though an ordinary man to-day would find it hard to move, welcomes Patroclus eagerly, and begs him to be seated.

Patroclus stood,[2] refusing, and spoke thus. " I cannot sit, Zeus-nurtured, venerable prince, and you will not persuade me. I was sent by one who claims respect, and whose anger is to be feared, to ask who is this man you have brought back wounded. I recognize him ; I see for myself, it is Machaon, shepherd of the people. And now I will go back with my news, to tell it to Achilles. You know yourself, Zeus-nurtured, venerable friend, what kind of man he is ; severe, and apt to blame, even when perhaps there is no fault.

Of course Patroclus has run to Nestor's hut, and now his loyalty to Achilles, his anxiety not to exceed his mandate, is struggling with his great respect for this Zeus-nurtured, venerable prince, and with his longing to be one of the Greeks again. But Nestor does not mean to let him go. The old diplomatist, as we have seen, knows on occasion how to hold his tongue; he also knows how to speak. What Patroclus needs, if he is to be used, as the old man intends, for an appeal to Achilles, is a little time, away from that great indignant presence. So Nestor talks. What is said matters less to him than the fact that he can keep Patroclus waiting. He will talk of his own youth and fire the young man's fancy ; but, above all, he will win time. The heart of Patroclus will do the rest.

" Why should Achilles care ? " he asks.[3]   " Is he sorry that the Achaeans are wounded ?   Well, he does not know the full tale. Listen. Diomed is wounded, and Odysseus and Agamemnon. And now Machaon. And what does Achilles care ? Is he waiting till the ships are burnt, and we are massacred in spite of all we can do ? I, for my part, am not the man I used to be . . . I wish I were as young and my strength as perfect as it

---

[1] XI. 632 ff.   [2] XI. 646 ff.   [3] XI. 655 ff.

was when we and the men of Elis had a quarrel about an ox-driving, when I killed Itymoneus. . . ."

What is Patroclus to do? He cannot leave this venerable Zeus-nurtured old man in the middle of a sentence. Yet Achilles is waiting, and the old man does not mean to stop. He will talk of the immense booty driven off to Pylos on that day. He will tell how glad his father Neleus was that his son had done so well in this first raid. He will tell how the heralds summoned the people in the morning, and how his father divided up the booty among the Pylians who had debts owing them from Elis—and there were plenty of them. Neleus himself, for instance, had had four horses, prize winners too, stolen from him by King Augeas. He had sent them to compete in races there, and the King had kept them, and sent back the hapless charioteer without them. Well, Neleus took full compensation on that wonderful day. And then . . . when you think the story is over, and Nestor will get back to Achilles, and round off his period, you are delighted (if you care for comedy) to find that Nestor does not think the time is ripe for letting Patroclus go. He is to wait and think about the wounded Achaeans, and think about the cruel obstinacy of Achilles, a little longer. So the story proceeds :—[1]

"So we divided all that booty, and we sacrificed to the gods throughout the city; but on the third day, they all came against us, men in great force, and their horses, in a great invasion. Among them were the two Molions. . . . Now there is a city called Thryoessa, a high hill town, far off on the Alphaeus, on the farthest boundary of sandy Pylos : to this they laid siege. . . ."

So it goes on.[2]

And Neleus would not let me arm for battle. He hid my horses away, because he said I was too inexperienced in war. But all the same, I was conspicuous among the horsemen, though I went on foot. . . .

The old man is getting nearer to Patroclus now; but he goes on as if unconscious—simply garrulous.

[1] XI. 706 ff.   [2] XI. 717.

There is a river called the Minyan river . . . there
we waited until morning, there we sacrificed [full informa-
tion on this point] and took our supper, all in our proper
divisions [you can trust Nestor to remember that detail],
and there were the Epeians eager to sack the city.   But
we surprised them ; at morning we gave battle, and
I was the first to kill a man and take his horses.   He
was a son-in-law of Augeas—married indeed his eldest
daughter Agamede, who knew all about drugs.

A pretty touch for the benefit of the physician and the nurse
who are listening.[1]

And they were utterly routed.   And I myself, like a
tempest, captured fifty cars, and killed two men in each.[2]

Of course Nestor, even now, can lift a cup quite easily
which two ordinary men would find it difficult to move
from the table ; so we must, I suppose, accept his story :
still . . . a hundred men and their fifty cars : it is a re-
markably even number.   But he did not kill the two
Molions ; their father, Poseidon, saved them.   However—
we pursued them . . . geographical details . . . and we
came back . . . and every one " prayed to Zeus among
gods, and to Nestor among men.   That is what I used to
be—but Achilles——" [3]

It is magnificent art, not futile garrulity.   The old man
sees that the time has come to pounce.   With a sudden
click of the mind Patroclus is aware that Nestor's story has
become important.   " But Achilles only, cares nothing
about his valour.   I think he will weep bitterly, but too
late, when the people have perished.   Dear boy " [4]—
ὦ πέπον—you see how it is done.   He could not have said
that at the beginning of the speech.   His artless talk has
given him this magnificent opportunity.   " Dear boy,
Menoitios charged you on the day when he sent you to
Agamemnon from Phthia . . . " then a digression because
he knows that Patroclus is already thinking for himself
about the old man's charge to him.   He remembers his
responsibility for Achilles while Nestor is saying—

[1] XI. 741.   [2] XI. 747 f.   [3] XI. 762.   [4] XI. 765.

Menoitios charged you on the day when he sent you
to Agamemnon from Phthia—because I and the bright
Odysseus were there in the hall, and heard his charge to
you.   We had come to Peleus' house, mustering men
throughout Achaea, land of lovely women.   And there
we found the hero Menoitios in the hall, and you, and
Achilles with you. . . .

Patroclus is to see in imagination the familiar household.[1]

There was Peleus, sacrificing, as it happened, to Zeus ;
and you two busy with the meat ; and we two standing
on the threshold.   Achilles leapt up in astonishment,
and took us by the hand, and bade us sit down, and
gave us all the hospitable entertainment that it is right
to give to guests.   But when we had had our pleasure of
eating and drinking, I began to speak and urge you to
come with us : you were very willing, and they both gave
you many injunctions.   Old Peleus enjoined his son
Achilles always to be first in valour and to surpass all
others.   [It is the common formula, already familiar.
Nestor is tactful ; he does not speak to Patroclus of the
more pregnant words about quarreling and loving kindness.]   And to you, in your turn, Menoitios, the son of
Actor, gave this injunction : " My child, Achilles is more
nobly born than you, but you are the elder.   In strength
he is far better than you, but do you speak soundly ;
advise him well, point him the road, and he will obey,
with a good issue."   That was the old man's charge to
you ; but you are forgetting.

Then comes the application.   Let Patroclus try to persuade
Achilles, "and if he is avoiding some secret of an oracle
that his mother has told him from Zeus,"[2] still let him
send Patroclus in his own armour to battle.   It may divert
the Trojans and give a respite to the Greeks.   " If he is
avoiding some divine oracle told him by his mother from
Zeus ! "   Nestor, though he was silent on the occasion of
the embassy, listened well.   He heard Achilles say, " My
mother told me it was death or honour ; "[3] and he thinks

[1] XI. 772 ff.   [2] XI. 794.   [3] IX. 410.

—he is wrong, but not absurd—he thinks that Achilles is held back by some knowledge about his own fate. He is quite mistaken, of course; but he has hit on that not unnatural explanation for the hero's conduct.

He does not understand Achilles; but he understands Patroclus. His reminder that Patroclus is responsible for his friend, does its work. "He spoke; and Patroclus stepped out running. . . . But when he came to the ships of Odysseus" [1]—Odysseus, Nestor's companion on the embassy—" where they had their place of assembly and of judgment, and where they had raised the altars of the gods" —to remind him and us that he was bound by every tie of loyalty to advise Achilles well—"there, Eurypylos met him," and Eurypylos too was wounded by an arrow from Paris. When he saw Eurypylos, Patroclus pitied him [2] and grieved for him. He asked, "Do you think the Achaean line will hold?" [3]

"No," said the wise Eurypylos. "No, Zeus-born Patroclus: the Achaeans cannot hold. They will reach the ships. All our best men are lying hit, and the Trojans still as strong as ever. But do you save me; take me to the black ship, cut out the arrow from my side; wash out the black blood with soft water, and sprinkle soothing drugs on it—the good drugs that you have been taught, they say, by Achilles, who was taught by Cheiron, the most just of all the centaurs. For Podaleirios and Machaon our physicians, one of them I think is wounded and in sore need himself of a doctor, and the other is in the field, standing against the bitter Ares of the Trojans."

Do you remember how Patroclus first responded to the call of his friend "like Ares"? [4] Do you not think Patroclus felt the meaning in the reference to the drugs that Achilles taught—Achilles, pupil of the most just centaur? Prayers go behind Infatuation, healing the hurt that she has done. So Patroclus, full of pity, tended Eurypylos.

[1] XI. 805 ff.   [2] XI. 814.   [3] XI. 819 ff.
[4] XI. 604, quoted above, p. 106.

CHAPTER III

THE STORMING OF THE ACHAEAN WALL

WE are discovering that the second movement of the "Iliad," like the first, was devised for our delight by a very cunning Muse. But we shall miss the Muse's pattern if we are thinking, as we listen, of archæology or history, of comparative religion or comparative philology, or of anything in fact, however excellent, except the story and the music.

The movement, which began when Zeus sent Strife with the battle-portent to the ships, when Agamemnon donned his armour, with its snakes and Gorgon, when Hera and Athene thundered in his honour, and when Zeus rained blood, is not yet finished. Its first chapter told how the great Greek chiefs, Agamemnon, Diomed, Odysseus and Machaon and Eurypylos, fought and were wounded, until Ajax alone was left as the chief bulwark of the Greek defence. Then, in a central panel, we saw Achilles roused from his indifference by the sight of the physician wounded, and Patroclus first at Nestor's hut, inspired with eagerness to take the field, then, as he ran back to Achilles, stopped again by pity for his wounded friend Eurypylos, whom he tended, as a physician taught by the pupil of Cheiron himself. The second chapter, which follows, corresponds, as we shall see in the pattern, to the first.

Look back, if you have patience, to the imagery of the first chapter. First, Zeus sends Strife, Agamemnon arms, and Zeus rains blood. Then the two armies meet like lines of reapers in a cornfield. Then, at the hour when a wood-cutter takes his dinner, the Trojans break. Agamemnon rages like a lion, like a fire in a high wind, mowing down the forest. Then Zeus sends Iris to Hector. Agamemnon, still like a lion, is wounded. He is like a woman in travail.

Hector is like a huntsman, setting his dogs at a lion or a boar. He is also like a great wind, scattering the foam. Diomed and Odysseus face him, like boars at bay. Hector is stunned and withdraws. Diomed, wounded by Paris, talks of mourning wives and of children orphaned. Odysseus, left alone, is like a boar at bay. He too is wounded, and he talks of a father and a mother unable to bury their dead son. Then Ajax come to the rescue, like a lion scattering jackals, like a torrent, carrying dead trees and rubble to the sea. Then Machaon is wounded by Paris.

Hector comes back and Zeus makes Ajax yield. Ajax is still a lion, driven off from a farm by javelins and torches. He is like an ass whom boys try to drive from a cornfield. Then Eurypylos is wounded by Paris.

Then, the first pattern completed, the interlude. Now comes the sequel, the second chapter of the pattern. First, a great torrent.

The present episode is to culminate in the moment when Hector crosses the Greek wall. Here, therefore, at the beginning, the poet reminds us that the wall was built against the will of the immortals and without sacrifice to them. The day was to come, after Troy had fallen and the Achaeans had gone home, when the gods would overthrow it :—[1]

Apollo and Poseidon brought the strength of the rivers against it. All the rivers that flow from mount Ida to the sea, Rhesos, Heptaporos, Caresos and Rhodios, Grenikos and Aisepos and the bright Scamander and Simoeis, where many shields of bulls-hide and many helmets and a race of god-like heroes fell in the dust. The mouths of all these rivers Phoebus Apollo turned together. For nine days he turned their streams against the wall. Zeus rained continuously that he might make

<hr/>

[1] XII. 18 ff.

the walls more quickly swim. The Earth-Shaker, himself, trident in hand, conducted the whole work, plunging
into the waves all the foundations of logs and stones
which the Achaeans laid with so much labour, and
levelling them by the strongly flowing Hellespont, and
covering the great shore with sand again when he had
blotted out the wall. Then Zeus turned the rivers back
to flow in the stream where formerly they poured their
beautiful water.

That is how this second chapter begins. The first began
with Zeus, Athene, Hera, Strife, and Battle-Havoc, with the
portents, the lightning and thunder, and the rain of blood.
The second answers it with Poseidon, Zeus, Apollo, overthrowing the wall with a great flood. And, to complete
the pattern, very notable in the first chapter was Ajax, like
a torrent sweeping dead trees and rubble from the mountains
to the sea.

This pattern has a purpose. Presently we shall hear of
a rebellion by Poseidon against Zeus, and later of Apollo
sent by Zeus with aid for Hector, to undo the sea-god's
work.

For the moment, however, look again at this new preface,
and notice how it repeats even the imagery of the first
chapter.[1]

This Poseidon and Apollo were to do in later days :
but on that day the battle and the battle-cry were raging
about the well-built wall like fire . . . and Hector was
still fighting, like a hurricane ; as when a boar or lion
among dogs and huntsmen. . . .

The great wind and the torrent, the boar and the lion
and the huntsmen are all of them effective reminiscences,
designed to make this panel a companion and a pendant of
the first.

But this boar, this lion, though surrounded by the dogs
and huntsmen, will not yield. " His own courage slays
him." [2]   That is Hector, the Hector of the tragic sequel.

_____

[1] XII. 40 ff.   [2] XII. 46.

Hector has already driven the Achaeans behind their defences, but he cannot cross the trench. The horses shy at
it. They stand on the edge neighing. The steep banks
and the stakes frighten them. So Polydamas, addressing
"the bold Hector,"[1] advises him to change his tactics, leave
the cars outside, and advance on foot. If Zeus is really
with them, they will beat the Achaeans so. On the other
hand, in the event of a retreat, the cars will be held ready
in good order to pick them up. Hector on this occasion
takes good advice. He will not always take it. His own
courage will slay him.

The Trojans dismount and advance to the attack in five
divisions.[2] They are led as follows, Hector and Polydamas,
with Cebriones, led the first division; secondly, Paris with
two others, the second; the prophet Helenus and the god-
like Deiphobus, two sons of Priam, led the third. But they
had with them as well a notable man, Asios, son of Hyrtakos,
the proud owner of a remarkable team of horses.[3] These
three led the third division. The fourth was led by Aeneas
with two others, and the fifth, the division of the allies, was
captained by Sarpedon, who was of course accompanied by
Glaucus.

Whatever may be thought of Hector's tactics, Homer's
strategy is clear. At one end of the pattern, Hector and
Polydamas; at the other, Glaucus and Sarpedon. In the
second and the fourth divisions, respectively, Paris, the
favourite of Aphrodite, balancing her son Aeneas. In the
centre, with two sons of Priam, the owner of fine horses,
Asios, son of Hyrtakos. This last is the only man in the
whole company so foolish as to disregard the warning of
Polydamas. He is not the last man in the "Iliad" to suffer
for that sort of vanity.

He would not leave his car and horses outside. He was
a fool, says Homer.[4] He was to fall ignominiously by the
hand of Idomeneus. But for the moment, this is what

happened.   He found a gate open—left open for stragglers
—and dashed through it, followed by his men, who shouted
and declared that the Achaeans could not stop them : they
would reach the ships.   They were fools, says Homer.[1]
At the gate they found two heroes waiting for them,
Polypoites and Leonteus, like tall oaks that stand the shock
of wind and weather because they are deep-rooted.[2]   That
is how they waited.   The Trojans, shouting round Asios,
rushed on, delighted to find the gates apparently unguarded.
And still the two men waited.   When the Trojans were
well involved, suddenly, from the gates, these two came
rushing at them, "like boars[3] that wait on the mountain
for a rabble of men and dogs : they rush sideways, breaking
down the brushwood as they go, cutting at the roots with
their tusks."   They fought very stoutly, trusting not only
their own strength but the people on the towers above, who
were hurling down great stones on the Trojans.   The stones
and weapons fell as thick as snowflakes, which a raging
wind shakes from the shadowy clouds in a great flood of
snow on the fertile earth.[4]

The picture has been criticized.   We shall look far before we find a better.   The Trojans are well caught.   Until
they were certain of their prey, the two great sentinels stood
waiting, as unmoved as two great oaks.   Then suddenly
they rushed at the invaders like boars in a mountain forest.
The stones and weapons from the defenders of the walls
above were falling like a sheet of snow.   Whether or not
we think the scene was patched up by a rhapsodist from
the epic stock-in-trade, we may find some satisfaction in
the new, delightful, use which somebody—we are inclined to call him Homer—has found for the old themes,
the similes of the boar, the forest-trees, the storm.   Notice
that in this new development the storm has become a
storm of snow.

Asios, son of Hyrtakos, at any rate, found the situation
convincing.   He protested to Zeus with an inconsequence
which is characteristic of the fool.[5]   "Zeus Father, you are,

[1] XII. 127.   [2] XII. 132 ff.   [3] XII. 145 ff.
[4] XII. 156 ff.   [5] XII. 164 ff.

it seems, indeed a lover of lies—because I said the Achaean heroes would not stop me . . . and look, they are fighting like wasps or bees whose home is a hole in a rocky road; they do not abandon the hive, but stay and defend their children against the robbers." Precisely, that is what the two good sentinels did. And the son of Hyrtakos no more convinced the mind of Zeus,[1] who was determined to give glory to Hector, than we, who would give to Homer his own glory, shall convince the critics.

Let us leave the critics—we shall not convince them— and turn back to Homer. After a brief catalogue of the exploits of the sentinels, we return to the activities of Polydamas and Hector. Of course we do. It is the old familiar design. Polydamas gave good advice to Hector. Hector took it, but Asios did not. An interlude for Asios and his folly. Then—[2]

> while they were stripping them—the unfortunate followers of Asios—of their gloriously gleaming armour, the youths who went with Hector and Polydamas, the most numerous and the best, the most eager to break through the wall and to burn the ships, were still standing by the trench, perplexed—because of a strange portent.

Let us make no mistake. This portent was a warning. Hector disregarded it, because he was a very noble patriot. But Homer says it was a portent sent by ægis-bearing Zeus.[3] The Trojans had good reason to shudder at it. It was an eagle flying with a snake in its talons, bloody and wounded, but alive and still able to bite. It bit the eagle, and the eagle dropped it with a screech and flew away. The eagle was Hector, for the moment the favourite of Zeus. The snake was the Achaean army. Homer has not forgotten the blazon on King Agamemnon's armour.[4]

So Polydamas, "advising the bold Hector,"[5] bade him withdraw.

> It is your habit, Hector, to blame me in the Assembly because I give good advice: because, you say, it is not

---

[1] XII. 173-174.   [2] XII. 195 ff.   [3] XII. 209.
[4] XI. 39, XII. 202.   [5] XII. 210 ff.

even decent for a man who is of the people to speak against you, be it in Council or in battle, but one should always only add one's weight to your authority.   But now I will tell you plainly what seems best to me.   Let us not go to fight the Danaans for the ships.   For this, I think, will come to pass as surely as this bird has come to the Trojans, in their eagerness to go over. . . . Though we break through the gates and wall, we shall not come back in good order from the ships : we shall leave many Trojans behind, killed by the Achaeans. . . .

Polydamas is right.   Hector, who took good advice before, rejects the warning.   He rejects it finely, with a noble gesture.   Had he taken it, he would have been a good example of caution, not a tragic hero.   Hector is fighting always for Troy and for his wife and children ; and yet he knows all the time that Troy will fall.   That is what makes him tragic, magnificent.   So here, Polydamas, common sense personified, tells him the plain meaning of the omen.   " Any good seer will interpret it in that sense." [1]

"Polydamas," says Hector, "this time I do not like your words.   You know how to think of something better to say than that." [2]

Does it not recall Agamemnon's attitude to Calchas ?

If you really mean what you say, the gods themselves have taken away your wits, for you are bidding me forget the counsel of the Thunderer Zeus, who promised me himself and confirmed it with his nod: and you are bidding me obey the birds on their outstretched wings—for which I do not care, nor pay any heed to them at all, whether they go to the right, to the dawn and to the sun, or to the left, to the darkness of the west.   Let us obey the counsel of great Zeus, King of all mortals and immortals.   One omen is best, to fight for the fatherland.   Why are you afraid ? . . . If we die, you need not fear, because you will not stand in the battle.   But if you stay away, or if with your

[1] XII. 228.   [2] XII. 231 ff.; cf. I. 106.

talk you prevent any man and turn him back from the battle, my spear will find you and you shall die at once.
Is it not well done? Do we not hear Agamemnon, certain of the Thunderer's favour? True, Zeus has promised Hector victory . . . until the sun shall set.[1] The gifts and promises of Zeus are like that. The sun will set for Hector. The bird will fly to the left, to the dark west. And Polydamas, the adviser, is no coward. Immediately after sunset Polydamas will give good advice again, and Hector will again reject it.[2] The Trojans will applaud him and call Polydamas a coward. But Hector will be thinking of Polydamas, and repenting his rejection of the good advice, when Achilles meets him at the Scaean gate.[3]

For the present Hector leads on, and the Trojans follow with a shout of assent. Zeus confirms them in their purpose by sending down from Ida a gust of wind which carries the dust they raise straight to the ships. So, "trusting in his portents and in their own strength,"[4] they tried to break through the Achaean wall. And the Ajaxes were there as two sentinels to defend it. The weapons of the defenders fell on them as thick as snowflakes "on a winter's day of storm, when Zeus determines to show his marvels to mankind He stops the winds and pours down snow continuously, until the peaks of the high mountains and the jutting headlands, the flower-clad plains and the fertile fields, are covered. Even the harbours and the coasts of the sea are snowed upon, but the waves still roll up and wash the snow away."[5]

Poseidon still the rebel. Possibly the sea-god will be helping the defence. Hector, like Asios, has disregarded good advice. Like Asios, he finds two strong men waiting for him. And the snow-simile, thus heightened in the repetition, points the parallel.

Hector has made his tragic, noble, choice, and is going forward. That is the moment chosen by the poet for

---

[1] XI. 209. [2] XVIII. 239 ff. [3] XXII. 100 ff.
[4] XII. 256. [5] XII. 278; cf. 156.

Sarpedon's famous apologue to Glaucus, the perfect exposition of the heroic view of tragic life.[1]

> The Trojans and bright Hector would not have broken through, had not Zeus roused his own son Sarpedon and sent him against the Greeks like a lion against cattle.   He was like a lion of the mountains, who has long been hungry and will have his prey from the farm, in spite of all the shepherds with their dogs and javelins.   He will have his prey, and take his chance of being hit and killed.   Such was god-like Sarpedon, and he spoke to Glaucus.   "Why are we honoured, Glaucus, in Lycia, and regarded by the people even as gods?   Because we are always first in the battle, leading the Lycians.   They can say 'Our princes are not men of little fame, who only eat and drink.   They are strong men and good.'   Dear boy, if you and I, by escaping safe from this battle, were likely to escape old age and death for ever, I should not be fighting in the front . . . But, as it is, let us go. . . ."

They advance.   Menestheus the Athenian sees them coming, and calls for help to Ajax.   Ajax brings Teucer with him.   The Lycians come on "like a black tempest."[2] Ajax kills a companion of Sarpedon, hurling a great rock down on him: he falls back from the tower, "like a tumbler."[3]   Teucer wounds Glaucus with an arrow: and Glaucus leaps down quickly, so that no Achaean may see that he is wounded.   Sarpedon grieves for his companion, but presses on.[4]   He invokes Athene, and grips the parapet of the tower with his strong hands.   It comes away.   He has made a path for the others.   He is wounded, but Zeus saves him from death.   He gives way a little, and calls to the Lycians to keep on fighting. They attack again, and the fight is equally balanced.   The two armies are like two men in a common field, disputing a narrow strip of boundary land, with measuring rods in their hands.[5]   The towers and ramparts are drenched with

---

[1] XII. 290 ff.   [2] XII. 375.   [3] XII. 385.
[4] XII. 392.   [5] XII. 421 ff.

the blood of Greeks and Trojans : but the fight is still equally poised. The armies are as nicely balanced as the scales of a true-hearted widow, who exactly weighs her wool, to earn a wretched livelihood for her children.[1]

These two men disputing in a field and this widow weighing her wool are new to us, and very homely, very touching. But they are after all only fresh modifications of the old themes. The widow was once a woman in travail. The men in the field are the kinsmen of the reapers and the donkey-boys.

So the fight continued until Zeus gave even greater glory to the son of Priam. Hector shouted to his men, and himself rushed forward, with a huge boulder which two modern men could not easily heave up with levers into a cart.[2] He carried it as lightly as a shepherd carries a lamb in one arm,[3] and he rushed with it against the gates. They broke, and bright Hector leapt in, like the swift night, gleaming in bronze, his eyes flashing like fire. He shouted again, and his men followed him through the gates. The Greeks fled to the ships.

So the chapter ends. Why are Hector and Sarpedon thus linked by the poet? Because Sarpedon is to be the tragic victim of Patroclus, and Hector, his avenger, is to meet Achilles at the Scaean gate.

[1] XII. 432 ff.   [2] XII. 495 ff.   [3] XII. 451 ff.

CHAPTER IV

THE EPISODE OF THE DIVINE REBELLION

HAVING brought the Trojans and Hector past the wall, Zeus became tired of the battle. He left the fighters to themselves, and looked away towards Mysia and the land of the Hippemolgi, who live on milk, and the just Abii. He did not suppose that any of the immortals would disobey him and interfere on either side. He was wrong. Poseidon, for whose intervention we have been prepared, was waiting for his opportunity. " He pitied the Greeks, and grew very angry against Zeus, as he sat watching on a high peak in the Thracian Samos." [1]

At once he stepped down from the craggy peak, moving swiftly : the tall mountain and the forest trembled under the immortal feet of Poseidon as he moved. Three strides he took, and with the fourth arrived at his goal, at Aegae, where was his glorious, golden, glittering, everlasting palace, in the depth of the waters of the sea. There he made ready his bronze-hoofed horses, swift-flying, with long golden manes ; and he himself put gold about his body, and took his well-made golden whip, and mounted his car and drove over the waves. The creatures of the sea came up from their hiding-places and gambolled as he went : they knew their king ; and the sea rejoiced and made a path for him. The horses flew very lightly, and the brazen axle was not wet beneath the car.

This is the sequel and the contrast to the picture of Poseidon as the destroyer of the Achaean wall. Nor has the poet forgotten that in his first great battle-story,

[1] XIII. 10 ff.

when Hector with the help of Ares was triumphant, and the Greeks were very hard pressed; when Diomed was tired, and Sarpedon (as here) just wounded, Zeus had allowed Athene to put on her armour and drive down with Hera from Olympus in a marvellous car:[1] nor how later, on the second day of battle, Hera had appealed, though vainly, to Poseidon,[2] and had afterwards been persuaded by Athene to drive down again to the rescue,[3] only to find that Zeus was at last in earnest and would not have his purpose frustrated any more. In this second movement, too, the poet means to have the Greek defeat postponed, and Greek honour vindicated by divine aid; but this time the rebel against Zeus is at once more cautious, more slow to move, and, when he moves, more powerful than Hera or Athene. The car in which Poseidon makes his journey over the sea is more brilliant even than the chariot of the Olympian queen. But we shall presently find Hera joining in Poseidon's rebellion, and with great effect.

This interlude of the divine rebellion begins, then, with Poseidon's marvellous sea-journey. Its first episode shows us Poseidon stirring up the Achaean heroes to resistance, and culminates when Idomeneus "like a flame"[4] and Meriones "like Ares,"[5] fall on the Trojans in a battle which the poet compares to a great storm on a very dusty day.[6] The end of this first chapter is thus indicated :—

So with two purposes, the two strong sons of Cronos made grief and pain for men and heroes. Zeus willed honour for swift-footed Achilles, and victory for Hector and the Trojans, but he did not wish the Achaean people to perish altogether before Ilion; he was only honouring Thetis and her great-hearted son. But Poseidon was stirring up the Argives; he had come to them, he had come secretly to their help, from the grey sea, because he

---

[1] v. 719 ff. Lines 768 ff. (the watcher, looking out over the sea) anticipate Poseidon's watchings in XIII. [2] VIII. 198 ff.
[3] VIII. 381 ff. [4] XIII. 328. [5] XIII. 330. [6] XIII. 336.

grieved to see them defeated by the Trojans and was very angry with Zeus. They were both of one race and of one fatherhood, but Zeus was the elder and knew more; therefore Poseidon roused the army secretly, taking the shape of a mortal man, and did not venture to bring succour openly.[1]

That marks the end of the first episode, in which Poseidon roused first the two Ajaxes, then others, then Idomeneus.

The second episode contains the exploits of Idomeneus and Meriones. One by one the leaders of the third Trojan division are disposed of. The second and the fourth divisions join the remnant of the third, without turning the scale. Poseidon helps the Achaeans more and more openly. Yet, on the whole, the Trojans hold their own. At the end, Hector has rallied the whole army, and is advancing very confidently to the attack, "like a hurricane driven by the thunderstorm of Zeus against the sea."[2] In the pattern, of course, this hurricane corresponds to the "storm of wind on a very dusty day,"[3] which marked the end of the first chapter.

There follows a third episode, linking this series with the main story, since it begins with Nestor, drinking in his hut, where he is still attending Machaon. The wounded heroes, Nestor and Odysseus, Diomed and Agamemnon, return to the field, if not to fight, at least to hearten the Achaeans. Poseidon, in the form of an old man, encourages King Agamemnon, then (forgetting his disguise) shouts with a noise which only a god could make, as loud as "nine-thousand or ten-thousand men in battle."[4]

Then Hera intervenes and plays her famous trick on Zeus. With Zeus asleep, Poseidon is left free to help the Greeks quite openly. The battle is frankly now a struggle between Hector and Poseidon, and the Trojan rout ensues . . . until Zeus wakes.

That is the main scheme of this great digression. First Poseidon stirring up the Achaean leaders; then the exploits

---

[1] XIII. 345 ff.   [2] XIII. 795 ff.   [3] XIII. 336.
[4] XIV. 147 ff. Notice that XIV. 135 = XIII. 10.

of Idomeneus ; then the return of Agamemnon and the other wounded heroes to the field ; then the great climax, in which Hera puts her lord to sleep and leaves Poseidon free to drive the Trojans back before him in confusion.

The main design is plain ; let us look at, the workmanship of the detail. Consider first the chapter which began with Poseidon crossing the sea in his miraculous car, then putting up his horses and going to the field, disguised, to stimulate the Greeks.

First, he found the Trojans pressing on "like a flame," or "like a wind-storm." [1] They thought they were to capture the ships and kill the best of the Achaeans. But Poseidon took the shape of Calchas and addressed the Ajaxes. He told them that in the other parts of the field he had no fear of the Trojans ; he only feared disaster "at the place where Hector is leading, mad, like a flame, boasting he is the son of mighty Zeus." [2] Yet Hector himself, if the Ajaxes stand and exhort the others, will be turned back "even if the Olympian himself is rousing him."

That is no casual utterance. In fact the Achaeans are to have no difficulty in dealing with the rest, " who come over in a crowd," [3] that is, with the three divisions led by Asios, Paris, and Aeneas respectively. The scheme of the whole episode depends on this distinction between Hector and the leaders of the other Trojan divisions.

What follows ? Poseidon hits the Ajaxes with his staff, giving them new strength and vigour ; then flies away "like a hawk after another bird." [4] And the heroes recognize him. The lesser Ajax, looking at his footprints, knew at once. " It is not Calchas, not a seer, a reader of birds. . . . Gods are easy to recognize ; I noticed the print of his feet and *knees* behind him as he went." [5] Knees? Yes, that sort of print is only left by birds and gods. Why did the poet choose this curious superstitious touch? Because a little while ago, we heard the favourite of Zeus exclaiming,

---

[1] XIII. 39. [2] XIII. 53 ff. [3] Poseidon's phrase, XIII. 50.
[4] XIII. 62. [5] XIII. 70 ff.

"You bid me to trust birds. . . . I have the warrant of a god, of Zeus himself."[1]   This god who has come to the Ajaxes in the likeness of a bird-reader, is in fact himself a bird—the hawk, not the eagle, but a great god, and the brother of Zeus.

Poseidon rallies other less distinguished heroes, Teucer Deipyros, Meriones, and others.[2]   For them he has a longer speech, with more reproach in it.   "Be brave, young men; be ashamed to yield.   If you shirk, defeat is certain.   O fie ! I never thought to see the Trojans so successful.   They used to be like frightened hinds, the natural prey of jackals, leopards, wolves; and now they are close to the ships—[3]

by the fault of a bad leader and a shirking people who, because they have quarreled with the leader, do not drive the Trojans from the ships, but stay there to be killed.   Why, even if the hero, the son of Atreus, King Agamemnon, is altogether and in truth to blame because he put dishonour on the swift-footed son of Peleus, that does not mean that we can shirk this battle.   Rather let us try to cure the hurt.   Good men's minds are curable— but as for you, you do not well to leave your valour, you, the best men in the army.

Therefore, good youths"—he ends as he begins[4]—"be ashamed to yield, and mend the breach where Hector has broken in."

So the young men rallied in two companies, one round each of the two Ajaxes—two phalanxes of men with which Ares and Athene could have found no fault.   They were the best picked men of the Greeks, standing in close order, ready for Hector and the Trojans, spear by spear, ox-hide pressed close to ox-hide, target to target, helmet to helmet, man by man.   The plumes of the helmets touched one another as they moved their heads, so closely were they marshalled.[5]

That is the first picture: Poseidon has not only formed a solid phalanx of resistance to the Trojans; for the poet's

---

[1] XII. 235 ff.   [2] XIII. 91 ff.   [3] XIII. 101 ff.
[4] XIII. 95, 121.   [5] XIII. 130 ff.

hearer he has set the incident in its proper place, as an episode in the main tragedy of Agamemnon and Achilles. Poseidon has interpreted and answered the natural feeling of the army losing spirit under defeat. Poseidon does not say that Agamemnon after all has done his best to make amends; he simply says, "No doubt your leaders are bad; no doubt Agamemnon is to blame for insulting Achilles; no doubt Achilles sets a bad example by shirking at this crisis. Your business is to fight because you are good men."

Presently we shall find the reference to Agamemnon very neatly justified. As for Achilles, look, before you criticize the poet's method, to the great moment when the Myrmidons are mustering round Patroclus, ready to return at last to battle. Achilles armed them. They were like wolves that worry a hind.[1] And Achilles, as he marshalled them in their five companies, reminded them that they had grumbled at him and had blamed him for his obstinacy, and had threatened to go home.[2] So Poseidon here implies that when Achilles shirks, the rest will think it an excuse for shirking. If you doubt that the poet is here preparing us for that great moment, see how the Myrmidons mustered, helmet by helmet, shield by shield, and man by man, "like a well-built wall."[3]

Poseidon came in his marvellous car. He encouraged the Ajaxes. They knew he was a god and they grew strong. He encouraged Teucer, Meriones, and others. He bade them fight well even if Agamemnon were a foolish leader: even if Achilles were a shirker. And they formed two solid phalanxes round the two Ajaxes.

Then the Trojans came on in a body, led by Hector, who leapt forward like a rolling boulder, broken away from a cliff by a mountain torrent.[4] It leaps and clatters down the hillside. It smashes through the wood. It runs straight on until it comes to the plain. Then it stops. So Hector stopped when he reached the Achaean phalanxes, and he yielded a little, but shouted loudly to his men, "Stand

---

[1] XVI. 156; cf. XIII. 103.
[2] XVI. 200 ff.
[3] XVI. 212 ff.; cf. XIII. 130 ff.
[4] XIII. 137 ff.

your ground : the Achaeans will soon give way—as surely
as I was sent here by the thunderous husband of Hera ! " [1]
" The husband of Hera " indeed, Zeus is to prove ; it is a
light touch, like the references to Poseidon in Book XII,
ominous for the sequel.

So the Trojans attacked, and Deiphobus sprang out first.
Meriones aimed at him, and hit his shield ; but the spear
stuck in the shield and broke, and Meriones went back
angry to the huts to fetch another spear. [2]

But the others fought, and the battle-cry rose, unquenchable. [3]   And Teucer, the son of Telemon, killed Imbrios,
husband of Priam's daughter Medesikaste, honoured by
Priam as one of his own sons.   He fell " like an ash
which is cut down by the bronze, and lays low its tender
foliage on the ground, on a high top of a mountain that can
be seen afar." [4]   Teucer stooped to take his armour ; Hector
aimed at him, but missed.   He hit Amphimachus, a grandson of Poseidon, and in his turn rushed out to spoil him.
Ajax hit Hector, but his armour saved him.   Still,
he had to yield, and the two bodies were taken by the
Greeks ; the body of Amphimachus was carried back to the
Achaean camp, but the body of the Trojan, the husband of
Priam's daughter, was snatched by the two Ajaxes (" as
lions snatch a goat from the hounds "), [5] stripped, and the
head thrown at the feet of Hector. [6]

It is surely Homer's own method ?   The first incident,
Meriones and Deiphobus, is of no great interest, though it
points to future events.   The second incident, Imbrios and
the rest, is touched with poetry, and is made relevant by its
poetry to the main tragedy.   Imbrios, like an ash cut down
on the mountain, is a second Simoeisios. [7] Yes, but he is
also a husband, married to a daughter of Priam, honoured
by Priam as a son, and after a short struggle over his body
and another body, his head is thrown at Hector's feet.   That
is how Homer works.   Three familiar themes, the felled tree,
the wife, the fight for spoils and bodies, are combined to
make the incident relevant and moving.

[1] XIII. 154.   [2] XIII. 165 ff.   [3] XIII. 169.   [4] XIII. 178 ff.
[5] XIII. 198.   [6] XIII. 205.   [7] IV. 473 ff., see p. 42.

The pattern is emerging very clearly. Poseidon roused the Ajaxes. He roused others (not without reference to Agamemnon and Achilles). The result: two Greek phalanxes, and Hector stopped in his career. Then Deiphobus met Meriones. Then Imbrios and Amphimachus were killed, and the head of Imbrios was thrown down at Hector's feet.

But Amphimachus was a grandson of Poseidon. The angry god for the third time makes his appeal to the Greeks. This time he meets and encourages Idomeneus—whom he encounters coming back from attendance on "a companion who was wounded." [1] Very strange in Homer not to add his name—but somehow moving. Idomeneus sets much store by loyal comradeship. That Idomeneus should be introduced precisely in that way is not an accident. It is designed to make us think again in passing of Nestor and Machaon, of Patroclus and Eurypylos.

To Idomeneus the Cretan, Poseidon comes in the guise of the prince Thoas, king of the Aetolians. This distinguished hero has the next place before Idomeneus in the Greek catalogue. [2] The poet knows his business.

To the question of the supposed Aetolian prince, "Where are the threats with which the sons of the Achaeans used to threaten the Trojans?" Idomeneus answers gloomily enough :—[3]

"Thoas, this time, so far as I can tell, it is no man who is to blame : we all know how to fight. . . . It seems, after all, it must be the pleasure of the masterful son of Cronos, that the Achaeans should perish without a name, away from Argos. But, Thoas, since you have ever been a fighter who could stand, and would exhort another if you saw him shirking—go on exhorting every man to fight."

Later in this same group of episodes we shall have Agamemnon saying, "It seems it is after all the pleasure of the son of Cronos. . . ." [4] But Agamemnon will not, like Idomeneus, say "Fight on." He will again propose evacuation. Once more there is a method in the poet's design.

[1] XIII. 211.   [2] II. 638, 645.   [3] XIII. 222 ff.   [4] XIV. 69.

It is like Homer first to make Poseidon tell the young
men—" If Agamemnon is a bad leader, that does not
exempt you " [1]—then to make Idomeneus say, " Zeus seems
to want our destruction ; so fight on ; " then at length to
introduce King Agamemnon saying, " Zeus seems to want
our destruction ; let us fly . . ." and to make a young man
(Diomed of course), with apologies for his youth, protest.

Thoas-Poseidon answers : " Get your armour ; let us see
what we can do.   If men will only unite and fight together,
even men in a bad plight can do great things." [2]   Is not this
reference to the value of good-fellowship in fighting relevant
to the whole " Iliad " ?   Well, when Idomeneus comes
shining in his armour like the lightning-flash of Zeus, he
meets his chosen comrade Meriones. [3]   It was for this that
the poet made Meriones lose his spear.   And when he saw
him, Idomeneus exclaimed : " Meriones, swift-footed son of
Molos, dearest of my companions." [4]   Do we not think of
Achilles and Patroclus ?   Listen again : " Why have you
left the battle and the fighting ?   Are you wounded, or have
you come with news for me ?   I myself have no mind to sit
in the huts ; [5] I am for fighting."

The dialogue which follows corresponds in the design to
the more famous dialogue of Glaucus and Sarpedon.   Of
course this pair of comrades is less tragic and less important
in the story than were Glaucus and Sarpedon, Polydamas
and Hector, Patroclus and Achilles ; and the interview is
pitched in a lower key.   Nevertheless the apologue about
the coward and the soldier in an ambush, and the confidence
of Idomeneus in his friend, are very noble.   " Let us not
stand talking then, like children, lest in indignation some one
scorn us.   Go and get your spear." [6]   So Meriones got his
weapon and went with his leader " like swift Ares." [7]

" Shall we fight on the right, or the left, or in the middle
of the battle ? "   " In the middle there are the Ajaxes and
Teucer ; men enough to give Hector pause, unless Zeus
himself sends a brand to fire the ships.   Ajax alone is as

[1] XIII. 121 ff., 226 ff. ; XIV. 69 ff., 110 ff.   [2] XIII. 237-238.
[3] XIII. 240, 246.   [4] XIII. 249 ff.   [5] XIII. 253-254.
[6] XIII. 293 ff.   [7] XIII. 295.

good as Achilles himself in such a fight as this, though no one can run like Achilles. Let us go to the left of the battle, to see if we shall give glory to another man, or another man to us ! " [1]

Were we not meant to think of Glaucus and Sarpedon ? So Meriones like Ares, and Idomeneus like a flame, fell on the Trojans ; and the battle was like a hurricane on a very dusty day.[2] And the two sons of Cronos pulled two ways ; but both caused grief and pain to men and heroes.

Once more, and for the last time, consider this—the first episode of the divine rebellion :—

Zeus looked away and Poseidon noticed it. He drove his car over the waves and came to Troy. The Trojans following Hector, were fighting like a flame, like a hurricane.

Poseidon went to the two Ajaxes disguised as Calchas. He encouraged them. The lesser Ajax recognized the god.

He encouraged Teucer, Meriones, and the "young men." Agamemnon might be a bad leader and Achilles shirk. Let the young men fight on.

They formed two phalanxes round the two Ajaxes.

The Trojans attacked, following Hector. He was like a boulder broken from a cliff by a torrent, crashing by leaps and bounds through the mountain forest to the plain ; then stopping. So Hector stopped when he reached the phalanxes: he cried, " we shall break them yet if Hera's husband really has inspired me."

Then Meriones fought Deiphobus, and left his spear in the Trojan's shield.

Then Teucer killed Imbrios, husband of Priam's daughter, like a son to Priam. He lay like a felled ash on the mountain ; they fought over his body. The Greek Amphimachus, Poseidon's grandson, also fell. The two Ajaxes seized the body of Imbrios, as lions seize a goat. The lesser Ajax cut his head off and hurled it at the feet of Hector.

[1] XIII. 307 ff., 312 ff., 327.
[2] XIII. 328, 330 335. So the panel ends as it began with wind and flame ; see XIII. 39 ff.

So Poseidon was angry and met Idomeneus, prince of the line of Cretan sea-kings. He was coming from attendance on a wounded friend.

Disguised as Thoas, prince of the Aetolians, Poseidon cried, "Where are our boasts?" Idomeneus answered, "Zeus it seems is bent on our destruction; therefore fight on."

It is the central doctrine of the heroic view of life.

Then Idomeneus met his companion Meriones. They exhorted one another. Idomeneus extolled the courage of his friend, most eminent when peril was most urgent. And they went together to join battle on the left, leaving the centre and great Hector to the Ajaxes. They went like Ares, like a flame. The battle was like a hurricane on a winter day.

So Zeus pulled one way, and Poseidon the other; but Zeus was the older and wiser, and Poseidon dared not work against him openly.

The second chapter naturally begins with the exploits of Idomeneus and his squire.

Idomeneus, though his head was already touched with grey, put terror into the Trojans. First he slew Othryoneus, lately arrived at Troy in the quest of fame in battle. He was asking to have Priam's loveliest daughter for his wife, without a bride-price. He had promised to drive off the Achaeans from Troy, and Priam had consented to the bargain. So he fought, and Idomeneus killed him, and boasted, "We Argives, if we made promises, should keep them. We would have promised you Agamemnon's loveliest daughter if you had sacked Troy for us! Come with me; let us make our agreement at the ships about the marriage. You will find us easy bargainers!" And he was dragging the man's body by the legs.[1]

Othryoneus corresponds in the pattern to Imbrios, Priam's son-in-law, but of course the effect is heightened. The grimmest humour takes the place of pathos. There is no tree simile here.

[1] XIII. 374 ff.

But the tree simile is not forgotten.

As the body of Othryoneus was dragged off, Asios, son of Hyrtakos, came to the rescue—" on foot, in front of his horses." [1]   We remember him well enough ; he was the first to drive through the gate, and would not leave his chariot behind at the trench.   He was too proud to take the advice of Polydamas.[2]

He comes to the rescue now " on foot in front of his horses : for his charioteer always held them in readiness behind him ; so close that their breath came on his shoulder." He came to the rescue of the body, but Idomeneus wounded him first :—

He fell as an oak or a white poplar or a high pine falls, cut down on the mountain by carpenters with newly sharpened axes, to be a ship's timber.   So he lay stretched on the ground before his car and horses, roaring, clutching at the bloody dust.   And his charioteer was suddenly driven out of his senses, which he had before.   He could not bring himself to turn the horses back and so escape the enemy's hands.   Antilochus, the son of Nestor, killed him and drove his horses off as booty.[3]

The folly of Asios is a preparation for the more heroic folly of Hector, in the sequel.   The tree simile is beautiful, but Homer is preparing us for something greater still. When Sarpedon falls to Patroclus, we shall hear of this comparison again, but in a nobler context.[4]   Sarpedon, too, will fall " like an oak or a white poplar . . . ;" he will also be like " a bull that a lion kills, a great-hearted tawny bull, which the lion has hunted from the herd of cows."   The whole effect is heightened.   The emotion we feel is due in part to the familiarity of both the images.

The fight goes on over the body of Asios.   Deiphobus aims at Idomeneus who is saved by his shield.   (Meriones, we remember, left his own spear broken in the shield of Deiphobus.)   But though Deiphobus misses Idomeneus, he wounds Hypsenor, and boasts that Asios is avenged.   " I have given him a companion ; he will go rejoicing to the

[1] XIII. 385.   [2] See p. 115.   [3] XIII. 389 ff.   [4] XVI. 482 ff.

realm of Hades, that strong gate-keeper." [1]   It is a bitter
reference to the havoc wrought by the two strong gate-
keepers when Asios and Deiphobus and their men drove in
through the open gate.[2]   Is not the touch like Homer?
Yet critics say that the tale of Asios and the two sentinels
at the gate is a patchwork botched up by some clumsy
rédacteur, to account for the presence of the chariot here!
Hades, the strong gate-keeper, refutes them.

But Hypsenor was wounded, not killed, and Antilochus
was indignant for his friend, and covered him with his shield
while his companions carried him away.   Idomeneus went
on to another triumph.   He had killed Othryoneus, who
was to have been the husband of Cassandra, loveliest of
Priam's daughters.   He had killed Asios, who fell like an
oak, or a white poplar or a high pine.   Now he killed a
third: it was the beautiful Alkathoos,[3] a son-in-law of
Anchises, who married Hippodameia, an eldest best-loved
daughter, in beauty, industry, and sense beyond all others
of her age.   That was why she was given in marriage to
Alkathoos, one of the best Trojans.   "But now Poseidon
subdued him at the hand of Idomeneus, putting a spell on
his bright eyes, and clogging his shining limbs : he could
not go back in flight, nor swerve ; but as he stood there
motionless, like a pillar of stone or a high-foliaged tree,
Idomeneus, the hero, struck him in the breast."

The fate of this third victim draws beauty from the fates
of the first and of the second.   For the suitor of Cassandra,
the husband of Anchises' daughter.   For the foolish Asios,
who was felled like a tree in the forest and whose charioteer
lost his wits and could not escape, the hero smitten by
Poseidon with a strange paralysis, unable to fly or swerve,
like a tree or a pillar of stone.   We have seen that the
comparison of Asios to a tree recurs with greater strength
and beauty for Sarpedon's death.   It is worth while to
look again at the last scene of Sarpedon's fight.   "Shall
I spare my own dear son?" cried Zeus.   "You may not
spare him," Hera answered, "but you may send his body

---

[1] XIII. 415.   [2] XII. 127 ff., see p. 116.   [3] XIII. 428 ff.

for burial to Lycia. His brothers and his kinsmen shall give him a funeral mound and a pillar of stone; that is the prize of honour of the dead."[1] Then Zeus rained blood, and he let Sarpedon die; and the hero lay like an oak or a white poplar, or a high pine, felled by carpenters on the mountain.

Like a tree or a stone pillar stood the beautiful Alkathoos, and could not fly. And Idomeneus boasted to Deiphobus:[2] "Shall it be three men for one? Come near me yourself, that you may see what a very son of Zeus is against you. Zeus was father of Minos, the first guardian of Crete, and Minos was the father of the noble Deucalion, my own father."

That completes the group of three. First Othryoneus, the bridegroom; then Asios, like a tree; then Alkathoos, the husband, like a pillar or a tree. And Idomeneus reveals himself, the very son of Zeus.

And the whole episode is touched with beauty by the themes which are to make the meeting of Patroclus and Sarpedon beautiful and tragic.

The next picture, still in the second chapter, brings a new Trojan division into action. Deiphobus wondered, should he stand alone, or get assistance.[3] He decided he would join Aeneas, son of Anchises, a member of a princely house which rivalled the house of Priam, destined to be the saviour of the Trojan line of kings. There is a hint of that story in the reference here to a quarrel between Priam and Aeneas. "Come, avenge your brother-in-law," says Deiphobus, "and forget your quarrel."[4] So Aeneas went with him against Idomeneus. But Idomeneus was not afraid like a child; he waited, as a wild boar on the mountain waits for a rabble of men, in a lonely place, eager to fight, his eyes flashing.[5] He called his friends to help him. "Aeneas is young," he cries; "if I were of his age, I would take my chance alone."[6] So his friends formed a phalanx round him; and the Trojan heroes formed a phalanx round Aeneas.

[1] XVI. 432 ff. 457.   [2] XIII. 446 ff.   [3] XIII. 455 ff.
[4] XIII. 463 ff.   [5] XIII. 470 ff.   [6] XIII. 485-486 ff.

The workmanship is ingenious. By the simile of the wild boar, Idomeneus is linked with the great heroes of Book XII.[1] As at the outset of his exploits we were told of his "grey hair" so at the outset of the encounter with Aeneas, he himself recalls his age.[2] As two phalanxes were formed about the Ajaxes, so here Idomeneus rallies a phalanx round him, and Aeneas rallies another.[3] But the poet cannot resist the patriotic addition that the group of Trojan leaders was followed by the common people "as a ram by sheep." [4]

Idomeneus has attracted against himself the leaders of no less than three of the five Trojan divisions. Homer's disposition is not casual. When the Trojans attacked in their five companies, Hector and Polydamas led the first, Glaucus and Sarpedon the fifth division; the second, third and fourth, were led respectively by Paris-Alkathoos-Agenor, Helenus-Deiphobus-Asios, son of Hyrtakos, Aeneas-Archelochos-Akamas. Idomeneus first attacked the third division: Asios fell to him. Alkathoos from the second division was his next victim, as he pressed on. Then Deiphobus called up Aeneas from the third. Now, in the phalanx that supports Aeneas against him, we find, as we should reasonably expect, Deiphobus and Paris and Agenor.[5] Against Idomeneus are the surviving leaders of these three divisions.

So they fought over the body of Alkathoos. But two great heroes were conspicuous, Idomeneus the Cretan, and Aeneas; "both like Ares." [6]

Aeneas aims at Idomeneus, who avoids the spear. Idomeneus himself hits Oinomaos. He withdraws his spear from the body, but goes back to safety slowly. His age is beginning to tell.[7] Deiphobus, still active against him, aims and misses; but he hits Askalaphos, a son of Ares. Ares did not know of it; he was sitting in Olympus, kept there like the other gods, by the fear of Zeus.[8]

They fight on over the body of Askalaphos. Deiphobus,

[1] See pp. 98 ff. [2] XIII. 361, 485. [3] XIII. 126 ff., 487 ff. [4] XIII. 492.
[5] XIII. 490. [6] XIII. 500. [7] XIII. 512 ff. [8] XIII. 521 ff.

as he stoops to spoil it, is wounded in the arm by Meriones, who "leaps forward like a vulture and snatches back his spear from the enemy's arm."[1] Why? Because at the outset Meriones left his spear in the shield of Deiphobus, and has not forgotten the humiliating moment. And Deiphobus was led away, by his brother Polites, from the battle.

But the others still fought, and the battle-cry rose un-quenchable. Aeneas killed Aphareus; Antilochus killed Thoon. The Trojans rushed to attack him as he spoiled the body, but Poseidon saved the son of Nestor. Adamas, son of Asios, attacked him, but Poseidon intervened again. He made the spear of Adamas stick in the shield of Anti-lochus like a burnt stake, and half of it broke off and lay smashed on the ground.[2] So Adamas went back without his spear; and Meriones stuck his own spear very firmly in the part which hurts men most—"that is where he stuck his spear."[3] Meriones is well avenged for the spear he left behind in Deiphobus' shield. The spear was so firmly stuck in the body of the unfortunate Adamas, that when Meriones withdrew it, he dragged Adamas after it, gasping, "following it as a cow that men have tied with ropes, and drag after them against her will,"[4] until at last Meriones went close up to him, drew the spear out, and he died.

It is a grim enough picture. The fighting, even of sub-ordinates, in this battle is no child's play, like the exploits of Diomed wounding an Aphrodite. But our business here is to notice the poet's craftsmanship. Who was this Thoon, killed by Antilochus? Who was this Adamas, killed by Meriones? They were two of the companions of the foolish Asios, son of Hyrtakos.[5] They were two of the company that rushed in shouting, thinking they would take the ships, and be the first men to get home by the easy route behind the Greek defence. With Asios in that entry, which they thought triumphant, went Iamenos and Orestes —both fell immediately in the struggle at the gate—and

---

[1] XIII. 531 ff. ; cf. 160 ff.   [2] XIII. 564 f.   [3] XIII. 568 ff.
[4] XIII. 571 ff.   [5] See XII. 139 f.

Adamas and Thoon and Oinomaos. So Oinomaos is the only
member of the group left unaccounted for by Homer?   Look
again.   Oinomaos was killed by Idomeneus himself so not
very long ago.[1]   Every one of that mad company has fallen.

Of the third division, which so proudly started the attack,
Asios and all his followers are gone; Deiphobus is
wounded; Helenus alone remains—and the moment
Adamas, the last of Asios' men has been disposed of,
"Helenus struck Deipyros with a great Thracian sword."[2]
He fell—"And Menelaus, son of Atreus, was seized by
grief, and stepped out brandishing a sharp spear, threatening the hero Helenus."[3]   Helenus shot an arrow at Menelaus, but it darted back from his breastplate, "as beans
jump off a winnowing fan,"[4] and Menelaus wounded
Helenus in the arm.
The last leader of this ill-fated division is disposed of.
But the pattern is not quite completed.   Peisander, an unfortunate man, attacks Menelaus. He is a son of the
Trojan who urged his fellows to kill Menelaus when he
went to Troy as an ambassador.[5] Homer does not mention the incident here.   But Menelaus remembers it.   Anyhow, this is what he shouts, when he kills his victim :—[6]

   "You shall leave our ships alone at last, proud
Trojans, you who never have enough of fighting! You
have no need of more shame and more disgrace, after
that shameful wrong you did me, base curs and womanly
cowards. You did not fear the counsel of Zeus who
guards the rights of hospitality, which will yet some day
destroy your city for you. You robbed me of my wife
. . . and now you are eager to set fire to our ships.   Some
day, though you are so eager, you shall be stopped from
your war-making.   Zeus, Father, they say that you are
wise above all other gods and men.   Yet all this is your
doing.   What favours you are showing to men of such

---

[1] XIII. 506, see p. 136.   [2] XIII. 576.   [3] XIII. 581 ff.   [4] XIII. 588-589.
[5] XI. 121 ff., 138 ff.   Peisander was hit on the breast and hurled out of his
chariot by Agamemnon, XI. 143, and his companion Hippolochus killed and
mutilated.   [6] XIII. 620 ff.

insatiate wickedness. Most men can have too much even of pleasure. They can have too much of sleep and love, too much of song and dancing. But these Trojans have never had enough of war!"

The appeal and protest to Zeus are important for the pattern. The first exploit of Idomeneus ended, we remember, with the boast that he was the very son of Zeus. Presently we shall find that Zeus himself can have too much of love and sleep. And the Trojans, when Zeus wakes, will have more than their fill of fighting.

That is the central panel of the Menelaus incident. First he wounds Helenus, who has aimed an arrow at him, in the bow-arm. Then he kills Peisander, son of his enemy, and appeals to Zeus. Now, thirdly, Harpalion, son of Pylaimenes, aims a javelin at Menelaus, but is wounded himself by an arrow from Meriones. His father [1] goes off with him, weeping. And Paris, very angry for his friend, aims at Euchenor, son of the prophet Polyeidos, who came to Troy, well knowing his fate, because his father had foretold that he should either die of disease at home or be killed in battle at Troy.[2] And the hero chose Troy. Thus a light reference to the Achilles *motif* ends the series of killings.

Look back at the pattern of this second chapter.

First Idomeneus killed Othryoneus, the would-be bridegroom. Then he killed Asios, son of Hyrtakos. Then the husband of Hippodameia, the beautiful Alkathoos, fell to him. And Idomeneus revealed himself as the very son of Zeus.

Secondly, Deiphobus appealed to Aeneas. Two phalanxes were formed, one round Idomeneus and the other round Aeneas. The phalanx of Aeneas contained the leaders of three Trojan divisions. One by one, the leaders of the third division, the division once led by Asios, son of Hyrtakos, were killed or wounded.

Thirdly, Menelaus wounded the sole survivor of that famous company. It was Helenus, the archer, and Menelaus hit him in the bow-arm. Then he killed Peisander,

---

[1] Here is a real inconsistency, Pylaimenes was killed by Menelaus, v. 576.
[2] XIII. 667 ff.

and appealed to Zeus. Then came the wounding of Harpalion, before the eyes of his father, by an arrow from
Meriones. And lastly, the archer Paris, the rival of Menelaus, the cause of the whole war, killed a man who came to
Troy although he knew that he would die there, a man
who chose to die in battle rather than stay at home and die
of disease.

So they fought like blazing fire. But Hector, dear to
Zeus, had not learnt it. He did not know that his
people on the left of the battle were being ravaged by
the Achaeans. Almost the victory might have gone to
the Achaeans; so much did the Earth-Holder, the Earth-
Shaker, inspire them, and also himself helped them with
his strength.[1]

Exactly. In the first chapter Poseidon stirred up first the
Ajaxes, then others, then Idomeneus. He did not take
active part in the battle himself. Now at the end of the
second, he is beginning to lend a hand himself.

But Hector did not know. He was still fighting in the
centre. He was busy with the Athenians, Ionians, Boeo-
tians, Locrians—a great list of them [2]—but above all with
the two Ajaxes, who worked together like a pair of oxen
ploughing with a good will.[3] But it is the lesser Ajax who
receives the fuller description here. That is because he
is presently to play a great part in the fighting.

Hector did not know. The result would have been
disaster for the Trojans, had not . . . of course, had not
Polydamas advised him to retire a little and rally the
whole army.[4] He assented. And he went to the left of
the battle, and looked in vain for the heroes who were
killed and wounded. He upbraided Paris unjustly: but
Paris answered that he had himself been fighting all the
time, and was prepared to go on fighting.[5]

So the Trojans rallied a great company round Hector.
They advanced on the Achaeans like a hurricane driven

---

[1] XIII. 673 ff.   [2] XIII. 685 ff.   [3] XIII. 703 ff.
[4] XIII. 723 ff.   [5] XIII. 769 ff., 775 ff.

down by the thunderstorm of Zeus to the plain : it falls on
the sea with a great roar. . . .[1] And Hector led them.
Ajax was not afraid. He challenged them. He shouted,
" It is not you, but Zeus who is defeating us. The time will
come when, as you fly, you will pray to Zeus and the immortals that your horses may be swifter than hawks to
carry you to your city." [2] As he spoke, two eagles came
flying on the right, and the Achaeans were encouraged.
But Hector mocked at the omen, and answered :—[3]

I wish I were as surely a son of Zeus, a child of Queen
Hera herself, and honoured by Athene and Apollo, as I
am sure this day brings evil for all the Argives. You,
Ajax, shall be one of the killed. . . . You shall feed the
dogs and the birds of the Trojans.

So he spoke, and led the way. His people followed with
a great shout of assent, and joined battle with the Achaeans.

Nestor, though he was drinking, heard the noise of battle.
He said to the son of Asklepios :—[4]

Think, bright Machaon, what can this mean ? The
shout of the young men at the ships is louder. Stay
here, and drink, until the lovely-haired Hekamede has
warmed your bath and washed the blood from your
wounds. I will go out, and see. . . .

The poet has brought us to that point. The moment
Hector had passed the wall, Poseidon began to rally a
Greek resistance. Two phalanxes formed round the Ajaxes,
but Hector still attacked, and boasted himself the favourite
of " Hera's husband." Then Idomeneus and Meriones,
inspired by the sea-god, drew against them three of the five
Trojan divisions. Still the battle raged, and the Trojans
would have broken, had not Polydamas and Hector come
to rally them. Thus Poseidon and the Ajaxes and the
rest of the Achaeans were now facing the whole army of
the Trojans, rallied by Hector, who still shouted that he
had Zeus with him. Homer means to fill the field again
with reinforcements. It remains for him to bring back into

[1] XIII. 795 ff.   [2] XIII. 817 ff.   [3] XIII. 825 ff.   [4] XIV. 3 ff.

the picture the major heroes of the Achaeans, wounded earlier in the day. So Nestor hears the shouting and goes out.

He meets, of course, the wounded heroes, Agamemnon, Odysseus, Diomed. " I fear," says Agamemnon, " Hector's threat to burn the ships is coming true. O fie! I fear the other Achaeans, like Achilles, are angry with me, and refusing to fight their best." [1] Exactly what Poseidon thought the Achaean young men might be tempted to do. [2]

"Only too true," says Nestor. " Zeus himself could not prevent our defeat now. The wall is down. The battle is confused, and one cannot see what the Achaeans are doing. All the same, let us think what can be done— if thinking can do any good. I do not ask you to go back to the field. Wounded men cannot fight." [3]

It was Nestor's notion, we remember, to make the wall and trench. He naturally takes a gloomy view. But at any rate his inference is this: " Things look bad. Therefore, let us think what can be done." Agamemnon's one thought is, of course, evacuation, and indeed, as things are, it is not a bad thought. The general is responsible for his men. " Let us get ready some of the ships, and be prepared to slip away at night." [4] But Odysseus, who by this time has every right to speak, breaks in with a heroic protest. [5] "A fatal counsel. Would you were leader of some other, some contemptible people, not of us to whom Zeus has given, it appears, the burden of hard battles as our gift, from youth to age, until each one of us shall perish. . . . Be silent. Do not let any Achaean hear you say what a King ought never to say." " Ah, but can anybody, young or old, propose a better course?" [6]

Diomed can. " I am young, I know. [7] But I am son of a good father, who was a rich man too, and a good spearman. Do not slight me, if I advise you. Let us go down to the battle, wounded as we are. We can encourage the others, even if we cannot fight." So he spoke, and they obeyed, and Agamemnon, the King, led them.

[1] XIV. 44 ff.   [2] XIII. III ff.   [3] XIV. 53 ff.   [4] XIV. 75 ff.
[5] XIV. 83 ff.   [6] XIV. 108.   [7] XIV. 110 ff.

It is a pretty sequel to Agamemnon's first Review, when he wished that Nestor were as young as he is wise ; when he slighted the father of Telemachus, and told young Diomed he was not the man his father Tydeus used to be. It is also a good sequel to Poseidon's exhortation, "Argive young men, fight on, even if your leader Agamemnon be to blame."

Anyhow Poseidon is delighted with the reinforcement. He takes the hand of Agamemnon and encourages him. Then, throwing off all disguise, he shouts as loud as nine or even as ten thousand men in battle, and the Argives feel their strength renewed.

At that moment Hera looked down from Olympus. She saw Poseidon helping her Greeks, and she rejoiced. She saw her husband seated on Mount Ida, and disliked him. And she formed a plan.

She dressed herself most exquisitely. She begged of Aphrodite, with a trumped-up story, a parcel of her charms, "love and desire and deceitful lovers' talk, which cheats the mind of the wisest," and put it with a smile into her bosom.[1] She went to Lemnos, and met Sleep, and cunningly invited him to help her. He hesitated. He remembered the old trouble about Heracles.[2] But she won him over with the promise of Pasithae, one of the younger Graces for his wife. Then she went to Zeus, and she charmed him as she never had charmed him before, and as none of his many mortal loves had ever charmed him.

At last he slept in her arms under a golden cloud on the mountain-top, which was covered with fresh grass and dewy lotus and hyacinth and crocus.[3] So Sleep went and told Poseidon. "You are free to help the Greeks with all your might. Zeus is asleep."[4]

Then Poseidon bade them give their best men the best weapons, and get their longest spears, and form their strongest phalanx. The wounded heroes saw to the best distribution of the weapons. They reviewed the army, and

---

[1] xiv. 115 ff.   [2] xiv. 247 ff., see p. 49.   [3] xiv. 347 ff.   [4] xiv. 357 ff.

Poseidon led them, his great sword shining like a lightning-flash. And Hector marshalled his Trojans. The strife which Poseidon made was more terrible than ever before. The sea washed up in a great wave to the huts and ships, and the Achaeans understood.[1] They shouted, and attacked.

> Never is the noise of the wave so loud, though it be stirred by the cruel blast of Boreas from the sea ; never the roar of fire so loud in the mountain glade, as it blazes and rolls on to burn the forest ; never the voice of the wind in the high-foliaged oaks so loud, though it roar very terribly in anger, as was the shout of the Trojans and Achaeans as they leapt on one another.

It is for this great culminating shock of battle that we have been prepared throughout the episode. The wind on the waves, the forest-fire, the wind in the forest trees, are all familiar. The shout of this battle is louder than them all.

Hector aimed first at Ajax and aimed well. But the spear was stopped by the two great belts from which hung the hero's shield and sword. Hector stepped back, angry that he had thrown his spear in vain.[2]

Is it not well done? The fighting of this series began with Meriones who left his spear in the shield of Deiphobus and was angry.[3]

Then Ajax seized a great stone, used as a prop under a ship. He sent it hurtling through the air, spinning like a top, and Hector fell, like an oak that crashes down beneath a bolt from Zeus : there is a smell of brimstone as it falls.[4] The tree simile, and the forest-fire, again.

But the Achaeans could not get at him to wound him. His companions came round him, "Polydamas and Aeneas and Agenor, and Sarpedon, leader of the Lycians, and Glaucus."[5] As we said, the five divisions of the Trojans are now fighting in one mass. But there is no leader of the third division left. So they fought, and Hector was carried swooning to his car, held in readiness for him, thanks to Polydamas. When they came to the river Xanthus, child

---

[1] XIV. 392 ff.   [2] XIV. 402 ff.   [3] XIII. 160.
[4] XIV. 414 ff.   [5] XIV. 425-426.

of Zeus, they laid him down and he recovered for a moment only to swoon again.[1]

The Argives leapt on the Trojans, and the lesser Ajax wounded his man. It was "Satnios, son of a Nymph, a blameless Naiad, who bore him to Enops, when he was a herdsman, by the river Satnioeis." [2] Polydamas, the greater Ajax, Akamas, each killed his man. Then Peneleos killed Ilioneus, "the son of Phorbas, owner of many sheep, the favourite of Hermes. This was his only son." [3]

Peneleos cut off the head of Ilioneus and showed it to the Trojans. We remember how the head of Imbrios was rolled at the feet of Hector.[4]

He held it up like a poppy-head and showed it to the Trojans, and he boasted: "Take my message, Trojans. Tell the dear father and the mother of the lordly Ilioneus to lament him in their halls. And the wife of Peneleos also will not be gladdened by the sight of her husband back home again, when the Achaeans go back in their ships from Troy."

Andromache and Hector. Peleus and Achilles.

With that incident the issue is decided. The Trojans break and fly. Tell us, Muses of Olympus,[5] who first won the bloody spoils? Ajax, the son of Telamon, from a great prince of the Mysians. Then Antilochus, two men; Meriones, two men; Teucer two, and Menelaus one. But Ajax the swift son of Oileus killed most, "for there was no man like him to pursue men in a rout, when Zeus had made them fly." [6]

When Idomeneus declared that the Ajaxes in the centre would give the Trojans trouble enough, he described the son of Telamon as the best man in the grappling, hand to hand, though he could not run, of course, like Achilles.[7] For running, we now find, the son of Oileus is the man. So the Trojans are put to flight. They run as far as the trench and over it. Outside, they stop, in panic and confusion, pale with terror, at their chariots. And Zeus wakes.

---

[1] XIV. 433 ff.   [2] XIV. 443 ff.   [3] XIV. 490 ff.   [4] XIV. 499 ff.; cf. XIII, 202 ff.
[5] XIV. 508.   [6] XIV. 521.   [7] XIII. 321 ff.

10

CHAPTER V

THE GREEK ROUT. PATROCLUS WITH ACHILLES. THE FIRING OF THE ACHAEAN SHIPS

ZEUS wakes, and the digression is at an end. We are not surprised to find that the pattern of the next episodes recalls the pattern of Books XI and XII.

Zeus, of course, is very angry. Hector, who ought to be triumphant, lies fainting, gasping, spitting blood, only half alive. The Trojans, panic-stricken, are flying before Poseidon. No wonder Zeus reminds his consort of the Heracles affair,[1] not without threats. She disarms him by a delicious feminine evasion.[2] Earth, Heaven, and Styx witness her oath: she did not bring Poseidon into the field. It is all Poseidon's fault. Even the King of gods and men is forced to smile at her effrontery. Still, he intends to stop this kind of thing for the future. "Fetch Iris and Apollo," he tells her. Iris shall send Poseidon out of the field. Apollo shall bring Hector back, and give him strength. Hector shall burn the ships. Achilles shall send out Patroclus, and Patroclus, after killing many Trojans, "and among them my own son, the bright Sarpedon," shall be killed by Hector. Then Achilles shall return. From that time the Trojans shall be beaten until Troy shall fall. But they shall triumph until the promise given to Thetis is fulfilled.

Hera darted from Ida to Olympus, swift as the thought in a man's mind, when he thinks about his travels and says to himself, "I was there, and I was there."[3] One feels the poet's happiness at being back from his digression to the

---

[1] xv. 25.   [2] xv. 36 ff.   [3] xv. 80 ff.

main story. It is reflected in the high spirits of this mischievous goddess. When she sits down in Olympus and
professes to be warning all the gods and goddesses how
hopeless is resistance to their lord and master, she is actually trying to push Ares into trouble.[1] She lets fall a reference, so casually, to his son, Askalaphos—dead in the
field. We suddenly remember. The simple Ares would
have rushed off to avenge him, had not Athene very sensibly
restrained him.

However, Hera did not fail to send Iris and Apollo to
her husband. "Go, swift Iris," says the Thunderer, "to
Poseidon. Bid him desist, and not cross me in future, who
am older and greater than he." She rushed down the
mountain-side as swift as a snowstorm or cold hailstorm,
driven down from the clouds about the summit by the blast
of the North wind.[2] Poseidon yields, but not without protest.
He will bow to Zeus, as his elder brother, in this matter.
There are Furies, Iris has reminded him, who wait on an
elder brother's curse.[3] But if Zeus intends to save Troy
against the will of the other gods, their anger will be incur-
able. However, he plunges under the sea, and the Achaeans
have to do without him.

After that Zeus sent Apollo with the miraculous aegis to
encourage Hector. He swooped down like a hawk, the
swiftest of birds.[4] Poseidon, we remember, went off like a
hawk when he had encouraged the two Ajaxes.[5] Hector
by this time was recovering his breath, able to sit up.
Apollo put fresh strength in him. And Hector went back
to the battle, running lightly like a horse that has fed well
and grown restless and broken out of its stable. Like a
noble lion that suddenly appears and turns back a band of
hounds and huntsmen who are chasing a stag or a wild
goat, so Hector turned back the Greeks.[6]

The comparisons are familiar, and therefore have, of course,
been criticized. Paris has been compared to this same brilliant restive horse,[7] and Ajax to this lion. It is true enough.

---

[1] xv. 164 ff.   [2] xv. 158 ff.   [3] xv. 204.   [4] xv. 237.
[5] xiii. 63.   [6] xv. 263 ff.   [7] xv. 281.

Hector, in this renewal of his youth, combines the beauty of Paris with the strength of Ajax.

Thoas, the King of the Aetolians, on the Greek side, grasps the situation. It was in the form of Thoas that Poseidon met Idomeneus, and encouraged him. Is Hector back in the field? "It is not without Zeus," cries Thoas, "that this thing has happened." The best plan is to withdraw the mass of men, while a phalanx of the best heroes make a screen behind which they can reform the line. So Ajax, Teucer, Idomeneus, and the others waited, while the rest withdrew.

The Trojans came on, Hector and Apollo leading. Apollo held the aegis which the smith Hephaestus made for Zeus to carry into battle.[1]

> So long as Apollo held it quietly in his hands, so long both sides kept shooting, and the people were falling ; but when he looked down and shook it downwards against the swift-horsed Danaans, and himself gave a very loud shout, he put a spell on their spirits in their breasts and they forgot their courage.

The Greeks were like a herd of cattle or a flock of sheep, terrified in the night by two wild beasts.[2] Such comparisons are usually kept for the Trojans. That the Greeks should be like sheep reveals the gravity of the new situation. Many Greeks fell, and Hector shouted—[3]

> Leave the booty. Go on to the ships. If any man shirk I will kill him, and his kinsmen and kinswomen shall not bury him. The dogs shall tear his body in front of Troy.

Is not that relevant to the sequel?

Apollo made the road easy for the Trojans. This time they drove their horses in. Apollo shook the aegis and a great stretch of the wall—not the whole, but the length of a spear's throw [4]—collapsed as easily as a sand-castle which boys playing on the beach first build then overturn with

---

[1] xv. 318 ff.   [2] xv. 323 ff.   [3] xv. 347 ff.
[4] xv. 358 ff. "He *bridged the trench* for the length of a spear's throw, and *overthrew the wall*." Surely not the whole wall, but the wall at that part of the circle?

their hands and feet for fun. Is not Homer, as well as
Hector, the father of Astyanax?

But Nestor prayed to Zeus, and the Father thundered.
He did not mean to destroy the Achaeans utterly. Still,
the Trojans leapt on all the more eagerly when they heard
the thunder. As a great wave, lashed by the wind, washes
over the side of a ship, they swept across the wall. At last
they were fighting at the ships.

Patroclus, meanwhile, throughout this battle, had still
been waiting on Eurypylos, his wounded friend. He heard
the shouting now, and he knew that it came from the ships.
"He groaned aloud, and struck his thighs with his hands,
and grieved and said, 'Eurypylos, I cannot stay.'" The
phrases are worth remembering.[1] He must go to Achilles.
Perhaps he may persuade him. A friend's advice is a good
thing.

By this time the Greeks had reformed their lines, and the
two armies had joined battle. Neither could move the
other. The fight was as straight and even as the measuring
line of a clever carpenter cutting a straight timber for a
ship.[2] We know this carpenter. His timbers are the
bodies of dead men.

Hector and Ajax too were pitted equally against each
other. The one could not drive his enemy off. The other
could not get at the ships, to fire them.

Ajax hit Kaletor, Hector's cousin, as he was bringing
fire to the ships, and Hector shouted to rally his men.
Hector aimed at Ajax, but missed him, and hit Lycophron,
his servant. Ajax called to Teucer, "Dear Teucer, where
are your bow and arrows, given you by Apollo?"[3] Much
good the bow and arrows will be now that Apollo is against
him.

Teucer shoots, and hits Polydamas, it is true. But when
he aims at Hector, Zeus breaks his bowstring. "O fie!"[4]
he cried. "It was a new bowstring. A god is making
us helpless." "Dear boy," said Ajax, "Get a spear

[1] xv. 397 f. (cf. 113).   [2] xv. 410 ff.   [3] xv. 440.   [4] xv. 467 ff.

and shield. Let us fight on." So Teucer obeyed, and
stood by Ajax again. But Hector shouted,[1] "I have
seen with my own eyes. It is easy to see when Zeus is on
one's side. Fight on. Who dies, let him die. There is
no shame in dying for a fatherland. What does death
matter, since our children and our homes and property are
safe, if only we can drive the Achaeans away?" But Ajax
shouted very nobly too,[2] "It is death or victory now. It
is not to a dance, but to battle, that Hector is inviting you.
There is no better plan than to fight on." They fell again
to their fighting and their killing. Among the victims was
Melanippos, a good Trojan, who had been a herdsman once
abroad, but had returned to fight when the war came.[3]
Antilochus wounded him and leapt on him as a hound
leaps on a hind that the huntsman has wounded;[4] but
Hector drove him off; he fled, though he was brave, like a
wild beast that has killed a hound or a herdsman among
his cattle.[5] The Trojans were now like ravening lions.[6]
They were fulfilling the design of Zeus. Zeus was waiting
for the prayer of Thetis to be accomplished, waiting to see
the flash of fire from the burning ships. After that he
meant to turn the Trojans back.

Hector raged like Ares, like a destructive fire in the
forest on the mountains.[7] He foamed at the mouth and
his eyes flashed terribly. But the Greeks stood like a rock
resisting wind and waves.[8] He could not break them.
He leapt on them, blazing with fire. He was like a wave,
fed full by the wind, that crashes down on to a ship: the
wind roars in the mast, and the sailors are terrified.[9] So
the Achaeans were distracted. He was like a lion—[10]

Like a lion that falls with baleful purpose on a herd
of cows, very numerous, feeding in a meadow-pasture:
their herdsman is a man who has not learnt yet how to
fight with a wild beast bent on the killing of a cow. He
walks always with the first or the last cows of the herd,
but the lion leaps in the middle, and eats a cow. . . .

[1] xv. 487 ff.   [2] xv. 502 ff.   [3] xv. 547 ff.   [4] xv. 579 ff.   [5] xv. 587.
[6] xv. 592.   [7] xv. 605.   [8] xv. 618 ff.   [9] xv. 624 ff.   [10] xv. 630 ff.

Again the wave on the ship, and the herdsman, and the lion among the herd. But with what heightened effect! This time the victim is the Mycenean Periphetes, son of Copreus, the notorious herald, who used to go on messages to Heracles from King Eurystheus.

At last the Achaeans had to give up the first ship. But they kept their ranks, and Nestor still appealed to them to fight for their honour and their wives and children. As a suppliant he begged them to fight well.[1] But Ajax could not bear to go back with the rest. He strode from deck to deck, jumping with an iron-shod ship's pole, twenty-two cubits long, like a trick-rider, managing four horses, leaping from horse to horse.[2] Nor was Hector less forward. He darted out "like an eagle, swooping on a flight of birds, geese, cranes, or long-necked swans, that are feeding by a river.[3] He rushed straight on to the ships. Zeus thrust him forward from behind, and made his people follow.

The fight was desperate. The Achaeans said to themselves that they would rather perish than fly; and every Trojan's heart was hoping for the burning of the ships and the massacre of the men. Hector seized the prow of the first ship, the ship that brought Protesilaos to Troy—the first man to land, the first to fall. Then they fought hand to hand, with battle-axes, swords, short spears : weapons went crashing to the ground : the earth ran with blood. Hector still held fast, and called for fire to burn the ship. " Bring fire !" he cried. " Zeus grants us the destruction of these ships, that have done such harm because of the old men's cowardice. They would never let me fight at the ships before. They always held me back. But if Zeus made them foolish then, he is inspiring us to-day and bidding us go forward." [4]

Ajax at last had to give ground a little. But he still kept fighting, and still shouting to his men : " There is nothing behind us now, everything depends on our right hands." And he wounded man after man, as they tried to fire the ships. Twelve men he hit. . . .[5]

---

[1] xv. 660. [2] xv. 679 ff. [3] xv. 690 ff.
[4] xv. 718 ff. [5] xv. 746.

And Patroclus was standing by Achilles, the shepherd of the people, weeping hot tears, like a black waterfall that trickles darkly down the face of a sheer rock. And the swift-footed bright Achilles, when he saw it, pitied him.[1]

So had Patroclus pitied Eurypylos, when he met him coming in wounded from the battle. When Machaon was carried home, Achilles " saw and noticed." [2] Homer did not say " he saw and pitied him." Here, for the first time, Achilles, " when he saw it, pitied him." At the end, when he first sees Priam, Achilles will " see and marvel." Then, after the old man has spoken, he will " pity his grey head and beard."

Why are you all in tears, Patroclus, like a little girl that runs along by her mother and begs to be picked up, clutching her dress and stopping her, though she is in a hurry, and looking up at her in tears, to make her pick her up?[3]

It is the old delightful trick of style. " Why all in tears . . . and looking up at her in tears. . . ." If this little girl be Homer's child, is she not also a sister of Nausicaa and of Astyanax and of the children who build castles on the sand and then destroy them " with their hands and feet, for fun "?

" Why are you crying?" Achilles goes on. " Is it bad news from home? Menoitios is still alive, they say, and Peleus is still living among his Myrmidons. We should grieve indeed for both of them, if they were dead."[4] A little later Achilles will be grieving not only for himself, but for Peleus: he will be wondering if Peleus is alive or dead. At this moment he has no notion that he is on the brink of his life's tragedy. But the full value of this exquisite psychology is lost if you suppose that the great interview with Priam was no part of the poet's design.

What? Can it really mean that you are being sorry for the Argives; for their destruction at their ships, because

---

[1] XVI. 1 ff.   [2] XI. 599; contrast XVI. 5, XXIV. 483, 526.
[3] XVI. 7 ff.   [4] XVI, 14 ff.

of their own fault? Tell me plainly, do not hide it from me, so that we may both know.

"Are you really being sorry for the Argives?"[1] Think of Nestor's question to Patroclus, when Achilles sent his friend to ask about Machaon, "Why should Achilles be sorry for the sons of the Achaeans?" And again, when Patroclus saw and pitied Eurypylos, he spoke to him, "being sorry."

With a deep groan, Patroclus, that good driver of horses, answered him. "Achilles, son of Peleus, first of the Achaeans, do not be angry: for the trouble that has overcome the Achaeans is so very great."[2] Patroclus speaks as nature prompts him, but his formula of address is itself an argument. Remember, it implies, that you are the son of Peleus, and that, after all, you are an Achaean yourself. All our bravest men are wounded, Diomed, Odysseus, Agamemnon, and—Eurypylos.[3] And the physicians with their drugs are doing what they can to cure them . . . "but you, Achilles, will do nothing and nothing can be done with you." That is the effect of the word ἀμήχανος and of the sudden repetition of the name Achilles.[4]

After this, the first paragraph of his appeal, there follow two quick sentences. First—[5]

As for me, may I never be taken by an anger like this which you hug so jealously, terrible, making your virtue into a scourge for you. What good will you be to men who are yet to be born if you do not save the Achaeans from disgrace and ruin.

Patroclus knows his friend's passionate desire for honour after death. Then, as if to take back the honourable title "son of Peleus"—[6]

You have no pity. Your father is not the horseman Peleus. Thetis is not your mother. The grey sea and the sheer rocks are your parents because your mind is ruthless.

Then the appeal that Patroclus at least may be allowed to go, beginning thus, as if Patroclus were reminded of old

---

[1] XVI. 17; cf. XI. 656, 815.   [2] XVI. 21.   [3] XVI. 27.
[4] XVI. 29.   [5] XVI. 30 ff.   [6] XVI. 33 ff.

Nestor's theory by his own mention of the goddess Thetis, and as if he could not bear to think that the true explanation is a lack of heart :—[1]

> Or if the reason be some secret word that you alone know and are avoiding, something told you as from Zeus by your lady mother, then at any rate send me at once and let the Myrmidons go with me. . . . Let me take your armour, that the Trojans may think I am you, and give way, if it be only for a moment.

So he spoke as a suppliant, in his great folly. It was for his own death that he prayed.[2]

The answer of Achilles[3] shows that he has been deeply moved by one phrase of the appeal :—

> Zeus-born Patroclus, what have you said? It is no secret, no prophecy told me by my mother from Zeus. I know of no such prophecy for which I care. . . .

He means that, although he knows about his early death, that would not keep him idle.

> It is this agony[4] that assails my heart and spirit, that a man should make his equal of no account and take away his prize of honour simply because he has the power to do it. That is what hurts me terribly, because for that I have suffered such grief in my soul. The girl, whom the Achaeans gave me . . .

He goes on with the old story, as violently as if Agamemnon had made no effort to conciliate him. The critics cannot understand it. Have they never been angry and obstinate themselves?

> King Agamemnon treated me as if I were an outlaw, a nobody, with no honour. . . . But we will let that rest —treat it as something past—one cannot cherish anger incessantly for ever. I said I would not cease my feud until the battle-cry and the battle reached my ships. But do you put on my famous armour about your shoulders and lead out the Myrmidons to fight. Lovers they are of battle.

---

[1] XVI. 36 ff.   [2] XVI. 45.   [3] XVI. 49 ff.   [4] XVI. 52 ff.

That shows how glad he would be to go himself. But he is still too proud and angry.

Look, the Greeks are hemmed in at the sea in a very narrow place, and the Trojans so confident, and Troy so safe. They would be running, they would be filling all the passages with their dead, if Agamemnon were but kind and fair to me.

Yes, at that moment, if Agamemnon came himself and offered amends, Achilles, we believe, would go out and fight. But as it is—

The Trojans are fighting round our army. It is not Diomed's spear that is busy to-day. It is not Agamemnon's voice that I hear from that well-hated head encouraging his men.

It is murderous Hector's voice, encouraging the Trojans that breaks on the air around us. The plain belongs to the Trojans with their battle-cry. They are beating the Achaeans in battle. All the same, Patroclus, fall on mightily and save the ships. Prevent them from burning the ships and taking away all chance of a dear home-coming. . . .

For whom? He does not say "for the Achaeans." But that is really what his words imply.

Then he adds the warning which shows that he now has more of calculation, less of passion, though much passion still, in his mood. Patroclus is not to drive the Trojans too far. If he did, the Greeks might not feel the need of Achilles, might not restore Briseis nor offer splendid gifts for reconciliation. Three times Achilles repeats the injunction.[1] And as he repeats it, we perceive a new thought working in his mind. "What if Patroclus himself should not come back?" So he says first, with the thought of his own honour uppermost, "When you have driven them from the ships, come back. So I shall still have the girl restored, and get splendid gifts of honour." Then, a second time, "If the husband of Hera honours you, do not be too eager

---

[1] xvi. 88 ff.

to fight on without me.   It would lessen my honour if you did."   That covers a real anxiety for his friend.   When the warning is given for the third time, the anxiety is openly expressed.   "Do not go on to Ilion, for fear some God may intervene.   Apollo the Far-Worker loves the Trojans dearly.   Turn back when you have saved the ships, and leave the fighting in the plain to others."   Then he covers his emotion by a violence which is, of course, illogical, excessive, and belied by his own conduct at this moment.   Is not that Homer's way of making Achilles say, "Come back safe.   I care so much for you?"   What Achilles actually says is this :—[1]

I wish, by Zeus the Father and Athene and Apollo, that not a single Trojan now alive might escape death, and not a single Argive, if we too only might escape destruction, and might capture Troy together.

It is fantastic.   But it means, though Achilles would never have said it, "Come back safe.   I care for you more than for all the Greeks and Trojans in the world."

While the two friends were talking, Ajax was struggling, giving ground, but always fighting.   Panting and covered with sweat, he still frustrated Hector and the Trojans.   Let the Muses tell,[2] as Homer bids them, how fire came to the ships.

Hector stood close to Ajax, and struck his ashen spear with a great sword.   He struck it in the shaft, behind the spear-head, smashing it right through.   There stood Ajax, brandishing the broken stump of the shaft, and the bronze head fell to the ground with a clang a long way off.   Ajax knew it in his noble heart for the working of the gods, and shuddered.   He saw that it was Zeus the Thunderer who was cutting altogether the sinews of his fighting and was willing victory for the Trojans.   So he gave way before their weapons.   And they threw the untiring fire on the swift ship, and inextinguishable flame was kindled on it.

[1] xvi. 97 ff.   [2] xvi. 112 ff.

It was for the sake of this moment that Teucer, not so very long ago, was foiled by Zeus, and had his bowstring, a new bowstring, mysteriously snapped. " It is Zeus," he cried, " who is cutting the sinews of our fighting." " My good lad," answered Ajax, " get a good spear and leave your bow and arrows." [1] And now the spear of Ajax himself is broken.

As the first ship took the flame, Achilles struck his thighs and spoke to Patroclus :—[2]

> Up, Zeus-born Patroclus.   Up, good driver of horses. I hear the whistling of fire at the ships.   They may destroy them.   They may be cutting off escape.   Quick, put you on my armour.

Was it not also for the sake of this great gesture that Patroclus, when he heard the shout of battle from the hut of Eurypylos, struck his thighs with the flat of his hands and said " Eurypylos, I cannot stay, although you need me " ?

[1] xv. 467 ff.   [2] xvi. 125 ff. ; cf. xv. 397.

CHAPTER VI

THE ARMING AND THE EXPLOITS OF PATROCLUS

PATROCLUS armed.[1] He put on all the armour of Achilles, the greaves, the breastplate, the silver-studded sword, the great stout shield, the helmet with its terrible nodding plumes : only he did not take the ashen spear of Peleus. No one but Achilles could wield that. It was a famous spear, and had been given to Peleus by Cheiron on Mount Pelion.[2] So Cheiron, the great healer, and the hero's father, are linked again.

This episode of the arming forms a small panel in the design, more simple than the arming of Agamemnon, yet more impressive. Because, for the tragedy, the snakes and the Gorgon on Agamemnon's armour matter so little. It is more simple also, but less impressive, than the arming of Achilles, because the armour of Achilles is to be a worthy symbol of his life and destiny.

The horses were yoked by Automedon, " whom Patroclus honoured most after Achilles." Two of them were the immortal pair, Xanthos and Balios—[3]

a pair swift as the wind, born to the South Wind by the Harpy Podargê, as she fed in a meadow pasture by the stream of Ocean.

With them he put a trace-horse, Pedasos, a mortal horse " which Achilles brought back with him when he took the city of Eetion." [4] It was from that city that he took Briseis. It was there that he showed respect for the dead body of his enemy, Andromache's father, and took Andromache's mother prisoner, but released her for a ransom. And it was

---

[1] XVI. 130 ff.   [2] XVI. 143.   [3] XVI. 149 ff.   [4] XVI. 153.

there that he took the harp to which he would sing in his proud loneliness about the fame of heroes—while Patroclus waited until he should have finished his song.   Not a hint of all these reminiscences from the poet.   Simply, " Pedasos, brought back by Achilles when he took the city of Eetion, a mortal horse to run with these immortal horses."   But one reason why Pedasos matters to us is that he was taken at this city.

Achilles himself reviewed the Myrmidons.   They were like wolves that have been worrying a stag : they come down to a stream and gulp its black waters greedily, and belch out blood which mingles with the water.   So violent were the Myrmidons.[1]   And Achilles himself marshalled them, urging on the horses and the spearmen.

There were fifty Myrmidon ships and fifty men from each. Achilles chose five leaders whom he trusted.   First, Menesthios,[2] son of the river Spercheios, whose mother Polydora was a mortal, daughter of Peleus, wedded openly to a mortal man but secretly to the river-god ; and secondly, Eudoros,[3] son of a mortal woman, Polymela, who was beautiful and had inspired the love of Hermes when he saw her in the dance of Artemis : so Hermes lay with her in an upper chamber secretly, and she bore him this fine son : but the hero Echecles took her as his wife, and cared for her child as if he were his own.   Thus the leaders of the Myrmidons have caught something of the beauty and the tragic mixture of mortality and divinity that belong to their great leader. Their poetic relevance to the main theory is like that of Simoeisios and Imbrios and those others, sons of nymphs and rivers.

The third leader was Peisander, the best spearman ; the fourth was Phoenix, the old horseman, whom we know ; the fifth Alkimedon, the noble son of Laerkes.   Achilles marshalled them all and spoke to them.   He reminded them how they had blamed him, called him hard-hearted, and threatened to go home if he would not let them fight.[4] Now they shall show their courage.

---

[1] XVI. 156 ff.   [2] XVI. 173 ff.   [3] XVI. 179 ff.   [4] XVI. 200 ff.

They formed a phalanx, as well made as a strong wall, spear close to spear, helmet to helmet, man to man.[1]   We have already spoken of the cunning with which the poet has led up to every detail.[2]   Now see what happens.   When they were all prepared, with Patroclus and Automedon, two hearts beating as in one bosom, ready to lead them :—

Achilles went to his hut,[3] and opened the lid of a beautiful and cunningly wrought chest, which silver-footed Thetis had put on his ship for him to bring to Troy : she filled it with shirts and woolly rugs and cloaks to keep the cold winds from him.   There, he had a fine wrought cup.   No other man drank bright wine from it, and Achilles himself did not pour libation from it to any other god than Zeus the Father.   He took it from the chest and cleaned it first with brimstone and washed it in a lovely stream of water, then washed his own hands, and poured into it bright wine.

Then he stood in the middle of his fenced enclosure and made libation of bright wine, looking up to the sky : and Zeus, who delights in Thunder, did not fail to see. And he said :—

"Zeus, King Palasgian, of Dodona, dwelling afar, Lord of tempestuous Dodona, where your Selloi dwell, your interpreters, with unwashed feet, making their bed on the ground.   You have heard my prayer that I have prayed. You have honoured me, and greatly crushed the sons of the Achaeans.   Fulfil now also this my prayer. . . ."

It is a worthy climax to the long series of appeals to Zeus with which the battle has been punctuated.   It is a worthy link in the long chain of prayers from the prayer of Chryses to the prayer of Priam.   And the cup ?   Was it not for the sake of this moment that Nestor was provided with the great and beautiful cup, which only he could lift, for the healing of Machaon ?[4]

So Achilles prayed that his servant might have glory, and might come back safe with his companions and the armour.   Zeus heard, and granted half the prayer, but half

---

[1] XVI. 212 ff.   [2] P. 127.   [3] XVI. 221 ff.   [4] XI. 632 ff., see p. 107.

he refused. And Achilles, when he had finished, went back to the hut, put the cup in the chest, and came out again, because he still desired to watch the battle. But Patroclus, the great-hearted, was followed by his men into the fight.

Patroclus and his Myrmidons poured out "like wasps on the roadside which boys provoke, as is their foolish way." [1] Asios, son of Hyrtakos, the fool, protested, not very long ago, to Zeus, " Look how these Greeks defend themselves, like wasps : they insist on fighting for their wives and children." [2] So the Myrmidons are like wasps, provoked by mischievous boys, so that : " Even if a passing traveller disturbs them by accident, they fly out, every one of them, and fight for their children." These mischievous boys are the same who built the castles on the sand.

Patroclus shouts, " Be brave, that we may honour Achilles, and make Agamemnon know his Infatuation in dishonouring the best of the Achaeans." [3] He is going out to fight for Achilles' honour, not his own. For a time he will remember Achilles' warning. Presently he will forget.

The Trojans thought it was Achilles, and were terrified and looked round for a way of escape. Patroclus killed Pyraichmes—fire-spear—and drove the Trojans back from Protesilaus' ship. It was left half-burnt. But the fire was out and the Trojans fled.

As when Zeus lightens and breaks up a cloud, and in the sudden flash of lightning the peaks and promontories and valleys are seen in a bright light, so the Greeks were suddenly relieved and heartened.[4]

It is a simile which we have heard before, repeated with a nobler application. But here it is to be the first of a great series.

The Greeks were heartened. But it was not yet a rout. Man killed man, and the Trojans tried to extricate themselves. First Patroclus, then the other great Greek chieftains killed their man. They were like ravening wolves

----

[1] XVI. 259 ff.   [2] XII. 167 ff., p. 117.   [3] XVI. 270 ff.   [4] XVI. 297 ff.

II

attacking sheep or goats, left unguarded on the mountain by a careless shepherd.[1]

The " careless shepherd " makes us think of Hector ; and, of course, " Ajax was aiming at the son of Priam." Hector escaped the blow by the skilful use of his shield. He knew the art of fighting. He saw that the fight had turned against him. But he stood his ground and tried to save his companions.[2] Both for good and evil that touch is relevant to Hector's destiny.

Then Zeus and the storm again.[3] As a cloud sweeps into the sky out of a bright clear upper air from Olympus, when Zeus is preparing a tempest, so the Trojans were chased from the ships, not in good order. Hector was carried off by his swift horses, and left behind the people, who were checked in their retreat by the trench. As we said, it was not the whole trench, but a stretch of it that Apollo levelled. Many chariots were now broken at the trench. And Patroclus drove straight on after Hector.

Then a third time Zeus and the storm.[4]

> As on a stormy day in autumn, when all the earth groans beneath the weight of the tempest, when Zeus pours his rains most violently on men who in Assembly give unjust judgments, distorting justice because they have no regard for the gods: when rivers are full and torrents carry down with them the hills in an avalanche, rushing headlong from the mountains to the sea with a loud roar, and the works of man perish. So the Trojans fled in the rout.

Patroclus would not let them get near the city. He kept cutting off the fugitives and heading them towards the ships. He killed first one man, then a second, then a third; then six others, in quick succession. And Sarpedon . . .[5] Is not the pattern well made?

First Patroclus called to his men. They fought, and we heard the simile of Zeus scattering the darkness with his

---

[1] XVI. 352 ff. ; cf. 156 ff.   [2] XVI. 363.   [3] XVI. 364 ff. ; cf. 297 ff.
[4] XVI. 384 ff.   [5] XVI. 419 ff. ; cf. 268 and 472.

thunderstorm and lightning. Then more fighting. Then
the simile of Zeus and the storm again. The chariots are
wrecked at the trench, and again we hear in its full splendour,
the theme of the storm from Zeus, sending flood and disaster
on the unjust. Then more killing by Patroclus, and—
Sarpedon, son of Zeus, called to his men :—

"Respect one another, Lycians, whom are you flying?
I will face this man, whoever he may be." He leapt down
from his car, and so did Patroclus. The two heroes faced
one another. They were like two vultures, fighting on a
high crag.[1] And Zeus, the son of Cronos, when he saw them,
pitied them.[2] That is the climax of the Zeus-similes. The
Father spoke to his consort and his sister, Hera. Would
not she too pity his son? Should he set Sarpedon down,
safe home, in Lycia? Her answer is that, if Zeus breaks
the rules, others will break them.[3] Sarpedon is a mortal
man, and his time has come. All Zeus may do is to have
the body carried off by Sleep and Death to Lycia for burial.

And Zeus bowed to the argument, and rained blood for
Sarpedon's death.[4]

The heroes were left to their fates. First Patroclus hit
Thrasymelos, Sarpedon's squire. Then Sarpedon, missing
Patroclus, hit Pedasos, the mortal trace-horse. Automedon
cut the traces, and the fight went on. Sarpedon missed
again, and Patroclus hit Sarpedon.

He fell like an oak, a poplar, or a pine-tree, cut down on
the mountain to be made into a ship's timber.[5] He lay
outstretched in front of his car and horses, groaning and
clutching at the dust. As a great-hearted brown bull is
picked out from the herd of cows and killed by a lion, and
dies, roaring angrily, so Sarpedon was angry as he died,[6] and
called to his friend Glaucus: "Glaucus, dear boy, be brave.
First rally the other chiefs, then fight yourself for my body.
I shall be a reproach to you always, if they spoil me." Were
we not justified in our thought that the scene of the bull and
lions on the Shield was poetically relevant to the scene of

---

[1] XVI. 427 ff. [2] XVI. 431. [3] XVI. 440 ff.
[4] XVI. 459. [5] XVI. 482 ff. [6] XVI. 485 ff.

fighting, where Fate dragged a dead man's body by the legs?[1]

Glaucus was helpless.   He had been wounded in the arm by Teucer.   But he could still pray to Apollo, and Apollo heard him.   So he rallied first the Lycian chieftains, then the Trojans, Polydamas, Agenor and Aeneas, and then Hector.   To Hector he had a word to say.   Hector had talked as if the allies were not doing their duty.   "Ah, Hector, have you quite forgotten your allies?"[2]   So Hector, deeply moved, and angry for Sarpedon, rallied to Glaucus.

On the other side Patroclus called to the Ajaxes.   "Here lies the man," he cried, "who was first to cross the trench. He is dead.   Now, if we fight, we can put dishonour on his body, and spoil him."[3]   So they fought about the body, and a great shout rose, and Zeus sent night on the battle.[4]

And soon there will be fighting for the body of Patroclus.

The Trojans fought hard.   Epeigeus, one of the best Myrmidons, was killed.   He was a suppliant, like Phoenix.[5] He had killed a man and suffered exile, but was hospitably received by Peleus and the silver-footed Thetis.   So, when he fell, Patroclus, grieved and angry for his dear companion, darted upon the Trojans "as straight as a swift hawk, scattering daws and starlings."[6]   He killed a man, and the Trojans withdrew the length of a spear-throw, "as far as a man can throw a hunting spear in the games or in battle."[7] But Glaucus was the first to turn, and he killed great-hearted Bathycles, pre-eminent among the Myrmidons for riches and prosperity.[8]   Again a touch, like the reference to the exiled suppliant, which makes the fighting relevant to Peleus and Achilles.

So the Trojans rallied again, but Meriones killed Laogonos "the priest of Idaean Zeus, who was honoured as a god by the people."[9]   That completes the introduction to the following episode :—

Aeneas aimed at Meriones, who adroitly evaded the blow. "You are a dancer, I see!"[10] cried Aeneas, "but my spear

---

[1] See p. 7.   [2] XVI. 538.   [3] XVI. 556 ff.   [4] XVI. 567.   [5] XVI. 570 ff.
[6] XVI. 582.   [7] XVI. 589 ff.   [8] XVI. 595-596.   [9] XVI. 604 f.   [10] XVI. 617.

would have stopped your dancing, had I hit you." "You may boast," answered Meriones, "but you too are a mortal man, and can be killed." Then Patroclus, "What, good Meriones? It is not words that will drive the Trojans from this body. Battles are won by fighting. Words are for the Council. Do not talk, but fight."[1]

The incident is the prelude to his tragedy. Presently he will himself be boasting, "I see you have tumblers in Troy!"[2] Presently he will die because he forgets "the wise word" of Achilles.[3] For the moment, ominously, we hear again the noise of the woodcutters at work on the mountains.[4] Such was the noise the fighters made, as they struggled about the body of Sarpedon, as persistent as flies round pails of milk in spring-time.[5]

And all the while Zeus watched them.[6] Should he let Patroclus die at once, or give him yet another moment of glory? He would give him one more victory.

Zeus gave victory once more to Patroclus. Hector was first to see that the scales of Zeus had turned against him.[7] Again a touch of contrast with his future blindness. He mounted his car, and called his men to retire. The Lycians fled in the rout, and the Greeks took the armour from Sarpedon's body. Then Zeus bade Apollo fetch the body for him. He took it up and washed it in the water of a flowing river, and anointed it.[8] Sleep and Death came and took it home for burial in Lycia.

But Patroclus was infatuated. He pursued the Trojans to Troy. Had he remembered the word of the son of Peleus, he would have escaped the evil fate of death.[9] "But the mind of Zeus is ever stronger than the minds of men, and it was Zeus that day who put a spirit of daring in his breast." He killed nine men. Troy would have fallen to him, had not Apollo stood on the wall to save it. Thrice Patroclus leapt at an angle of the wall, and thrice Apollo thrust him back. But when for the fourth time he rushed on like a daimôn, Apollo shouted terribly, "Yield, Patroclus ׀

[1] XVI. 627 ff.   [2] XVI. 750.   [3] XVI. 686.   [4] XVI. 632 ff.   [5] XVI. 641 ff.
[6] XVI. 644 f.   [7] XVI. 655 ff.   [8] XVI. 678 ff.   [9] XVI. 686 ff.

The sack of Troy is not for you, nor for Achilles, who is better far than you ! " And Patroclus went a long way back, avoiding the wrath of the Far-Shooter.[1]

Then Apollo went to Hector, who was waiting with his charioteer Cebriones at the Scaean gate, and sent the two against Patroclus. Patroclus dismounted, aimed a huge boulder at Cebriones, and mocked at him as he fell from the chariot. " Ah, I see you have tumblers in Troy."[2] And he ran at the body, like a lion that has been wounded in a raid on a farm. " His own courage killed him."[3] Over the body Hector fought with him. They were like two lions on the mountains, both hungry, quarreling for the body of a hind.[4] We have had similes of a lion and a bull, a lion and hounds, a lion and a hind. To crown the series, here are two lions, Hector and Patroclus. They pulled at the body. Hector had it by the head, Patroclus by the legs. The Greeks and Trojans fought round them. The battle was like the encounter of two winds in the mountain forest, when the oak and the ash and the long-leaved cornel are crashed together, and there is a great noise of the breaking of the branches.[5] We have heard before of the wind in the mountain forest. Now there are two winds fighting.

And all the while, as the weapons rang and the spears and arrows flew round him, Cebriones lay on the ground, " great and greatly lying : he had forgotten his driving " :—[6]

So long as the sun was bestriding the midst of the heaven, so long they shot their weapons at one another, and the people were falling. But when the sun was turning to the hour of the loosing of cattle, then beyond their portion the Achaeans were victorious. They dragged the body of the hero Cebriones out from among the weapons, out of the battle-tumult of the Trojans, and stripped him of his armour. And Patroclus leapt on the Trojans with evil purpose. Thrice he leapt on them like swift Ares, shouting terribly : and thrice nine men he slew. But when for the fourth time he rushed on like a

[1] XVI. 702 ff., see p. 46.   [2] XVI. 751.   [3] XVI. 752-753.
[4] XVI. 756 ff.   [5] XVI. 765.   [6] XVI. 776 ff.

daimôn, then to Patroclus appeared the end of life. Apollo met him in the battle, terrible: and he did not see him as he came. . . .

Apollo struck him on the back.   Down fell his helmet, the helmet of Achilles.   It had never been in the dust before: now Hector was to wear it.   For Hector too was soon to die.   The spear broke in Patroclus' hand.   His shield and shield-belt fell from his shoulders.   Apollo loosed his corselet.   He stood confused, and Euphorbos, the beautiful young son of Panthoos, wounded him in the back.

But he was still alive, and was going back to safety, when Hector overtook him.   They were like a lion and a boar who fight for a small spring of water.[1]   Hector boasted, "Ah, much good your friend Achilles does you, who bade you not return without the spoils of Hector."[2]   But Patroclus answered, "Boast if you will.   It is the son of Leto and Euphorbos that have killed me.   You are only the third. And you will die yourself very soon, at the hand of that same Achilles, son of Aeacus."[3]

He died, and Hector spoke to the dead man.[4]   "Patroclus, why prophesy my death?   Who knows if Achilles, son of lovely-haired Thetis, shall perhaps be struck first by my spear, and lose his life?"

So he spoke, and drew the brazen weapon from the wound; as he drew it out, he trod on the body, and pressed it down away from the spear.   Then at once, with the spear in his hand, he strode after Automedon, the god-like squire of the swift-footed son of Aeacus, eager to wound him.   But the swift immortal horses which the gods had given as a splendid gift to Peleus, carried Automedon away.[5]

The gifts of the gods to Peleus we remember.   They were splendid.   He had riches and a kingdom, and a goddess for his wife.   But he had no son to tend him in his old age. One son he had, Achilles.   But he was not tending Peleus. He was here at Troy, troubling Priam and his children.

---

[1] XVI. 823.   [2] XVI. 837 ff.   [3] XVI. 849 ff.   [4] XVI. 859 ff.   [5] XVI. 862 ff.

CHAPTER VII

THE HOME-COMING OF THE BODY OF PATROCLUS

THE second movement of the poem is nearing its close. We shall soon embark on the last and noblest movement, the culminating tragedy of Hector and Achilles. But first there is the defence by Menelaus and the Ajaxes of the body of Patroclus. How perfectly this last panel of the series fits into the pattern, we shall see if we look back for the last time at the path by which we have travelled.

Zeus sent Strife with the battle-portent. Strife shouted. Agamemnon shouted. Agamemnon armed. And Zeus rained blood.

Until mid-day the fight was equal. The armies mowed each other down like lines of reapers in a cornfield. Strife rejoiced. But at the hour when the woodcutter is tired of felling trees, and takes his dinner, the Achaeans broke the Trojan line.

Agamemnon did great deeds. He was like fire. He was like a lion. Zeus saved Hector from him, and sent Iris to the Scaean gate with warning and encouragement for Hector.

Agamemnon did great deeds, but at last was wounded. Then Hector ordered an advance. He was like a huntsman setting hounds at a lion or a boar.

Hector did great deeds, but Odysseus and Diomed rallied, like boars turning on the hounds. They fought well, but Hector was saved by his helmet, Apollo's gift. Diomed was wounded, and Odysseus left alone, like a boar surrounded by the hounds and huntsmen. He too was wounded. Should he fly? No, he would call for help. Menelaus and the two Ajaxes joined him. Ajax, the son of Telamon, appeared to the Trojans like a lion scattering jackals that have been worrying a hind. Menelaus led the wounded Odysseus away, and Ajax, left alone, was like a torrent sweeping rubble and dry tree-trunks down to the sea.

Meanwhile Hector, who had gone to another part of the field, was facing Idomeneus. Machaon, the physician, was wounded here by Paris, and was taken off by Nestor. Hector came back to rally the Trojans against Ajax.

Ajax went back slowly, like a lion, like an ass, driven out of a cornfield, but only after he has finished eating, by the cudgels of small boys.

And Achilles sent Patroclus to the hut of Nestor to inquire about Machaon.

The Greek wall was no longer to stop the Trojans. In the sequel, after Troy had fallen, Poseidon and the other gods were to destroy it in a flood. For the present the fight raged round it. Hector, urging on his men, was like a lion or a boar among huntsmen.

But the horses shied at the trench. Polydamas advised, and Hector agreed, that the chariots be left outside. So the Trojans advanced on foot in five divisions.

Asios, son of Hyrtakos, alone drove in, through an open gate. He found two sentinels ready for him, and lost many men. He protested feebly to Zeus. These Greeks, he complained, defend themselves like wasps.

Zeus sent an omen of an eagle and a snake. Polydamas warned Hector that it was bad. But Hector answered, "the best omen is to fight for one's fatherland." Zeus sent a wind, which carried a dust-cloud to the ships of the Achaeans. And the Trojans went gladly to the attack.

The battle was violent. The Ajaxes were strong in the defence. The weapons fell as thickly as the snow which Zeus sends to cover all the earth. The land is covered by it, but on the sea-coasts the waves keep washing it away.

The Trojans would not have got in, had not Zeus inspired Sarpedon, who was like a lion. He spoke to Glaucus.

"Why are we princes honoured? Because we are good fighters. Were not death and old age certain, I might shirk. As it is, let us go." Glaucus was wounded. Sarpedon grieved, but went on. He dragged down part of the battlements.

The fight was equal. It was like the quarrel of two men for a narrow strip of land. It was as exactly poised as the scales of a careful widow, weighing out the wool for her day's work.

Then Zeus gave glory to Hector, who broke down a gate with a huge boulder, and leapt in, like the night, like fire.

Hector once in, Zeus looked away. Poseidon came, in a marvellous sea-journey, to inspire the Greeks. He spoke to the two Ajaxes and others. The Achaeans formed two solid phalanxes and the Trojans were held.

Teucer killed Imbrios, who fell like an ash, cut down on the mountain. Hector too killed a man, and there was a fight over the two bodies. The head of Imbrios was thrown at Hector's feet.

Poseidon spoke to Idomeneus, who had been waiting on a wounded friend. Idomeneus met Meriones, and the two, remembering how much better are two men together than two single fighters, entered the battle.

So Zeus and Poseidon pulled both ways.

Idomeneus killed, among others, Asios, son of Hyrtakos, who fell, like an oak or a poplar or a pine, in front of his useless chariot. His charioteer lost nerve, and he too was killed.

After more fighting, Idomeneus killed the beautiful Alkathoos. He was struck with confusion by Poseidon so that he could not escape. Like a tree or a memorial pillar he stood, and was so cut down.

Aeneas rallied the Trojans, and two bands fought over the body of Alkathoos. After more fighting, in which Aeneas and Idomeneus were protagonists, Deiphobus killed Askalathos, a son of Ares. But Ares did not yet know of his death. So they fought on over the body.

Yet more fighting, with Aeneas conspicuous. Then Menelaus became prominent. He wounded Helenus and killed

Peisander. He boasted, and appealed to Zeus. "They say that you are wise : yet all this is your doing. These Trojans have never had their fill of fighting."

Hector, meanwhile, in another part of the field, was facing the two Ajaxes, who were like two oxen ploughing together. He did not know that the Greeks were winning on the left. But Polydamas advised him to withdraw and reform his lines. He agreed and the Trojans rallied. But Ajax still challenged them boldly. "Soon you shall be praying to Zeus for your horses to be swifter than hawks in flight." Zeus sent an eagle on the right, and the Greeks rejoiced. But Hector scorned the omen and pressed on.

The battle was joined again with loud shouting. Nestor, though he was waiting on Machaon, could not bear to hold aloof. He had to go, at least to view the struggle. His mind was troubled as is the sea when the wind is still uncertain. He met Agamemnon, Odysseus, Diomed, all wounded, Agamemnon in despair, Odysseus still resolved, Diomed still full of fire. Diomed led them back to the field. They could at any rate encourage their men. Poseidon cheered them on, and the Greeks fought well.

Then Hera helped them. She borrowed the charms of Aphrodite, and persuaded Sleep to be her ally. At last Zeus slept in her arms. The battle between Hector and Poseidon raged more violently than fire or wind or sea.

In the Trojan rout that followed, Ajax, the son of Telamon, did great deeds. So did others. Menelaus killed Hypsenor, shepherd of the people. But Ajax, son of Oileus, killed most in the rout.

Zeus woke, and sent Iris to Poseidon, who retired unwillingly. Apollo, with the aegis, joined Hector, and drove back the Greeks in panic. "Leave the booty, and go on to the ships," cried Hector, "I shall kill any man who shirks." Apollo levelled a great stretch of the wall, like a sand-castle, built and overturned by children playing on the beach. Nestor cried to Zeus, who thundered : but the Trojans pressed on all the more. They drove on like a great wave of the sea, and the Greeks fell back to the ships.

And Patroclus, who was waiting on Eurypylos, could not
stay.   He left his friend, and ran back to Achilles.

Hector and Ajax fought an equal battle for the ships.
Teucer joined Ajax, but Zeus snapped his bow-string, and
Teucer cried " Zeus cuts the nerves of our fighting."   But
Ajax answered, " Good lad, get a spear ! "   Hector shouted,
triumphantly, " Zeus is on our side.   Let those who die, die.
All is well if we can only drive out the Greeks."   But Ajax
splendidly answered, " Up Greeks.   It is not to a dance,
but to a fight, that Hector is inviting you."
    The battle grew more and more violent.   The Trojans
were now like lions.   Zeus looked for the flash of fire from
the ships.   Hector was raging like Ares, like fire, with
foaming mouth and flashing eyes and helmet.   The Greeks
stood like a wall, but the Trojans came on like a great
wave, like a lion.   At last the Greeks gave up the first ship,
but retired in good order, Nestor still exhorting them.   Ajax,
with a great ship's pole, leapt forward, from deck to deck,
still keeping Hector off.   Hector leapt out like an eagle.
    So at last the first ship was fired.   And Hector cried
again, " See Zeus is with us."
    And Patroclus stood before Achilles, weeping like a
little girl that clutches at her mother's skirt.   And at length
Achilles let Patroclus go.

We have seen how the exploits of Patroclus, his arming,
his killing of Sarpedon, and his own death at the hands of
Hector, gain significance from this noble introduction.   We
are now to notice how the pattern is completed by the
interlude between the death of Patroclus and the arming of
Achilles.
    Menelaus saw Patroclus fall,[1] and came to the rescue of
his body.   That is why in the earlier fighting Menelaus
three times suddenly emerged into the foreground.[2]   First
he appeared, with the two Ajaxes, for the rescue of Odysseus.
Then, when Poseidon helped the Greeks, great deeds were
done first by the Ajaxes, then by Idomeneus, then by

[1] XVII. I.   [2] XI. 463 ff., XIII. 581 ff., XIV. 516 ff.

Menelaus. Again, in the Trojan rout, great deeds were done by Ajax, son of Telamon, by Menelaus, and by the lesser Ajax. Now, in the sequel first Menelaus, then Ajax and the rest. Menelaus, not a great fighter, but a brave and gentle hero, stood over the body as a mother cow defending her calf.[1] " She stands by it, lowing. It is her first calf. She has never borne young before." And Euphorbos, the beautiful son of Panthoos, who first wounded Patroclus, challenged him. " Ah, the pride of you sons of Panthoos," cried Menelaus, " Did not Hypsenor die when he dared to face me ? "[2] " I will avenge him," cried Euphorbos. But Euphorbos fell. His lovely head, elaborately dressed with gold and silver, "like the graces," was drenched in blood. He was like a flourishing olive-shoot that a man nurses tenderly in a place where there is abundance of water. All the breezes blow on it, and it grows luxuriantly, until a sudden blast of tempest uproots it and lays it low on the ground.[3] It is the old tree-simile again, but the effect is new. Presently we shall hear from Thetis that she reared Achilles like a plant in the orchard corner.

So Menelaus killed Euphorbos. He was like a lion[4] that the dogs and huntsmen dare not approach, until Apollo sent Hector against him. Then he looked round for help to Ajax.[5] Hector and the Trojans came on. Menelaus retired, like a lion chased by the dogs and the huntsmen. But he went unwillingly.[6]

Together Menelaus and Ajax stood against Hector, who gave the spoils of Patroclus to his comrades to take home to Troy. Ajax was like a lion defending his young.[7]

So the little panel is completed. Menelaus was a mother cow with her calf. Ajax is a lion defending his young.

Glaucus, the friend of the dead Sarpedon, upbraided Hector,[8] using phrases which recall the old complaints of Achilles against Agamemnon. "Why should we allies

---

[1] XVII. 4 ff.   [2] XVII. 24 ; cf. XIV. 516 ff.   [3] XVII. 50 ff.   [4] XVII. 61 ff.
[5] XVII. 102. The whole scene in XI. 400 when Odysseus is rescued by Ajax and Menelaus is the preparation for the present crisis. As usual the first panel and the last of a series answer one another.
[6] XVII. 109 f.   [7] XVII. 132 ff.   [8] XVII. 142 ff.

fight for you? You did not help Sarpedon. What advantage do we get from fighting well? We will go home. If we could only get Patroclus' body, they would give Sarpedon's body back for burial. But you are a coward, afraid of Ajax!" "It is not Ajax," answered Hector. "It is Zeus. But for all that, let us go together." He shouted to the Trojans and their allies. He ran after his men, who were carrying to Troy the spoils of Patroclus, the armour of Achilles, and began to put it on himself.

Zeus meditated. "You think nothing, Hector, of death, which is very near you. But I will give you glory, because you shall not return to Andromache." Zeus nodded, and fitted the armour to Hector's body. So, flashing in the armour of Achilles, Hector shouted to the allies, " It is not for the sake of your numbers that I entertain you and spend the substance of the city on you. It is for the defence of Troy. Defend the city whose food and wealth I have spent on you. Fight on, and either die or be saved. That is the lovers' talk of war. Whoever takes the body of Patroclus shall share the spoils with me, and take half my glory." [1]

Again the son of Telamon splendidly answered with a cry to the Greeks. "It is not now for the body of Patroclus, but for our lives that I fear. Shout, Menelaus, for help." And Menelaus shouted, " You who sat at Agamemnon's table, help." Ajax, the son of Oileus, Idomeneus, Meriones, and others joined them. Thus the old pattern, Menelaus, and the Ajaxes, and Idomeneus, recurs.[2] The Trojans came on like a tidal wave.[3] The Achaeans stood firm. Zeus sent a mist on the battle. And the Greeks gave ground until Ajax rallied them, "like a boar that easily scatters the dogs and huntsmen on the mountains." [4]

They fought, and the Trojans would have fled had not Apollo roused Aeneas. They fought, and many were killed : but more Trojans than Greeks, because the Greeks fought in good order, helping one another. They fought over the body of Patroclus in the mist. Elsewhere in the field the

[1] XVII. 220 ff.   [2] XVII. 237 ff., 256 ff.   [3] XVII. 263 ff.   [4] XVII. 281 ff.

sun shone brightly.   But they, the best, fought in the mist, in trouble.   Two heroes had not heard that Patroclus had been killed, Thrasymedes, and the son of Nestor, Antilochus.[1]

They fought, and the body was dragged both ways, like a hide, stretched for tanning.[2]   It was a fight with which Ares and Athene could have found no fault.   But Achilles did not know.[3]   He thought Patroclus would yet come back alive.   He did not think he would sack Troy without him —no, nor with him : his mother had told him so much as that.   But he did not know that his friend was dead.

The Greeks thought "better to die than yield."   So thought the Trojans.   And while they fought, the horses of Achilles wept.   They stood as still as a gravestone.[4] Automedon could not make them move.   And Zeus reflected.[5]   "Why did we give you to a mortal ?   There is nothing more wretched than a mortal man of all that breathes and moves on earth.   But Hector shall not drive you."   So Zeus inspired them to rush off with Automedon, who could not stop them.

Athene, in the shape of Phoenix, roused Menelaus.   She gave him the persistence of a fly.   Apollo, in the form of Phaenops, "dearest to him of all the allies," encouraged Hector.   Zeus lightened.   The Trojans took heart and advanced.   The Greeks were routed.   Ajax exclaimed "We are defeated !   Zeus, if thou wilt destroy us, destroy us in the light !"[6]

And with this cry for light, which Zeus heard and answered, Ajax thought, "Achilles must be told. . . . Menelaus, look for Antilochus, the son of Nestor.   Send him with the news to Achilles."[7]   Menelaus went, like a lion who has tried all night to snatch a cow from the farm, but has failed.[8]   He went unwillingly, and he begged Meriones and the Ajaxes to remember the kindness of Patroclus.   "He knew how to be pleasant to all when he was alive.   And now he was dead."[9]   So he found Antilochus and told him, then returned to Ajax and the body.

[1] xvii. 366 ff., 377 ff.   [2] xvii. 389 ff.   [3] xvii. 401 ff.   [4] xvii. 434 f.
[5] xvii. 443 ff.   [6] xvii. 645 ff.   [7] xvii. 652 ff.   [8] xvii. 657 ff.   [9] xvii. 670 ff.

Ajax bade Menelaus and Meriones lift the body.   The Trojans attacked like hounds that leap out before the huntsmen on a wounded boar.   But the boar turns on them, and they fall back in terror.[1]   So the Trojans fell back when the Achaeans turned on them.   Their colour was changed.   Not one of them dared to come forward and fight for the body.

So the heroes carried the body back to the ships.   Just behind them the battle raged, as savage as a fire which suddenly attacks a city: it runs and blazes, and houses collapse in the great glare: and the strength of the wind roars over it.[2]   So, as they carried the body, they were followed close behind by the noise of horses and of spearmen.   But like mules which put out their great strength and drag a log or a great ship's timber down the mountainside along a craggy path, their spirit, as they press on, afflicted by the labour and the sweat: so were they zealously carrying the body.[3]   And behind them the two Ajaxes held back the Trojans as a wooded headland, running sharply into the plain, stops the strong rivers, and turn their waters back into the plain.[4]   So the two Ajaxes kept the Trojan battle back.   But the Trojans pressed on them hard, and most of all Aeneas and bright Hector.   As a flight of starlings or of jackdaws rises with a loud chattering when a hawk is seen approaching, bringing death to the small birds,[5] so the youth of the Achaeans went back before Hector and Aeneas with a cry, and forgot their fighting, and many good weapons fell round and about the trench of the Danai as they fled.

Have not the similes of the boar and the huntsmen, of the hawk and the starling, of the wind-fed fire, of the mountain torrent, and, above all, of the tree cut down in the forest, acquired a new and more tragic meaning?   Would not these comparisons, and indeed the whole pattern, be ruined, if we cut away the earlier, less striking, panels of the magnificent design?

Behind the body, as it was carried home, the battle raged

---

[1] XVII. 725 ff.   [2] XVII. 787 ff.   [3] XVII. 742 ff.
[4] XVII. 746 ff.   [5] XVII. 755 ff.

like fire. But Antilochus came to Achilles. And Achilles was already thinking what was true. He was remembering what before he had forgotten, " My mother told me that the best of the Myrmidons would die while I was still alive . . . the son of Menoitios is dead." [1] Then Antilochus came, and told him. [2]

The son of noble Nestor came near him, pouring hot tears, and told his grievous story. "Oh me, son of wise Peleus, very sad is the news that you shall hear. I wish it were not true. Patroclus is lying on the ground, and they are fighting now about the body. It is stripped naked. Hector of the gleaming helmet has the armour."

Achilles poured dust on his head and comely face and beautiful garments, and himself lay in the dust, "great and greatly lying." [3] The slave-women whom he and Patroclus had together taken, were grieved and cried aloud and ran out round Achilles, beating their breasts, while Antilochus held the hero's hands for fear he should kill himself. And Achilles groaned aloud :—[4]

And his lady mother heard him, as she sat in the midst of the sea by her old father. She wailed, and the goddesses gathered round her, all the Nereids that there were in the depths of the sea, Glauke, Thaleia and Kymodoke, Nesaia, Speio and Thoê, and the ox-eyed Haliê. . . .

So the exquisite list goes on. The Nereids too beat their breasts, and Thetis led them in lamentation :—[5]

Sister Nereids, listen, that you may hear and may all know well the sorrows that are in my heart. Ah me, for my unhappiness ! Ah me, for my sad child-bearing ! I bore a son, noble and strong, eminent among heroes. He ran up like a shoot, and I nursed him like a young plant in an orchard corner, then sent him out in the beaked ships to Ilium to fight against

---

[1] xviii. 9 ff.   [2] xviii. 18 ff.   [3] xviii. 26.
[4] xviii. 37 ff.   [5] xviii. 52 ff.

the Trojans. But I shall not welcome him again, re-
turning home to the house of Peleus. And even while
he lives and sees the light of the sun, he is suffering,
and little good can I do by going to him. Yet I will
go, that I may see my dear child and learn from him
what is the sorrow that has come to him though he
held back from battle.

Does not this complaint of Thetis owe something of its
power upon our hearts to the memory of the day when
the heralds came and fetched Briseis, and when Achilles
prayed on the beach, and his mother heard him as she
sat in the depths of the sea by her old father? It is
Homer's method to begin his third and final series with
repetition and development of themes from the first series.

So now, as then, Thetis rises from the sea, and comes
to Achilles. She takes his head in her hands, and speaks
to him. "Why do you weep? Has not Zeus fulfilled
your prayer?"[1] "He has fulfilled it, mother, but what
pleasure is there in it, since my friend Patroclus is dead?
Patroclus whom I honoured above all my comrades, even
as myself. I have lost him, and Hector has the armour.
I no longer wish to live unless I first kill Hector." "Then
you will not live long. Your own death comes to you
soon after Hector's." "Now, now at once, may I die.
I was no use to Patroclus—and to the others. I am a
mere hulk, cumbering the ground. Would that Strife
and Anger might perish from the earth and from the
heavens. A quarrel is so sweet at first[2] . . . but afterwards . . . I will go and find Hector. I will die when
Zeus wills. Not even Heracles escaped his fate.[3] So I
shall die when my time comes. But first I shall win
glory. The Trojan women shall be made to weep for
Patroclus."

"Do not go at least until I come again in the morning
with new armour for you."

So she leaves him. She sends the Nereids back into
the depths of the sea, and goes herself to Olympus.[4]

---

[1] XVIII. 73 ff.   [2] XVIII. 107 ff.   [3] XVIII. 117 ff.   [4] XVIII. 146.

Is it not clear that we have here a deliberate repetition on a nobler scale of the scene in which Achilles prayed to his mother on the seashore, and the goddess took his prayer and laid it on the knees of Zeus in Olympus?

Meanwhile the body of Patroclus was being carried home. Thrice Hector seized it by the leg.[1] Thrice the Achaeans drove him off. He was like a lion that the shepherds cannot keep away. Then Iris, sent by Hera, came to Achilles. "Help Patroclus." But he had no armour. He could not go into the field. At least he could stand at the edge of the trench and shout. The light that shone from his head was like the glare of fire-signals lit at night in a beleaguered city.[2] He shouted, and so did Pallas. Their voices were like the voice of a trumpet from a city besieged.[3] Thrice Achilles shouted and three times the Trojans fell back.[4]

So they brought the body in and laid it on a bier, lamenting.

And among them was Achilles, weeping hot tears, when he saw them laying on the bier, slain by the sharp bronze, his faithful comrade whom he had sent out with horses and with chariots to the battle, but did not receive again safe home.[5]

And the sun set, and the Achaeans rested from fighting.

The sun set, and the Trojans held an assembly, in which the wise Polydamas again advised them well.[6] He alone could see before and after. He was the comrade of Hector, born in the same night, and as much above Hector in counsel as Hector was his master with the spear. "Let us go back to Troy," he said, "since Achilles will be fighting now." Hector scoffed at the advice, and the Trojans, fools that they were, applauded Hector.

We have seen the interview of Achilles and his mother. We have seen the bringing home of the body of Patroclus.

[1] XVIII. 155 ff. [2] XVIII. 207 ff. [3] XVIII. 219 ff.
[4] XVIII. 227 f. [5] XVIII. 237 ff. [6] XVIII. 249 ff.

After that, like a central panel, came the episode of the Trojan meeting and of Hector's fatal courage.   The pattern is to be completed.

All night the Myrmidons and the Achaeans mourned Patroclus, and Achilles led them.   He laid his murderous hands on the breast of his companion.   He roared like a noble lion whose cubs a hunter has stolen from the forest lair.   The lion in its grief and rage scours the forest looking for the robber.[1]

We see that the panel fits the pattern.   We also see that when Homer made Menelaus search for Paris like a beast that has lost its prey,[2] and again when he made Menelaus fight for the body of Patroclus like a mother cow defending her calf,[3] and made him leave the body very reluctantly like a wounded lion driven off from a farm by burning torches ;[4] and yet again, when he made Ajax fight for the body like a lion fighting for its cubs,[5] he was holding in reserve another and a nobler lion-simile. That is how Homer worked.

Again, at this great moment of Achilles' sorrow for his friend, the poet gives a hint—it is no more than a hint—of the greater sequel, when he shall remember first Patroclus, then his father Peleus, and shall pity Priam.[6]

> I told your father I would bring you safely home : and now you are lying here dead.   I myself shall die here with you.   I shall not go home.   My father and my mother will not welcome me on my return.   I will not bury you until I have brought Hector's armour, Hector's head, to you.   I will kill twelve Trojans for your burial.   The Trojan women, whom you and I together took captive, shall weep for you night and day. . . .

The Myrmidons washed the body and anointed it, and wrapped it from head to foot in linen, and put a white cloak over it.[7]   And all night Achilles lamented.

---

[1] XVIII. 318 ff.   [2] III. 449.   [3] XVII. 9.   [4] XVI. 61.
[5] XVII. 132.   [6] XVIII. 324 ff.   [7] XVIII. 350 ff.

Zeus spoke to Hera.[1] " You have roused Achilles,"
he says. " These Greeks are surely your own children."
But she answered, " Son of Cronos, even mortals care for one
another. Shall not I, who am a goddess, care for my
friends ? "

Is not the pattern well wrought ? First Thetis and her
son : then the bringing home of the body : then the interlude of the Trojan Assembly, Hector's folly : then the
mourning and the washing of the body—to which, by the
way, the washing of Sarpedon's body [2] was not surely quite
irrelevant?—then the Olympians again. Thetis went up
to Olympus, to the brazen strong, immortal house of
Hephaestus, beautifully wrought and cunningly adorned.
And Grace, the goddess, wife of the skilful workman,[3] welcomed her, and called Hephaestus to her. He greeted her
respectfully, affectionately. Was it not Thetis who had
hidden him from the wrath of Zeus, when Zeus was angry
with him for abetting Hera in the Heracles affair? [4] So when
she had told her story,[5] " I wish," said Hephaestus, " I could
as surely hide your son away from death as he shall surely
have fine armour." He was still remembering how Thetis hid
him from the wrath of Zeus. He forged in a bright fire
a shining suit of armour. He put on the shield, the earth
and sea and sky, the sun and stars and ocean. He put on
it also all the life of men, at peace and in war : marriages
and feasts, harvest-home and ploughing : vintage and song
and dancing : battle and murder and sudden fear and death.
Read the description again,[6] and you will see how much it
has gained in beauty and significance from the earlier
panels of the poem.

But the eyes of Achilles, when his mother brought him
the armour, blazed more violently than before, like a flash
of lightning beneath his eyebrows. Yet he was glad to
have the gifts of the great metal-worker.

[1] xviii. 356 ff. [2] xvi. 678 ff.
[3] xviii. 382 ; cf. Hera's promise to Sleep, xiv. 267.
[4] xviii. 394 ff. ; cf. Sleep's reminiscence, xiv. 250 ff. These touches link
the two Olympian scenes. But the theme of Thetis as the saviour of
other gods is first exquisitely sounded at vi. 123 ff.
[5] xviii. 429 ff. ; cf. 59 ff. [6] See p. 7.

BOOK III

THE MUSE'S DESIGN : FINAL MOVEMENT

CHAPTER I

THE ARMING OF ACHILLES AND THE END OF THE QUARREL

THE second movement of the "Iliad" began with the sending of Strife by Zeus to the Achaean ships, with the shout of Strife, which put courage into the hearts of the Achaeans, and the arming of their leader Agamemnon. It began with a fight which was equal until the hour at which "the woodcutter on the mountain takes his dinner, because he is tired of felling the tall trees." As we have seen, the movement ends with the bringing home of the body of Patroclus, drawn in by the hard-pressed Achaean heroes, who are like mules laboriously dragging a felled tree-trunk down from the mountains. It ends with a shout from Achilles, heartening the Greeks and putting terror into the Trojans. And finally, as it began with the arming of Agamemnon, so it ends—or rather, the transition between the second and the third movements is marked—by the exquisite interlude of the making of divine armour for Achilles by Hephaestus.

The first movement of the "Iliad" ended with the repentance of Agamemnon, and the rejection by Achilles of the suppliant Achaeans. That rejection involved Achilles in his tragedy, which has now overtaken him. The end of the second movement finds Achilles, with his prayer for vengeance and for glory abundantly fulfilled, but with his friend Patroclus sacrificed. The final act of his tragedy is not yet consummated. He is to seek comfort in atrocious vengeance, and to' learn, by suffering, that he and all his enemies are human. But Hector, who has reached the height of glory and of self-confidence, is to be the tragic victim of his vengeance. Accordingly, just as the first movement ended with the tragic rejection by Achilles of the Achaean prayer, so the second movement ended with the rejection by Hector, of the good advice which might have saved him and his people from disaster.

The final movement, which begins when, with the dawn of a new day, Thetis brings down the armour for Achilles, is not introduced, as was the second movement, by a fresh Prelude. It is, indeed, closely linked by the design with the concluding scenes of the second movement. Nevertheless, the making of the armour marks a pause between two chapters of the tragedy, and a new series of episodes which begins with the new day is characterized by a new spirit. Here the poet uses all his resources. His effects are fuller, nobler than ever. But we shall see that, if we have mutilated the first two movements of the poem, we shall have robbed this last and noblest movement of its finest effects.

Achilles shouted terribly from the trench. The body of Patroclus was brought home, and Achilles went with it, weeping: The sun set, and the Trojans held their assembly. But Achilles led the lament for Patroclus, and bade his companions wash and anoint the body. So all night they mourned for Patroclus.

Then Zeus spoke to Hera. Then Thetis went to Olympus, and Hephaestus made the armour.

In the morning, when Thetis brought the armour to Achilles, his first thought was for the body of his friend :—[1]

Mother, the arms that the god has given are such as works of the immortals are likely to be ; such as a mortal

[1] XIX. 21 ff.

man could not have made. Now I will arm myself.
But I am grievously afraid that, while I fight, the flies
may come to the brave son of Menoitios, and creep in
by the wounds that the bronze has made, and breed
maggots. . . .

" My child," said Thetis, " I will see to that. But do you
call the Achaean heroes to Assembly,[1] and renounce your
quarrel with Agamemnon." So she poured ambrosia and
nectar into the nostrils of Patroclus, to keep the body fresh.

And the glorious Achilles went along the beach of
the sea, shouting terribly, and roused the Achaean heroes.
Even the men who before used to stay behind at the
ships, the helmsmen and the bread-stewards, went to the
assembly then, because Achilles had come out. . . .[2]

That is the pattern : the body, the Trojan Assembly, the
Olympian episode and the armour, the body again and the
Greek Assembly.

Diomed and Odysseus came together, limping, for they
were wounded. Agamemnon, still weak from his wound,
came last. Achilles rose. It would have been better, he
said, that Briseis should have died on the day when he took
Lyrnessos, than that Agamemnon and he should have quarreled. But he renounces his wrath. Let Agamemnon
give the signal for battle. Not a word of compensation.
Agamemnon, seated, and at first not certain of his audience,[3]
" It is right that a man should stand when the people listen
to him. But do not interrupt me. I was wrong : yet it
was not I, but Infatuation. Even Zeus was once her victim :
so was I. But I will make amends. Achilles shall have
great compensation. . . ." " Give me the gifts, if you will,
but now fight ! There is a great work still undone."

But Odysseus, common sense personified, reminds him
that men cannot fight on empty stomachs.[4] Let the army
eat, and meanwhile let Agamemnon make his reparation
publicly to Achilles, and swear a solemn oath that he has
not touched Briseis, but sends her back as she came to him,
unharmed.

[1] XIX. 34 f.   [2] XIX. 40 ff.   [3] XIX. 79 ff.   [4] XIX. 155 ff.

"Excellent," cries Agamemnon, "I will do it all." But Achilles will not eat while his friend lies unavenged.

The great Achaean Assembly corresponds in the main pattern to the Assembly scenes of the first two books. The sacrifice and the solemn oath-taking which follow recall in the design the sacrifice and the oaths of Priam and Agamemnon in the earlier series. So the presents are taken to the hut of Achilles, and Briseis is brought back. The assembly panel thus completed, we return to the lament over the body. When Briseis saw Patroclus, she wept for him. "You comforted me, Patroclus, and now you are lying dead."[1] And the women mourned and beat their breasts, for Patroclus . . . no, each for her own sorrow.[2] The Achaeans begged Achilles to eat, but he would not. "No, leave me—except the sons of Atreus, and Odysseus and Nestor and Idomeneus and Phoenix." And again Achilles led the lamentation. "You, Patroclus, used to prepare my food, and now that you are dead, I will not eat. No worse than this could happen to me . . . no, not the news of my father's death. He is weeping now for the lack of his son: and I am here at Troy, for the sake of hateful Helen. Not the news of my own son's death: whom I thought that you would comfort, and would share my inheritance with him. As for my father, if he still lives, he is very near to death, as he sits and waits to hear that I am dead."[3]

So they all wept, thinking of their own people at home.[4] And Zeus pitied them, and sent Athene with nectar and ambrosia to sustain Achilles.[5]

So the pattern is completed, and the hero's thought of his father, still linked with his mourning for Patroclus, prepares us for the final scene with Priam.

The Myrmidons armed. The white plumes of their helmets shone in the sun like snow.[6] Achilles armed. The earth was aglow with the sunlight and the gleaming bronze. But Achilles gnashed his teeth: his eyes flashed fire: in

[1] XIX. 287 ff.   [2] XIX. 302.   [3] XIX. 315 ff.
[4] XIX. 339.   [5] XIX. 352.   [6] XIX. 357 ff.

his heart was intolerable pain.[1]   His helmet shone like a star.   His shield flashed like a watch-fire that sailors see high up above them in the hills when they cannot make the shore.   His armour was as light as feathers on him.   He took his father's famous spear.   It is a heightened repetition of the arming of Patroclus.   Patroclus had put on the armour of Achilles, but could not wield the spear : and he bade Automedon yoke the immortal horses. . . .[2]   So now, Achilles put on the armour lightly, and took the famous spear, and the horses, yoked by Automedon and Alkimos, stood ready.   And he reproached them with the death of Patroclus.[3]

Xanthos bowed his head to the ground, and Hera gave him the gift of speech.   "It was not our fault.   It was a god and his fate that killed him.   Apollo slew him and gave glory to Hector.   You also will die very soon at the hands of a god and a man."

"I know.   But I will not cease from battle until I have given the Trojans their fill of war."

[1] XIX. 364 ff.   [2] XVI. 140 ff.   [3] XIX. 400 ff.

CHAPTER II

THE BATTLE AND THE TROJAN ROUT

THE Trojans too were arming.   And a third Assembly was summoned.   Zeus sent Themis to summon an assembly of the gods.   All crowded to Olympus.   The rivers came, and the nymphs.   And Poseidon himself obeyed the summons.   "What is the reason for this great Assembly?   Is it Troy again?"

"I care for them," Zeus answers.   "I care for them, though they perish."[1]   And He who formerly held back the gods from the battle, bids them all go down and fight. He fears that Achilles, in his present fury, may sack Troy before its time.   So the gods went down to war: on the one side Hera and Athene and Poseidon, Hermes and Hephaestus: on the other, Ares, Phoebus, Artemis and Leto, Xanthus the River-God, and Aphrodite.

The battle raged, Athene shouted at the trench and on the shore.   Ares shouted from the citadel and at the river Simoeis.   Zeus thundered, and Poseidon shook the earth, the mountains and the city and the ships.   Hades himself was terrified at the convulsion.   God fought against god. Apollo fought Poseidon, Ares Athene, Hera Artemis, Leto Hermes, and Xanthus fought Hephaestus. . . .   But Achilles looked for Hector.[2]

For this hero in his anger all the gods of Olympus are a mere foil and background.

Apollo made Aeneas face Achilles, who was like a lion, enraged, and lashing itself to greater fury.[3]   "Why do you face me?   Priam will not reward you with the kingdom.

[1] xx. 21.   [2] xx. 48 ff., 75 ff.   [3] xx 164 ff.

187

Do you not remember how I chased you once from Ida, when I caught you there?"   "Do not try to frighten me with words. We know our origin. You are the son of Thetis and of Peleus. I am a son of Aphrodite, and my father is a son of the great house of Dardanus, the son of Zeus. That is my origin: but it is Zeus alone who gives or takes away men's valour. Let us not talk idly, like children, nor scold, like quarrelsome women. Let us fight." [1]

They fought, and Aeneas would have perished, had not Poseidon rescued him to save the Trojan dynasty.

And Achilles shouted to the Greeks, and Hector to the Trojans. But Apollo bade Hector hold back, and avoid Achilles. Did not the episodes of Diomed and Idomeneus contribute something to this greater tragedy?

Achilles leapt on the Trojans, shouting terribly. He killed first, Iphition,[2] son of a nymph, a naiad, whom his mother bore beneath the snowy Tmôlos to Otrynteus, sacker of cities. He killed also Demoleon and after him Hippodamas, who roared in his agony like a bull which youths are dragging with ropes to be sacrificed to Dionysus.[3] Then he met Polydoros, youngest son of Priam. Priam had tried to keep him from the fighting, but the boy trusted in his swiftness, and Achilles caught and killed him.[4]

When Hector saw it, he could not hold aloof. He rushed forward, and Achilles, when he saw him, leapt on him. "Here is my man. . . . Come closer, that you may die." "Do not try to frighten me with words. I know you are a good fighter, and I much worse. But the issue lies on the knees of the gods."[5] He hurled his spear, but Athene puffed it away. Achilles leapt on him, but Apollo carried him away. Three times Achilles leapt. Three times he beat the air with his weapon. Then, for the fourth time,[6] Achilles rushed on, like a daimôn, and shouted with a terrible cry, "Dog, you have escaped again, though death came near you. Apollo, whom you pray to, has saved you.

[1] xx. 181 ff., 200 ff.   [2] xx. 382 ff.   [3] xx. 403 ; cf. XIII. 571 f.
[4] xx. 406 ff.   [5] xx. 434 ff.   [6] xx. 445 ff.

But I shall meet you again and kill you, if I also have a god to help me." And Achilles went after other victims.

Did not the episode of Diomed contribute something?

Again Achilles killed or wounded four of the enemy. And the fifth who fell to him was the son of Alastor, who seized his knees and begged for mercy. He was a fool for his pains. It was not a kindly man he met that day.[1] Like a fire that is rolled by the wind through the woods on a mountain, Achilles raged,[2] like a daimôn; and the earth grew dark with the blood. As oxen tread out barley on the threshing-floor, so the horses of Achilles trampled the bodies and the weapons. The car and the horses and the hands of the son of Peleus dripped blood.

Were not the earlier episodes designed for this?

When they reached the river Xanthus, the Trojans were divided. Half fled towards the city; half were driven into the river by Achilles. He leapt in after them, and killed the men, like fishes. But twelve young men he took alive, to be sacrificed for the honour of Patroclus. He bound them with the straps that they wore for the adornment of their shirts,[3] and gave them to his servants to take back to the ships. Himself, he went on killing.

Then he met a son of Priam, young Lykaon, whom he had captured once before.[4] He had caught him in his father's orchard, cutting young branches from a wild fig-tree, to make rails for his chariot. And Achilles had accepted ransom, and had spared his life and sold him to a son of Jason. But a friend — none other than Eetion [5]—had bought him and had sent him to a place of safety, whence he had escaped and made his way again to Troy. Eleven days he had been happy with his friends, since his return. And now, on the twelfth day,[6] a god put him into the hands of Achilles, who was to send him, all unwilling, to the House of Hades.

---

[1] xx. 466 ff.   [2] xx. 490 ff.   [3] xxi. 30 f.   [4] xxi. 34 ff.; cf. xi. 101 ff.
[5] Ἴμβριος Ἠετίων xxi. 43, xiii. 178 ff.
[6] For this effect, cf. i. 493, xxiv. 31, 665 ff.

"I clasp you by the knees, Achilles. Zeus-nurtured prince, I am as your suppliant. Respect my supplication. Pity me. I broke my fast with your bread, when you took me prisoner. You sold me across the sea for the worth of a hundred oxen. Now set me free again for three times that ransom. It is the twelfth day only since I reached home after such suffering. Zeus must hate me that he has put me into your hands again. My mother must have borne me to live only a little time. My brother was Polydoros whom you have just killed. Spare me. It was not my mother's womb that bore Hector, who has killed your strong, kind friend!"[1]

But it was not a voice of kindness that answered his appeal.[2]

"Poor fool, show me no ransom. Give me no talk. Before Patroclus met his day of destiny, my heart was glad to spare the lives of Trojans. Many I took alive and sold for a price. But now not one shall escape death; not one of all the Trojans whom the god puts in my hand; and above all, not one of Priam's sons. Nay, die, my friend. Why do you weep? Patroclus died, and he was far better than you. Do you not see how tall I am, how beautiful? A noble man is my father, and a goddess my mother. Yet death and violent fate will come for me, be it morning, evening or noon, when one shall take my life from me in battle with his spear or with an arrow from his bow."

"Die my friend."[3] Achilles kills his victim, yet even in this crisis of his agony and wrath, he is at one in his mortality and in this strange friendship with his enemy.

The moment passes, and Achilles flings the body of his victim to the fishes.[4] And the River-God grows angry.

After that comes a companion picture to the meeting with Aeneas. Achilles leapt on Asteropaios, son of Periboia and the river Axios. Asteropaios faced him, and Achilles asked "Who are you, who dare thus to stand against me? It is the sons of unhappy men who meet my valour."[5]

[1] XXI. 74 ff.   [2] XXI. 99 ff.   [3] XXI. 106.   [4] XXI. 122.   [5] XXI. 150 ff.

"Great-hearted son of Peleus, why do you ask my origin? I come from Paeonia, a fertile land, far off, and I lead the Paeonian spearmen. This day is the eleventh since I came to Troy. My birth and origin is from Axios, the broad river, father of Pelegon, that famous spearman. And he, they say, was my own father. Now, bright Achilles, let us fight."

They fought, and he wounded Achilles. And the spear of Achilles stuck fast in the bank of the river. Three times Asteropaios tried to drag it out. The fourth time, when he tugged with all his might, it broke.[1] But Achilles leapt on him with the sword, and boasted.[2] "You say you are the son of a River-God? I am a very son of Zeus. My father Peleus was a son of Aeacus, and was not Aeacus the son of Zeus himself? You have a river to help you? Much good may your river do you! Not Achelôus, no, nor Ocean, the father of the rivers of the world, can fight against the son of Cronos and his thunderbolts."

And he drew the spear from the bank and left him, dead, food for the fishes, and still went on killing. The River-God grew more angry, and protested. But Achilles went on killing, rushing on the Trojans, like a daimôn.

And the River-God cried to Apollo.[3]

But Achilles leapt into the water; and the river rose about him, and flung the bodies to the dry land, roaring like a bull.[4] It swept Achilles from his feet, but he saved himself by clutching at a branch of an overhanging tree. He swung himself to land, and leapt away, with the eyes of an eagle.[5] Even Achilles was afraid. The river overflowed its banks and pursued him. He was like a farmer who has been irrigating his orchard, when suddenly the flood sweeps down on him.[6] And he cried to Zeus, "Is this to be my death? My mother said I should die at the hands of Apollo. Would that even Hector had killed me. A good man would have killed a good man then. But to die so shamefully, like a boy, a swineherd, caught by a mountain torrent![7]

[1] XXI. 176 ff. [2] XXI. 184 ff. [3] XXI. 228. [4] XXI. 237.
[5] XXI. 252. [6] XXI. 257 ff. [7] XXI. 273 ff.

But Poseidon and Athene came to him and comforted him with the promise of his glory. He should yet kill Hector.

The whole plain was full of the rushing waters.   Xanthus called to Simoeis for aid.   Then Hera called to Hephaestus. Let fire fight against the waters.[1]   And the plain was filled with fire, until the river cried for mercy, and Hera called Hephaestus off.

The gods fell to it again.   Athene wounded her old enemy Ares.   And when Aphrodite took Ares by the hand, to lead him from the field, Athene tumbled both of them over together.[2]   So the precious pair, the two great plagues of mankind, the two causes of all this mischief, were ig-nominiously handled by the great Greek goddess.

Then Poseidon challenged Apollo.   But Apollo would not fight him.[3]   He respected that great god.   Homer has not forgotten Diomed and Apollo.

Hera spilt the arrows of poor Artemis, the huntress : and her mother Leto picked them up.   For Hermes too was modest,[4] and would not fight the great goddess, mother of Apollo and of Artemis.   And, while Artemis flew off dis-tressed to heaven, Apollo went to Troy.   He feared for the safety of the walls.[5]

Because Achilles was still fighting terribly.   As the smoke that goes up from a burning city is a sign of sorrow for men, so Achilles laid suffering and sorrow on the Trojans.[6]

The Trojans fled before him to the city.   And Priam watched them.[7]   He bade his people hold the gates open for the fugitives.   And Apollo, taking the shape of Agenor led Achilles away, so that the Trojans might escape.   He led him on and away until all but Hector had escaped. Then he revealed himself to Achilles.

Then Achilles came, like a race-horse, after Hector.[8] And Priam saw him.   He was like a brilliant, ominous dog-star.[9]

[1] XXI. 331 ff.   [2] XXI. 426.   [3] XXI. 461 ff.
[4] XXI. 497 ff.   [5] XXI. 516 f.   [6] XXI. 522 ff.
[7] XXI. 526.   [8] XXII. 22 ff.   [9] XXII. 25 ff.

CHAPTER III

THE VENGEANCE OF ACHILLES FOR PATROCLUS

IT is with Priam that the pattern of the last great episode begins. As Achilles ran like a race-horse towards Hector, who stood waiting for him at the Scaean gate, Priam was first to see him.[1] To the old man's eyes he was like a blazing autumnal star, like the hunter Orion's dog, brilliant, but deadly. Homer has not forgotten how the She-Bear on his hero's shield " moves round in her place, but always watches Orion." [2]

Priam beat his head, and cried aloud in supplication to his son.[3] But Hector stood his ground, still eager to fight Achilles.

" Hector, dear child, do not wait. The son of Peleus will kill you. He is a better man than you, and hardhearted. Ah, if the gods hated him as I do, he would soon feed the dogs and vultures. How many of my sons he has killed or sold to slavery : and now, Lycaon and Polydoros —has he taken them alive, or are they dead ? If they still live, we can ransom them for gold and bronze. If they are dead, more sorrow for me and for their mother : but the rest of the people will not grieve so much, unless you too are to die. So come in, dear child; save the Trojans and the Trojan women ; do not give this great glory to the son of Peleus ; and think too of your own life. And lastly, pity me, who have seen so much of sorrow, and in the end . . . my own dogs will tear my body to pieces, when I lie, an old man, disgraced and killed in shame." [4]

---

[1] XXII. 25 ff.　　[2] XVIII. 488-489.　　[3] XXII. 33 ff.　　[4] XXII. 37 ff.

But Hector would not listen.[1] Then his mother bared
her breast, and begged him to remember. "Hector, my
child, be touched, and pity me. . . . Remember, and come
in to do your fighting : if he kills you, I shall not have you
here to mourn you in your funeral couch, you, the dear plant
of my own nursing, nor your wife. The dogs of the
Achaeans will feed on you." [2]

So both of them prayed and wept in supplication.[3] But
he would not listen. He waited for Achilles, like a moun-
tain-snake, guarding its hole in the rock, glaring, ready to
fight the traveller, because it has fed on poisonous herbs.[4]
And as he waited, he leant his shield against a jutting angle
of the wall, and meditated.[5]

Ah me, if I go in through the gates and behind the
ramparts, Polydamas will be the first to reproach me,
because he bade me lead the Trojans back to the city at
the beginning of this dreadful night, when the glorious
Achilles roused himself; but I would not listen. Indeed
it would have been far better. But now, since I have
destroyed the people through my folly, I am ashamed to
face the Trojans and the Trojan women with their trailing
robes; for fear some baser man than I may say "Hector,
because he trusted his own strength, has destroyed the
people." So they will say, and for me it would be far
better to face Achilles and to kill him before I go, or else
be killed by him before the city gloriously.

What if I set down here my metal-studded shield and
my strong helmet, and propped my spear against the wall,
and went unarmed to meet the noble Achilles, and promised him that Helen, and with Helen all the wealth
which Alexander brought with him to Troy, the source
of all the quarrel, should be surrendered to the sons of
Atreus to take home? What if I promised to divide
among the Achaeans all the other treasures that our city
holds, and laid a solemn oath on the Trojans to hide nothing but bring everything to the division? No, no; why
entertain such thoughts? I might go to him, and yet he

---

[1] xxii. 77.   [2] xxii. 82 ff.   [3] xxii. 90 f.   [4] xxii. 92 ff.   [5] xxii. 99 ff.

would not pity me, nor at all respect me, but would kill me naked as I was, and helpless, like a woman, once I had put off my armour.   There is no room for talk between him and me, as between girl and boy at an oak or by a rock, talking as lovers together, girl and boy. Better to fight.   Let us know at once to which of us the Olympian means to give the glory.

So Hector thought, and Achilles came on like Ares: the flash of his armour was like a blazing fire, like the light of the rising sun.[1]   Hector trembled and fled.   Achilles pounced on him as a hawk on a dove.[2]   Past the watch-tower and the wild fig tree[3] he pursued him, until they came to the two springs of the Scamander, where the wives and daughters of the Trojans used to wash their shining clothes in peacetime, before the Achaeans came.[4]   They were like race-horses,[5] but the race was for no ordinary prize.   They were running for the life of Hector.

Three times they completed the circle of the city, and the gods were watching them.[6]   Zeus remembered Hector's sacrifices, and inclined to save him.   But Athene cried " He is a mortal man, and his death is fated.   Would you save him from it ? "   Zeus yielded, and let her go from Olympus to the help of Achilles.[7]

Still Achilles pursued Hector, like a hound that chases a hind.[8]   As in a nightmare the pursuer cannot catch his victim, nor the victim get away, so Achilles could not come up with Hector, nor could Hector escape.[9]   But Apollo for the moment gave him strength and saved him : and Achilles motioned with his head to the Achaeans to keep the ring, not to shoot and so rob him of his glory.

But when at last they came for the fourth time to the springs, the Father stretched his golden scales, and put in them two fates of the death that lays men low, one for Achilles and the other for horse-taming Hector, and took the scales by the middle and weighed them.   Hector's day

[1] xxii. 135.   [2] xxii. 138 ff.   [3] xxii. 145.
[4] xxii. 147 ff.   [5] xxii. 157 ff., 162 ff.   [6] xxii. 165 ff.
[7] xxii. 185 ff.   [8] xxii. 188 ff.   [9] xxii. 199 ff.

of destiny turned the scale, and sank to the home of Hades, and Phoebus Apollo left him.[1]

Do we not feel the value of our old familiar formula ? " Three times he shouted and attacked : but the fourth time, when he rushed on like a daimôn, Apollo met him. . . ."

But it was Athene, as our pattern has already suggested, who at this juncture intervened for the discomfiture of Hector. She bade Achilles rest, and herself, in the shape of Deiphobus, went to Hector, pretending to bring him help at the entreaty of his parents.[2]

So Hector, encouraged, went to meet Achilles, and proposed a compact.[3]   Let the victor in the fight give up the body of his enemy for honourable burial.   " Talk not to me of agreements," said Achilles, "No oaths between lions and men."

Do not this meeting and this interchange of speeches gain value from the meetings and the talk of Diomed and Glaucus, of Patroclus and Sarpedon ?

Achilles aimed at Hector and missed him, but Athene gave back the spear into his hand.   Hector did not see it, and boasted.   So Patroclus had not seen Apollo when he met him in the battle.

Hector aimed, and did not miss the shield of Achilles, but the weapon glanced off harmlessly from the shield. Baffled and angry, Hector called to the supposed Deiphobus for another spear.   But Deiphobus was not near him. Hector understood.[4]   " O fie !" he cried, "the gods have deceived me.   I am to die.   But before I die, I will do a great deed bravely : " and he drew his sword and swooped on Achilles, like an eagle.[5]   But Achilles, blazing with his shield and spear like the evening star,[6] met him and thrust his javelin through Hector's throat.

It was for the sake of this great moment that Achilles at the outset of the encounter was compared to the star that hunts with Orion and to a hawk that swoops on the small birds.

[1] XXII. 208 ff.   [2] XXII. 239 ff.   [3] XXII. 254, see p. 206.
[4] XXII. 295 ff.   [5] XXII. 308 ff.   [6] XXII. 317 ff.

Hector fell, and Achilles boasted, now for the first time, naming Patroclus to his enemy.[1]

Hector, you told yourself, when you stripped Patroclus, that you would be safe: you thought nothing of me, because I was far away. Fool! He had left behind him a champion far better than you at the ships, even myself. And I have loosed your knees. As for you, the dogs and birds shall shamefully tear your body, while he shall be honourably buried by the Achaeans.

Then Hector prayed to him as a suppliant,[2] appealing to his love of his own parents, but got back for his prayers only the cruel answer which made him say, " You have a heart of iron." [3] So Hector died, prophesying that, for all his valour, Achilles very soon should die in his turn at the hands of Paris and Apollo at the Scaean gate.

" Die," said Achilles. " I will take my own fate, when it is the will of Zeus and of the other gods to bring it on me." [4]

Achilles drew his spear from Hector's body, and stripped him of his armour. The rest of the Achaeans ran up and marvelled at the beauty of their dead enemy, then plunged their spears into his flesh. Not one of them who did not wound him over again.[5] He was so easy to handle now. But Achilles cried, " Let us pursue the rest of the Trojan army : " then, as he spoke, he remembered Patroclus, lying still unburied :—[6]

There is¹ lying by the ships a body, unwept, unburied, Patroclus, whom I shall not forget so long as I myself am among the living, so long as my knees shall move : and if they forget the dead in the realm of Hades, I shall remember even there my dear companion. So, come, young men of the Achaeans, let us sing a paean and go to the hollow ships, and take this body with us. We have won great glory, we have killed bright Hector to whom the Trojans used to pray in their city, as if he were a god.

[1] xxii. 331 ff. [2] xxii. 338 ff.
[3] xxii. 357. For Achilles' answer see p. 206.
[4] xxii. 358 ff., 365-366. [5] xxii. 370-371. [6] xxii. 378 ff.

Is that the end of the story? Our study of the hero's character alone would justify us in rejecting such a notion: and the poet's normal method of arranging his design in panels makes us certain.

Priam, we remember, saw Achilles rushing against Hector, and begged Hector to come in. But Hector would not listen. Hecuba implored him to take cover: but he stood his ground. Andromache did not know.

Then the two enemies met, and at length Patroclus was avenged. The panel must be completed. Achilles, in his passion for revenge, devised a shameful handling of the body.[1] He tied it to his chariot, and dragged it behind him in the dust, as he drove away across the plain. And the mother Hecuba saw it, and screamed and tore her hair.[2] And the father Priam saw it, and cried aloud; he begged his people to allow him to go down in supplication to his enemy, to pray him in the name of Peleus to be merciful.[3] And Hecuba lamented.[4] But Andromache did not know.[5] She was heating the bath for her husband, when he should come back from the field. She did not know that Athene had slain him at the hand of Achilles very far from her baths.[6] Suddenly, she heard the cry of Hecuba, and ran to the wall, and saw for herself. She swooned, and as she fell, her marriage-veil, given her by Aphrodite on the day when Hector brought her from the city of Eetion,[7] fell from her. And when her breath came back to her, she mourned for Hector, and Astyanax, and again for Hector.[8]

Is not this the device of the same poet who, at the beginning of his first battle series, made Helen talk with Priam on the walls, and wonder at the absence of her brothers, who were dead in Sparta, then, at the end of it, made Hector meet first Hecuba, then Andromache and the child Astyanax?

Meanwhile Achilles had come to his ships and huts. Three times he drove his car round the body of Patroclus,

---

[1] XXII. 395 ff.   [2] XXII. 405 ff.   [3] XXII. 408 ff.
[4] XXII. 431 ff.   [5] XXII. 437 ff.   [6] XXII. 445.
[7] XXII. 470 ff.   [8] XXII. 477 ff., 484 ff., 508 ff.

then laid his murderous hands on the breast of his dead friend, and swore an oath that he would perform his promise, sacrifice twelve Trojan prisoners at the funeral pyre, and give Hector's body to the dogs.[1]

For the present he made a funeral banquet for his men, but himself refused to wash or eat until the morning, when he would burn the body of his friend. So the men took their supper, and went off to rest, but the son of Peleus went out to the shore of the sounding sea, and lay there groaning, but slept at last, and saw the spirit of Patroclus in his sleep.[2]

It is worth while to notice what the vision of Patroclus has to say. Patroclus is not concerned with thoughts of vengeance. He does not talk about the twelve young Trojans who are to be slaughtered at his funeral pyre. He only wants the last rites to be paid him quickly:[3] "Are you asleep, Achilles? Have you become forgetful? You did not neglect me when I lived. . . . Make my funeral with all speed. Let me pass through the gates of Hades. Because the ghosts of the dead keep me off, and will not let me go with them across the river. . . . Give me your hand, because I shall not come back again from Hades, when once you have given me the rites of fire. We are no longer to live, and no longer to take our counsel by ourselves, away from our companions. The fate which was mine from my birth has opened for me and swallowed me. And it is your fate too, godlike Achilles, to die here at Troy." Then this :—[4]

Do not lay my bones, Achilles, away from yours, apart : let us lie together, as we were reared together in your home at Phthia, when Menoitios brought me as a little child to your country from Opoeis, because of a fatal killing, on the day when I had killed the son of Amphidamas, in my childishness, not meaning it, in a fit of anger—about knuckle-bones. Then Peleus welcomed me in his home and reared me carefully and named me your servant. So let one urn take the bones of both of us.

[1] XXIII. 20 ff.   [2] XXIII. 59 ff.   [3] XXIII. 69 ff.   [4] XXIII. 83 ff.

Phoenix has already shown us Achilles as a little baby.[1] This is a companion picture, not irrelevant, I submit, to the sequel when the son of Peleus meets and accepts, as a suppliant, the father of the man who killed his friend.

In the morning solemn rites are duly paid to the body. First Meriones leads men and mules to the mountains to cut down wood for the funeral pyre and mound.[2] As they mount the spurs of Ida, then fell tall oaks, then make their way back home with the logs through the underwood, we hear again the music of the woodcutter-similes.

After the dedication of the lock of hair, which the hero had hitherto reserved for his native river Spercheios, but which he now gave to Patroclus, in the certainty that his own death was very near; after the funeral feast and the placing of the body on the pyre; after the "evil deed"[3] of the sacrifice of Trojan captives, Achilles cried to Patroclus:—[4]

"Give you good greeting, Patroclus, even in the halls of Hades. Now I fulfil for you all that I promised. Here are twelve good sons of the great-hearted Trojans, all of them eaten by the fire with you. But Hector I shall not give to the fire. I shall give him to the dogs."

So he spoke, threatening. But Aphrodite, daughter of Zeus, kept off the dogs from Hector's body and anointed it with rosy oil, ambrosial, by day and night, that Achilles might not injure it as he dragged it through the dust.[5]

At first the pyre would not burn. But Achilles prayed to Zephyr and to Boreas.[6] The two winds, summoned by Iris, came and blew up the flame. All night long they blew, and all night Achilles poured libations of wine from a golden bowl and called on the spirit of Patroclus. As a father mourns for his son, who was a bridegroom and is dead, so Achilles mourned Patroclus.[7]

Is not that also relevant to the final scene of the epic? Are not our hearts being prepared by Homer for the mission of King Priam?

---

[1] See p. 78.   [2] XXIII. 114 ff.   [3] XXIII. 176.   [4] XXIII. 179 ff.
[5] XXIII. 185 ff.   [6] XXIII. 194 ff.   [7] XXIII. 220 ff.

Next morning the ashes of Patroclus were collected, and laid up in a pot of gold in the hut of Achilles.[1]   A circle was traced out for the mound beneath which in due course the ashes of Achilles should lie with the ashes of his friend. Then Achilles did honour to Patroclus and showed that he himself was reconciled with the Achaeans by the lavishness and gentle courtesy with which he celebrated funeral games.[2] If you cut out from the epic this description, which forms a panel in the pattern between the mourning for Patroclus and the supplication of King Priam, you destroy not only the balance of the composition, but the logical development of the hero's own psychology.   Throughout this scene of the games, Achilles is the peacemaker.[3]   He has something now of the gentleness of his dead friend.   For the Trojans he has as yet no thought of pity, no imagination.   But where Achaeans are concerned he has travelled far from the spirit of his quarrel with Agamemnon.

That is the main effect of the funeral games, which are also used by the poet to round off the story of the lesser Achaean heroes.   Nestor's sage advice to Antilochus for the chariot-race,[4] and the happy sequel in which Achilles gives a prize to Nestor,[5] delightfully recall the day when Nestor's wisdom met with a poor hearing.   When Antilochus protests at the award to the unfortunate Eumelos of the prize which he can reasonably claim for himself: " You have plenty of gold, Achilles ; give Eumelos some other present, not my prize," [6] we hear an echo of the far-off talk about Briseis.   Achilles now sets the example of good sense and generosity which the other heroes are not slow to follow.   So later on, when Antilochus is beaten in the running by Odysseus, he accepts defeat so beautifully that Achilles finds an extra prize for him.[7]

It was Antilochus who brought Achilles the first news that his friend was dead.

Finally, when a prize is offered for the throwing of the javelin, and Agamemnon himself stands up to try his skill, Achilles stops the contest, and gives the prize at once to

---

[1] XXIII. 252 ff.   [2] XXIII. 237 ff.   [3] XXIII. 491 ff.   [4] XXIII. 306 ff.
[5] XXIII. 615 ff.   [6] XXIII. 549 ff.   [7] XXIII. 785 ff.

the man with whom he has so lately and so tragically been at issue.[1]

So at last night came again, and the rest of the company slept. But Achilles lay awake and thought of Patroclus, and in the morning resumed his miserable rite of vengeance, dragging Hector's body three times behind his chariot round the funeral mound of Patroclus, then leaving it again to lie in the dust, where it was tended by Apollo. And the gods pitied Hector, and would have sent Hermes down to steal the body away, had not Hera and Poseidon in their hatred of the Trojans still prevented it. So for eleven days the tragedy was enacted.[2] But on the twelfth day Phoebus Apollo protested, and Zeus sent Thetis to her son for the last time, to touch his heart and to bring him back the human pity, which Apollo said he had quite lost.[3]

Finally, Iris went to Troy, to Priam.[4] She bade him go and ransom Hector. Hecuba begged him not to go,[5] but he answered, " If it had been a prophet who had given this message, I might not have heeded it. But this was told me by a god. . . . I will go, for I will gladly let Achilles kill me, if first I have once taken my son again in my arms." [6]

A cart is loaded with treasure. Libation is poured to Zeus with prayer for a good omen. In answer, a great eagle appears, and the old man starts on his adventure. Then Zeus sends Hermes, beautiful, " like a young prince," [7] to escort this tragic king, whose sons Achilles has killed. It is no accident that Hermes comes to Priam with the beauty of the young men who lie dead, with the beauty of Achilles, whose servant he pretends to be.[8] Nor is it accident that Hermes, thus pretending, says to Priam : " You are old, sir : you remind me of my father." [9]

So at last they came to the hut of Achilles. Hermes opened the door, and Priam passed in.[10] He lay at the feet of Achilles as a suppliant, and prayed to him by the name we have heard so often, " Son of Peleus, remember your

---

[1] XXIII. 890 ff.   [2] XXIV. 31.   [3] XXIV. 44-45.   [4] XXIV. 143 ff.
[5] XXIV. 200.   [6] XXIV. 224 ff.   [7] XXIV. 347.   [8] XXIV. 396.
[9] XXIV. 371.   [10] See p. 207.

own father." [1]   And both remembered, Priam remembered Hector, and Achilles remembered both Patroclus and his own father Peleus.   Then Achilles spoke to the suppliant of the two jars which stand on the threshold of Zeus.[2]   It is no irrelevant parable, but the central doctrine which gives nobility to Homer's vision of our tragic life.   So the enemies look at one another first with pity,[3] then with admiration : [4] and Achilles, who had vowed to feed the dogs with the body of the man who killed his friend, not only gives the body back for burial, but promises twelve days [5] of truce to let the rites be well and honourably done.

Priam went back to Troy with the body of his son.   The city came out to meet him.   Andromache and Hecuba and Helen led the mourning.   For the last time mules and woodcutters went up to the mountain [6] and the last funeral pyre was kindled and put out.[7]   Hector was buried with all honour.

[1] XXIV. 486.   [2] XXIV. 527 ff., see p. 208.   [3] XXIV. 516.
[4] XXIV. 631.   [5] XXIV. 667 ff.   [6] XXIV. 782 ff.   [7] XXIV. 787 ff.

THE PATTERN AND THE POET'S VISION OF LIFE

H OMER was, no doubt, retelling an old story, in which the characters as well as the events were to some extent already fixed. But he impressed on the ideas of his generation the stamp of his own genius, his own finer vision of life. The peculiar quality of his emotion springs from his sense that the nobility and the beauty of life are bound up with its frailty. The hero makes life splendid not in spite of, but because of his uncertain tenure. The commonplaces are the commonplaces of a fighting, feasting, quarrelsome but not ungenerous aristocracy. The use that Homer makes of them, his vision of the heroic life and character, are not traditional. He expresses his own vision in a thousand different ways; never perhaps more clearly than in Sarpedon's famous words to Glaucus :—[1]

Dear boy, if by escaping safely from this fight, we were likely to avoid old age and death for ever, I should not myself be fighting in the front rank nor sending you into the fight that gives men glory. But as it is, since, anyhow, innumerable fates of death stand waiting, which it is not possible for a mortal man to escape or to avoid, let us go to see if we shall give some man glory, or if some man shall give it to us.

The "Iliad" is pervaded by this sense that human greatness is linked with, and is in some degree the fruit of human weakness. That fact makes the last books indispensable to the effect of the whole poem as a work of art. Agamemnon, in his madness could not look " behind him and before

[1] XII. 322 ff.

him." He forgot for a time that he and Achilles and the
rest of them were mortal, human creatures, living a little
while on the edge of doom. Achilles also in his turn,
when Agamemnon repented and offered generous amends,
was proud and hard and so inhuman. And again, when
his friend Patroclus had been killed by Hector, the passion
of Achilles, tragic and noble as it was, the measure of his
love for his friend, passed beyond bounds, and made him
barbarous and cruel. Yet Homer, throughout the poem,
has taken pains to make Achilles more human, more sensitive than other heroes. He could not have borne to end
the story of the wrath and tragedy of Achilles with the
singing of a paean by the young Achaeans as Hector's body
was dragged behind the chariot of his enemy.

"We have won great glory, we have killed the
splendid Hector."

That is the crude heroic doctrine.[1] Life is short, and
killing men in battle honourable, and revenge for injury a
very pressing point of honour. Homer's vision was more
tragic, more profound than that.

The argument which we have traced from the pattern of
the poem confirms the argument from Homer's vision of
life. It was not for nothing that the poet chose to begin
his epic with the picture of an old man and a father, suppliant
before the son of Atreus. Agamemnon rejected the
suppliant, and the dishonour that he put on Chryses was a
prelude to the dishonour that he put on Achilles. Presently,
after the first great scenes of fighting, a band of suppliants
will come to Achilles with a message from Agamemnon.
They will be led by Nestor, here as before the promoter of
conciliation, and by Odysseus, Homer's type of common
sense :—

And they stepped along the beach of the plashing sea,
with many prayers to the Earth-Holder, the Earth-Shaker,
that they might easily persuade the great heart of the son
of Aeacus.[2]

---

[1] XXII. 391.   [2] IX. 182 ff.

Achilles rejected their prayer.   He was not satisfied to have his honour vindicated.   He must glut his pride by the sight of the Achaeans cooped up and massacred at the ships. Zeus granted his wish.   Another'spell of fighting and the first ship was fired.   Then Patroclus begged that at least, if Achilles would not go, he might be sent.   " He begged it as a suppliant," says Homer, " it was his own death that he prayed for." [1]

So Patroclus died, and Achilles at last went out to avenge his death on Hector.

When Hector turned to face Achilles, he proposed an agreement.   He thought the issue of the fight uncertain.[2]

" I may slay you or be slain.   Let us look to the gods. They will be the best witnesses and guardians of our compact.   I will not do your body sore dishonour if Zeus grant me to hold my ground and I take away your life. But when I shall have stripped you of your famous armour, Achilles, I will give your body back to the Achaeans."

" Talk not to me of agreements," answered Achilles. " There is no oath-keeping between lions and men. . . . There shall be no oaths between us until one of us has fallen and has sated Ares with blood."

When they had fought and Hector lay dying, Achilles, in the name of vengeance for Patroclus, declared that the dogs and birds should have Hector's body.

Then in his weakness Hector of the bright helm spoke to him.[3]   " As a suppliant I beseech you by your life, your knees, and your own parents, do not let the dogs of the Achaeans feed on me by the ships.   Accept the gifts of gold and bronze which my father and my queenly mother will give you in abundance, and give back my body home, that the Trojans and the wives of the Trojans may pay me the due rite of fire when I am dead."   But the swift-footed Achilles looked askance at him and said : " Pray not to me, dog, by my knees nor by my parents. I would the passion of my anger might move me to cut

---

[1] XVI. 46 λισσόμενος, μέγα νήπιος.   [2] XXII. 254 ff.   [3] XXII. 337 ff.

off your flesh and eat it raw, for all that you have done to me. There is no man that shall keep the dogs from your head, no, not if they brought me and weighed out ten times and twenty times the price of ransom, nor if Priam son of Dardanus were to offer me the weight of you in gold. . . ."

"I understand," said Hector. "You have a heart of iron." And he died, prophesying the death of Achilles in his turn at the hands of Paris and Apollo.

But it is an old man, like Chryses, praying like him in the name of a father, who comes as the last suppliant of the "Iliad" to the hut of Achilles :—[1]

> The great Priam passed within unnoticed, and stood near, and took hold of the knees of Achilles, and kissed the terrible and murderous hands that had killed many of his sons. As a man is at his wit's end and distracted, who has killed a man in his own country, and has come to a strange people to a rich man's house, and all who see him marvel ; so Achilles marvelled at the sight of god-like Priam ; and the others marvelled and looked at one another. And Priam, as a suppliant, spoke to him. "Remember your own father, Achilles, like unto the gods. . . ."

When Priam had finished speaking, Achilles "gently" put him away. And they remembered. Priam remembered Hector, slayer of men, and wept abundantly, as he crouched before the feet of Achilles. But Achilles wept for his own father, and then again for Patroclus.[2]

> Then the glorious Achilles, when he had finished weeping, pitied the grey head and the grey beard, and sprang from his seat, and raised the old man by the hand.

After that Achilles spoke, in words that are very memorable. Like the words of Sarpedon to Glaucus, they state the central doctrine of Homer's own heroic faith—if you like to call it faith : perhaps it would be better to call it a recognition of the fact of our common humanity.

---

[1] XXIV. 477 ff. [2] XXIV. 509 ff.

Alas, unfortunate![1]   Indeed the sorrows you have had
to bear are many.   And your courage—how did you dare
to come alone to the ships of the Achaeans, to face the
eyes of him who has killed your many good sons—your
heart must be of iron.[2]   But come, sit down.   Let us
leave our griefs, in spite of all, to lie in our hearts, in spite
of grieving.   There is no use in chill lamenting.

This is the fate that the gods have spun for us poor
mortals, to live in sorrow: the gods alone have none.
There are two Jars kept in the house of Zeus, full of the
gifts he gives, the bad gifts, and the other Jar of good.
He to whom Zeus the Thunderer gives a mixture, sometimes meets evil, sometimes good.   But he to whom Zeus
gives of those bitter gifts only, he makes utterly accursed.
Driven by evil famine over the glorious earth, he wanders
without honour from gods or mortal men.

So to my father Peleus the gods gave splendid gifts
from his birth up.   He surpassed all men in his prosperity
and wealth.   He was King among the Myrmidons, and
though he was a mortal a goddess was made his wife.
Yet on him too the gods laid an evil.   No race of princely
sons was born in his halls.   One son he had, born out of
season: and I, who am that son, instead of tending him
in his old age, sit here at Troy, very far from my father's
country, troubling you and your children.

And you, Sir, too—we hear that in other days you too
were happy.   Through all the country between Lesbos,
Phrygia and the great Hellespont, they say that you
surpassed all others, Sir, in wealth and in your sons.
And now, since this is the trouble that the heavenly ones
have given *you*, always to have about your city fights and
the killing of men, bear up.   Do not grieve incontinently.
You will do no good by grieving for your son.   You will
not raise him from the dead.   Before that you are likely
to live and suffer some fresh evil.

It was no accident, but a masterstroke of composition, that
made the " Iliad " begin with the wrong done by King Aga-

---

[1] xxiv. 518 ff.   [2] So Hector had said of Achilles, xxii. 357.

memnon to a suppliant father and end with the right done
by Achilles to the helpless Priam. Nor was it accident
that put a visit of a band of suppliants to Achilles at the
central crisis, when the hero had to choose between an offer
of conciliation and the obstinacy which involved him in his
tragedy.

It is the thought of his own father that makes Achilles
"know himself," and recognize in Priam's sorrow the common
human lot to which he himself is subject. He is thinking
of his father when he speaks of the best that we poor human
creatures can expect, as not perfect happiness, but a due
admixture of evil and of good. And the thought of his own
father makes him great enough to stop the battle, so that
Hector, Priam's son, may be honourably buried. It was
not for nothing, though Achilles would not listen at the
time, that Odysseus, as King Agamemnon's messenger,
recalled the words of Peleus, spoken when he parted from
his son :—[1]

My child, Athene and Hera will give you strength and
victory, if they will : but keep in check your great passion
in your breast, for loving kindness is better. Cease from
strife, which works evil, that the Argives, young and old,
may honour you the more.

The memory of those words was already working in Achilles,
though he did not know it, when he cried in his distress to
Thetis, " Would that strife and quarreling might perish from
the earth." [2]

Nor was it for nothing that old Phoenix, sent by Peleus
as the boy's guardian to Troy, told Achilles his own story :
how he quarreled with his father, and very nearly killed him
—but was saved from that; how he nursed his anger, and
at last, as a homeless exile, came to Peleus as a suppliant,
and was welcomed.[3] Phoenix went on to remind Achilles
that he, the glorious indignant hero, was once a baby in his
arms, slobbering wine on the old man's shirt.[4] That forcible
reminder of our poor mortality, which makes it seem

[1] IX. 254 ff.   [2] XVIII. 107.   [3] IX. 479.   [4] IX. 490.

14

ridiculous to stand upon our dignity, was a prelude to an apologue, worthy to rank with the story of the two jars of Zeus :—[1]

> Prayers also are the daughters of Zeus, though they are lame and wrinkled and blear-eyed. They go behind ruinous Infatuation, always dogging her. But Infatuation is strong and fleet-footed : she easily outruns them all, and arrives before them over all the earth, doing men harm. Then the Prayers come behind to cure the hurt. If a man respects these daughters of Zeus when they approach him, they do him much good and they hear him when he prays. But if a man refuses them and stubbornly rejects them, they go and pray to Zeus the son of Cronos that Infatuation may go with him, so that he be harmed and pay the penalty. But do you, Achilles, give the daughters of Zeus their honour.

The daughters of Zeus came to Agamemnon, in the person of the suppliant Chryses, and were rejected. They sent Infatuation to him, and both he and the Greek army suffered. They came again to Achilles, in the shape of Agamemnon's embassy, and were rejected. Achilles was infatuated by his pride and bitterness. He suffered hurt. But in the end these lame and wrinkled and blear-eyed goddesses came after Infatuation, healing—so far as healing was possible— the harm that she had done. The tragedy of the " Iliad," like the later Attic tragedies, ends in the peace not of exhaustion but of the healing of the human soul.

[1] IX. 502 ff.

A NOTE ON THE INFLUENCE OF HOMER'S TECHNIQUE

ONE reason why it is worth while to study Homer's method of composition is that he was the master of the later Greek poets. Rightly or wrongly the ancient critics regarded the " Iliad " as a model of artistic construction, and the technique of the later Greek poets only becomes intelligible when we understand the method of the first and greatest source of their inspiration.

Aeschylus, for example, called his dramas "slices from Homer's banquet," and I am convinced that it was from Homer—though, of course, the lyrical tradition is also important—that Aeschylus, in the main, learnt his technique. He adapted, in fact, to dramatic ends the devices of arrangement, symmetry and balance, which we have been studying in Homer. If Homer begins his invocation with the name of Achilles, son of Peleus, then names Zeus as the author of the tragedy, and ends his paragraph with the repeated name of "the divine Achilles," Aeschylus will begin and end the prologue of his Trilogy with the Watchman's prayer for a good end of troubles, and will place his first hint of the tragic splendour of his heroine at the centre of this same paragraph. If Homer frames his picture of the first day's fighting with the beauty and the pity of his Helen and his Andromache, Aeschylus will begin and end Cassandra's scene of tragic revelation with the thought of human pity. If Homer begins with the coming of the suppliant Chryses to the son of Atreus, and ends with the coming of the suppliant Priam to the son of Peleus ; if he begins his story with the blazing of the funeral pyres of the plague-stricken Achaeans, and ends it with the lighting of the funeral pyre of Hector ; Aeschylus will begin his Trilogy with Clytaemnestra's ominous cry of triumph, with the delusive fires of victory and the vain sacrifices and libations of the adulteress, and will end it with the holy cry of jubilee, the sacrifices, torches and libations of an Athens honouring the goddess who has brought at last the happy end of troubles, the answer to the Watchman's prayer.

Aeschylus understood the art of Homer.   His formal pattern, his habit of beginning and ending his paragraph of scene or play with repetition of the opening theme, and also his elaborate recurrent images, are a magnificent development of devices which are already characteristic, though more simply used, in Homer's epic composition.   The lyrical tradition, as we have said, is different.   The art of Pindar, for instance, treats words as elements in a musical design in which the aim is rather to conceal than to mark clearly the division between paragraph and paragraph, panel and panel.   In other words, the choral lyric, in its finest musical development, is, as the Greeks said, "a woven song," like an embroidery, with a complicated pattern, woven in one piece. Homer's art is described by Pindar—in the metaphor which has given us the curiously misleading modern word "Rhapsody"—as a singing of "stitched song."   That is to say, the narrative is made up of strips of story, stitched together, so as to make a perfect pattern.   Each strip, of course, is woven.   But the several parts are "stitched together," and the lines of division between the parts are left quite clear.

A full discussion of this point lies outside our present purpose. But if any student of Greek poetry cares to pursue the matter, he will find a good example of the transition between the "stitched" poetry of the epic and the "woven" song of the Dorian lyric in the Prelude to Hesiod's "Theogony."   And in the Second Nemean of Pindar he will find an example of a lyric deliberately framed—so far as choral lyric permits—in the shape of a stitched epic song.

Prose writers, too, Herodotus, and even Plato—though he hated Homer's morals, owe something of their form to Homer.

In the last book of the "Republic," for example, the recurrence of a theme already treated early in the dialogue has puzzled critics. It is Plato's conscious or unconscious tribute to the power of the great educator of the Greeks in poetry.   He copies Homer's technique at the very moment when he is denouncing Homer's influence.

The ancients understood the art of Homer.   So did Milton. He understood at any rate the value of devices precisely similar to those in which we find the master-key to Homer's method. "Paradise Lost" begins, as every one knows, with a reminiscence of the "Aeneid."   "Arma virumque," says Virgil, and "Of Man's first disobedience," Milton answers.   Every one knows that Virgil was referring to the "Iliad" and the "Odyssey."   His Roman epic, he implies, is to include a war of more importance than the

Trojan, and the sufferings of a hero more important in his destiny than Odysseus. It is perhaps not generally known that in his first great paragraphs Milton not only quoted Virgil, but adapted and transmuted by a more noble theme the very form of the first paragraph of Homer's "Iliad." Homer begins his prelude with the invocation of the Muse to sing the wrath of Achilles, son of Peleus, the fatal wrath which laid innumerable woes on the Achaeans. He reminds us that these woes were the fulfilment of the will of Zeus, then ends his paragraph as he began it with the great name of Achilles, now glorified by a bright epithet which links the hero with the god. So Milton bids the Heavenly Muse discourse

> Of Man's first disobedience and the Fruit
> Of that Forbidden Tree whose mortal taste
> Brought Death into the world, and all our Woe,
> With loss of Eden, till one greater Man
> Restore us. . . .

It is Homer's formula. For Achilles, son of Peleus, disobedient Man: for all the woes of the Achaeans, all the woe of lost humanity: and for the repetition, "glorious, divine Achilles," this nobler repetition, as by man came death, so shall one greater Man restore us. Nor is this all. Milton has not forgotten the use which Homer made of the name of Zeus. He has not finished weaving his great pattern with the names of man and God. "Of Man's first disobedience," and "one greater Man," and then :—

> if Sion's hill
> Delight thee more, and Siloa's brook that flowed
> Fast by the oracle of God, I thence
> Invoke thy aid. . . .

Then again—

> But chiefly Thou, O Spirit, that dost prefer
> Before all Temples the upright heart and pure,
> Instruct me, for Thou know'st . . .
> That to the height of this great Argument
> I may assert Eternal Providence,
> And justify the ways of God to Men.

When Chryses prayed to the Olympian Apollo, Lord of Chryse and of Killa and of Tenedos, he reminded him how he had roofed his shrine. Milton's prayer is to the Spirit of Knowledge that prefers the upright heart and pure before all temples. But his pattern and his vision of our life alike draw something of their splendour from the inspiration of the poet whose more tragic creed bids his soldier cry in battle "Zeus, if thou wilt destroy us, destroy us in the Light."

INDEX